Blooming Good

National Council
Of
State Garden Clubs, In[c.]

D1315186

This cookbook is a collection of our favorite recipes,
which are not necessarily original recipes.

Published by: Favorite Recipes® Press
P. O. Box 305142
Nashville, Tennessee 37230

Copyright© National Council of State Garden Clubs, Inc.
4401 Magnolia Avenue
St. Louis, Missouri 63110

Library of Congress Number: 91-42752
ISBN: 0-87197-325-1

Printed in the United States of America
First Printing: 1992   25,000 copies

Welcome to Our World of Gardening

Within the lifetime of many of our members, we have witnessed the growth and development of the garden club movement from sparsely scattered pioneer clubs to a national and international organization which today holds the unique distinction of the largest group of organized gardeners in the world—The National Council of State Garden Clubs, Inc.

From a nucleus of 13 states in 1929, the Council grew to encompass all 50 states and the National Capital Area. Eight geographical Regions were established to facilitate the work of the National Council. International affiliates now total 216.

The Headquarters Building is located in St. Louis on 6½ acres adjacent to the Missouri Botanical Gardens. Here is the hub that disseminates the work of the Board of Directors, the Schools... Flower Show, Landscape Design and Gardening Study and the Member Services Department that provides member clubs a vast array of pamphlets, slides, videos, program ideas and books on various gardening related subjects. *The National Gardener* is the official publication of the organization.

Our membership is typically American in scope and has no counterpart in any other country.

Garden Clubs are obviously devoted to the pursuit of growing flowers, shrubs, trees, fruits and vegetables, and landscaping home grounds. Additionally they are involved with civic projects and are concerned with environmental issues and the protection and conservation of our natural resources.

The Object of National Council is to coordinate and further the interests and activities of its membership together with similar affiliate organizations in other countries. Local clubs have complete freedom and flexibility in their activities. Youth garden club sponsorship is an important function of many local clubs. Scholarships are available yearly for Advanced College studies.

A "strong force" is the proper description for its membership of 51 federations with approximately 300,000 members and National and International Affiliates numbering 200,000.

We present this "Gardeners 500" collection to celebrate the culinary skills of our members as they share favorite recipes and regional specialties for your enjoyment. They're BLOOMING GOOD!

Violet Dawson

Acknowledgements

NATIONAL COUNCIL OF STATE GARDEN CLUBS, INC.
ELECTED OFFICERS

Mrs. James C. Dawson—President
Mrs. Graem Yates—First Vice-President
Mrs. John M. Michie, Jr.—Second Vice-President
Mrs. J. E. Barnette—Third Vice-President
Mrs. Charles O. Smith Jr.—Fourth Vice-President
Mrs. Robert E. Larkin—Recording Secretary
Mrs. Thomas F. Wipperman—Treasurer

National Council Board of Directors
National and International Affiliates

RECIPE BOOK COMMITTEE

Mrs. H. W. Ellinghausen, Chairman
Mrs. John Barba, Vice-Chairman
Mrs. Frank Folk, Editor
Mrs. Emil Walker, Horticulturist
Mrs. David Wright, Consultant

National Council of State Garden Clubs, Inc. members who so generously contributed recipes, designs and support to this National Council project.

ILLUSTRATIONS

Line Drawings by Botanical artists—Henrietta H. Tweedie and Roberta L. Simonds.

COVER

Watercolor Design by artist Mary Mitchell.

The cover design features the NCSGC gift to the AmeriFlora '92 of a 20-foot tall gazebo in a field of flowers. This celebrates the Quincentennial of Columbus' voyage in 1492.

EXHIBITION TABLE DESIGNERS

Page 9—Georgia McHugh
Page 35—Marge Purnell
Page 69—Mrs. Hal Bryant
Page 103—Deen Day Smith

Page 137—Barbara Bilby
Page 171—Jeanne Dabney
Page 205—Beverly Savage
Page 239—Elaine Piper

Contents

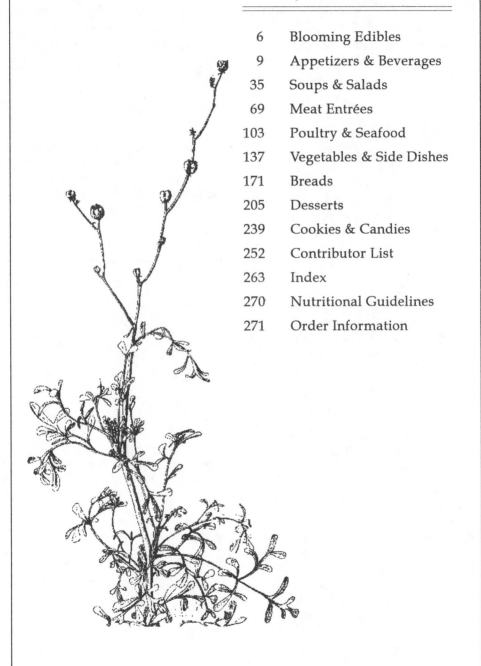

Blooming Edibles

People of all ages have enjoyed the beauty of flowers, from carefully tended formal gardens to the wild profusion of the countryside. Much of the world is also aware that flowers can please the sense of taste, and flower blossoms are boiled, crumbled, steeped and fried for use in teas, soups, salads and vegetable dishes in most other countries.

CRYSTALLIZED VIOLETS

Dip violet blossoms into egg whites beaten until frothy. Dip carefully into sugar, coating all surfaces well, and molding petals back to original shape with toothpick. Dry in 200-degree oven for 30 to 40 minutes or until sugar crystallizes. Place gently on racks to cool. Sprinkle again with sugar if areas appear syrupy. Store between waxed paper in airtight container for up to 1 year.

QUEEN ANNE'S LACE JELLY

Steep 15 large Queen Anne's Lace blooms in 3½ cups boiling water. Strain 3 cups of the infusion into saucepan with 3¾ cups sugar and 1 package Sure-Jell. Prepare jelly using recipe on Sure-Jell package.

Perhaps the blossoms most widely and traditionally used in cooking are violets. They are easy to crystallize for attractive and edible decorations and they also make beautiful jelly.

VIOLET JELLY

Pour boiling water into quart jar filled with violet blossoms; seal. Steep for 1 day. Strain into saucepan with juice of 1 lemon and 1 package powdered pectin. Bring to a boil; add 4 cups sugar. Bring to a boil and boil for 1 minute. Pour into small jars leaving a small amount of headspace; seal with 2-piece lids.

A similar recipe can be used to make jelly from almost any flower blossom, even the lowly roadside bloom of Queen Anne's Lace.

TYLER ROSE PETAL SALAD

Arrange the leaves of 2 Belgian endives on a chilled salad plate for 4 servings. Sprinkle with torn Bibb lettuce, pine nuts and the petals of 1 or 2 mature roses. Drizzle with a vinaigrette of 6 tablespoons raspberry vinegar and ½ cup light olive oil.

The petals of roses have long been candied and added to vinegars in Europe. Recently, roses have appeared in ice cream and salads even in this country. What could appeal to more senses than a beautiful rose petal salad?

Your grandfather may have enjoyed his dandelion wine, and real men today will like Dandelion Quiche—that is, once they try it.

DANDELION QUICHE

Mix ½ cup baking mix, 1½ cups milk, 6 tablespoons melted butter, 3 eggs and salt and pepper to taste in blender until smooth. Stir in ½ cup dandelion petals, 1 cup shredded cheese, 2 tablespoons sliced green onions and ¾ cup sliced mushrooms. Pour into 10-inch pie plate. Bake at 350 degrees for 45 minutes; cool for 10 minutes.

HONEYSUCKLE CHICKEN SALAD IN CANTALOUPE

Cut 2 cantaloupe into halves, discarding seed; cut pulp into balls, reserving shells. Combine 2 cups chopped cooked chicken with 1 cup seedless green grapes, ¼ cup slivered almonds and ⅓ cup mayonnaise in bowl. Fold in melon balls and 3 tablespoons honeysuckle blossoms and serve in drained cantaloupe shells.

Probably you remember the childhood pleasure of sucking the nectar from a honeysuckle blossom. The most recent version of that combines honeysuckle with chicken and fruit.

Flower eating has practical as well as aesthetic applications. A good solution to an over-plentiful squash harvest is to eat the blossoms. Some markets now sell courgettes, or squash with the flowers still attached.

MARIGOLD CHEESE BALL

Beat 3 ounces cream cheese, 1½ cups shredded sharp Cheddar cheese, 1½ teaspoons prepared mustard, ½ teaspoon Worcestershire sauce and ⅛ teaspoon cayenne pepper in mixer bowl until smooth. Stir in ¼ cup chopped marigold petals. Shape into ball and roll in ¼ cup marigold petals. Chill until serving time and garnish with whole marigolds.

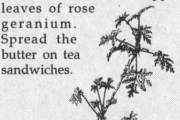

Try your own edible floral accents, using such blossoms as nasturtiums, chrysanthemums, day lilies, daisies, lavender and pansies. Remember that all blossoms must be free of pesticides. Remember, also, that not all flowers are edible. Flowers to avoid eating are azalea, crocus, daffodil, foxglove, oleander, rhododendron, jack-in-the-pulpit, lily of the valley, poinsettia and wisteria.

SAUTÉED SQUASH BLOSSOMS

Combine 3 beaten eggs with ½ cup flour and 1 or 2 teaspoons milk to make a thin batter. Season with salt and pepper. Cut off the bases of 24 squash blossoms and flatten. Dip in batter and sauté in ⅓ cup butter or olive oil in skillet until brown on both sides.

Another good way to introduce diners to flower power is in a cheese ball. After all, most people love anything mixed with cheese and spread on crackers.

FLOWER BUTTERS

Herbs have traditionally been used to flavor butter, but a more recent trend has been the use of edible flower petals. Try the petals of violets, roses, lavender or even the chopped leaves of rose geranium. Spread the butter on tea sandwiches.

Appetizers & Beverages

New England Tradition

New England

Connecticut • Maine • Massachusetts
New Hampshire • Rhode Island • Vermont

*S*mallest geographically of the Regions, New England combines sea and sky, rocks and marshes with spruce, pine and hardwood forests along with the charm of village greens and spires of small white churches. Civic beautification is a priority and the National Council Statue of Liberty Fund project had its beginning in Connecticut. Mrs. Thomas Motley, Jr. of Hyde Park, founding President of the Massachusetts Federation, went on to appointment as the first President of the "National Council of State Garden Club Federations" in 1929 and 1930.

A Vermont Menu

This menu is fun for children and adults alike to herald the early spring in Vermont, when days are warm, but nights are still wintry.

Hard-Boiled Eggs
Sour Dill Pickles   Sugar on Snow*
Plain Doughnuts
Beverage of Choice

New England Boiled Dinner

Tomato Bouillon*
New England Boiled Dinner*
Horseradish   Mustard Pickles
Indian Pudding*

*See index for recipes.

Appetizers

Taffy Apple Dip

Yield: 24 servings

**2 cups caramel ice cream
  topping**

16 ounces cream cheese, softened
¹/₃ cup chopped pecans

Blend ²/₃ of the caramel topping with cream cheese in bowl. Spread in serving dish with 2-inch side. Drizzle remaining caramel sauce over top; do not spread. Sprinkle with pecans. Chill for 2 hours or longer. Serve with apple wedges. Toss apple wedges with lemon juice and let stand for 5 minutes or store in a plastic bag in the refrigerator.

Approx Per Serving: Cal 146; T Fat 8 g; 46% Calories from Fat;
    Prot 2 g; Carbo 18 g; Fiber <1 g; Chol 21 mg; Sod 123 mg.

Hot Artichoke Dip

Yield: 20 servings

**1 4-ounce jar chopped
   pimento, drained**
**1 14-ounce can artichoke
   hearts, drained**
**2 7-ounce cans chopped green
   chilies, drained**

1¹/₂ cups mayonnaise
**1 cup shredded Monterey Jack
   cheese**
³/₄ cup grated Parmesan cheese

Reserve 2 teaspoons pimento. Combine remaining pimento with artichoke hearts, green chilies, mayonnaise, Monterey Jack cheese and ¹/₂ cup Parmesan cheese in bowl; mix well. Spoon into 1¹/₂-quart baking dish. Sprinkle with remaining ¹/₄ cup Parmesan cheese and reserved pimento. Bake at 325 degrees for 30 minutes or until bubbly. Serve with corn chips or tortilla chips.

Approx Per Serving: Cal 167; T Fat 16 g; 84% Calories from Fat;
    Prot 3 g; Carbo 3 g; Fiber <1 g; Chol 17 mg; Sod 371 mg.

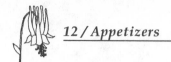

Bagna Cauda

Yield: 20 servings

*This is a low-calorie version of the Indian "hot bath" for vegetables
and is just right for low-fat diets.*

1   8-ounce can tomato sauce
1/4 cup salad oil
1 tablespoon anchovy paste

1 or 2 cloves of garlic, mashed
Tarragon and pepper or
   Tabasco sauce to taste

Combine tomato sauce, salad oil, anchovy paste, garlic, tarragon and
pepper in saucepan. Heat until bubbly and smooth, stirring constantly.
Spoon into chafing dish. Serve with bite-sized vegetables for dipping.

Approx Per Serving: Cal 30; T Fat 3 g; 82% Calories from Fat;
   Prot <1 g; Carbo 1 g; Fiber <1 g; Chol 0 mg; Sod 69 mg.

Zippy Horseradish Dip

Yield: 18 servings

*This recipe was a prize winner in the International Horseradish Festival
in Collinsville, Illinois.*

1 round 16-ounce loaf unsliced
   rye bread
1/2 cup prepared horseradish
2 cups sour cream
2 4-ounce cans deviled ham
1 1/2 cups mayonnaise
1/4 cup onion flakes

1 teaspoon dill
1 teaspoon Beau Monde
   seasoning
1 tablespoon parsley flakes,
   crumbled
Flowerets of 2 stalks broccoli
4 carrots, cut into 3-inch sticks

Cut off top of rye bread. Scoop out center, reserving shell; tear center
into bite-sized pieces. Combine horseradish, sour cream, deviled ham,
mayonnaise, onion flakes, dill, Beau Monde seasoning and parsley flakes
in bowl; mix well. Spoon into bread shell; place on serving tray. Arrange
torn bread and vegetables around shell.

Approx Per Serving: Cal 299; T Fat 24 g; 70% Calories from Fat;
   Prot 6 g; Carbo 17 g; Fiber 3 g; Chol 22 mg; Sod 420 mg.
   Nutritional information does not include Beau Monde seasoning.

*Cut azaleas will wilt when their stems are put into
warm water, which works well for many woody
plants, but they stay fresh and perky in cold water.*

Jezebel Sauce

Yield: 24 servings

This sauce will keep in the refrigerator for months. Vary the amounts of the various ingredients for a hotter or milder sauce.

1 10-ounce jar pineapple or
   apricot preserves
1 10-ounce jar apple jelly

1 2-ounce can dry mustard
1 5-ounce jar horseradish
1 tablespoon pepper

Combine preserves, jelly, dry mustard, horseradish and pepper in bowl; mix well. Serve over cream cheese with crackers.

Approx Per Serving: Cal 78; T Fat 1 g; 9% Calories from Fat;
   Prot 1 g; Carbo 18 g; Fiber <1 g; Chol 0 mg; Sod 9 mg.

Hot Chesapeake Mushroom Dip

Yield: 16 servings

$^1/_3$ cup grated Parmesan cheese
1 cup shredded Cheddar cheese
1 envelope Italian salad
   dressing mix

8 ounces mushrooms, chopped
$^3/_4$ cup mayonnaise
1 teaspoon cayenne pepper,
   (optional)

Reserve a small amount of Parmesan cheese and Cheddar cheese for topping. Combine remaining cheeses with salad dressing mix, mushrooms, mayonnaise and cayenne pepper in bowl; mix well. Spread in 9x13-inch baking dish. Sprinkle with reserved cheese. Bake at 350 degrees for 20 minutes. Cool for 10 minutes. Serve with crackers or chips.

Approx Per Serving: Cal 115; T Fat 11 g; 86% Calories from Fat;
   Prot 3 g; Carbo 1 g; Fiber <1 g; Chol 15 mg; Sod 194 mg.

Lumpy Dip

Yield: 15 servings

8 ounces Cheddar cheese,
   shredded
6 to 8 green onions, chopped
$^1/_4$ cup sliced almonds

10 slices bacon, crisp-fried,
   crumbled
$^1/_2$ cup (about) mayonnaise

Combine all ingredients in bowl; mix well. Chill for 24 hours. Serve with thin wheat crackers.

Approx Per Serving: Cal 149; T Fat 14 g; 82% Calories from Fat;
   Prot 6 g; Carbo 1 g; Fiber <1 g; Chol 24 mg; Sod 203 mg.

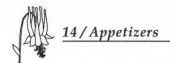

Pistachio Cheese Dip

Yield: 16 servings

8 ounces cream cheese, softened
3 tablespoons crumbled bleu
   cheese
1/2 cup half and half

1 tablespoon (or more)
   mayonnaise
1/2 cup chopped salted
   pistachios

Blend cream cheese and bleu cheese in bowl. Add half and half; mix well. Stir in mayonnaise and pistachios. Chill until serving time. Serve with crackers or chips.

Approx Per Serving: Cal 99; T Fat 9 g; 83% Calories from Fat;
   Prot 2 g; Carbo 2 g; Fiber <1 g; Chol 21 mg; Sod 118 mg.

Chutney Cheese Spread

Yield: 24 servings

12 ounces cream cheese,
   softened
2 cups shredded Cheddar cheese
8 teaspoons dry sherry

1 teaspoon curry powder
1/2 teaspoon salt
1 cup finely chopped chutney
2 tablespoons chopped chives

Combine first 5 ingredients in bowl; mix well. Spread in 10-inch dish. Chill until firm. Spread with chutney at serving time. Sprinkle with chives. Serve with wheat crackers.

Approx Per Serving: Cal 99; T Fat 8 g; 74% Calories from Fat;
   Prot 4 g; Carbo 3 g; Fiber <1 g; Chol 25 mg; Sod 203 mg.

Ramírez Hot Crab Spread

Yield: 32 servings

16 ounces cream cheese, softened
2 tablespoons milk
1 pound cooked crab meat
1/2 cup chopped green bell
   pepper

1/2 cup chopped scallions
4 teaspoons Worcestershire
   sauce
1/2 teaspoon salt
1/4 cup slivered almonds

Blend cream cheese with milk in bowl. Add crab meat, green pepper, scallions, Worcestershire sauce and salt; mix well. Spoon into 2 1/2-quart baking dish. Sprinkle with almonds. Bake at 350 degrees for 15 minutes or until bubbly. Serve with crackers.

Approx Per Serving: Cal 72; T Fat 6 g; 72% Calories from Fat;
   Prot 4 g; Carbo 1 g; Fiber <1 g; Chol 30 mg; Sod 121 mg.

Guacamole Mold

Yield: 35 servings

2 envelopes unflavored gelatin
¼ cup cold water
1 envelope chicken broth mix
    or instant bouillon
½ cup boiling water
2 large avocados
2 tablespoons lemon juice
2 cups sour cream
1 teaspoon Worcestershire sauce
2 teaspoons grated onion

½ teaspoon chili powder
Hot pepper sauce to taste
Salt to taste
1 lemon slice
1 tomato, chopped
3 green bell peppers, finely
    chopped
1   8-ounce can kidney beans,
    drained, puréed

Soften gelatin in ¼ cup cold water in small bowl. Add chicken broth mix and ½ cup boiling water; stir until gelatin and broth are dissolved. Set aside. Mash avocados with lemon juice, sour cream, Worcestershire sauce, onion, chili powder, pepper sauce and salt in bowl. Stir in gelatin mixture gradually. Spoon into 9 or 10-inch dish. Chill for 4 to 6 hours or until firm. Dip bottom of mold into hot water 3 or 4 times. Unmold onto serving plate. Place lemon slice in center. Sprinkle tomatoes in 1½-inch ring around outer edge of top. Sprinkle green peppers in 1-inch ring inside tomatoes. Spread remaining surface with beans. Serve with tortilla chips or corn chips.

Approx Per Serving: Cal 56; T Fat 5 g; 70% Calories from Fat;
    Prot 1 g; Carbo 3 g; Fiber 2 g; Chol 6 mg; Sod 70 mg.

Gala Pecan Spread

Yield: 16 servings

8 ounces cream cheese, softened
2 tablespoons milk
1   2½-ounce jar dried beef,
    finely chopped
¼ cup minced green bell
    pepper

2 tablespoons minced onion
½ teaspoon garlic powder
¼ teaspoon pepper
½ cup sour cream
½ cup chopped pecans
2 tablespoons butter

Blend cream cheese and milk in bowl. Add beef, green pepper, onion, garlic powder and pepper; mix well. Fold in sour cream. Spoon into shallow 1-quart baking dish. Toast pecans in butter in skillet. Sprinkle over beef mixture. Bake at 350 degrees for 20 minutes. Serve hot with crackers or crisp toast.

Approx Per Serving: Cal 112; T Fat 11 g; 84% Calories from Fat;
    Prot 3 g; Carbo 2 g; Fiber <1 g; Chol 30 mg; Sod 212 mg.

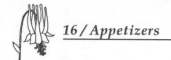

Salmon Balls

Yield: 24 servings

1   16-ounce can salmon, flaked
8 ounces cream cheese, softened
6 to 7 tablespoons lemon juice
2 green onions, chopped
2 tablespoons chopped parsley

¹/₄ teaspoon chopped garlic
¹/₄ teaspoon hickory smoke
¹/₂ teaspoon dillweed
¹/₄ cup chopped pecans

Combine salmon, cream cheese, lemon juice, green onions, parsley, garlic, hickory smoke and dillweed in bowl; mix well. Chill in refrigerator. Shape into orange-sized balls. Roll in pecans. Chill, covered, until serving time.

Approx Per Serving: Cal 69; T Fat 5 g; 68% Calories from Fat;
       Prot 5 g; Carbo 1 g; Fiber <1 g; Chol 20 mg; Sod 133 mg.

Avocado and Salmon Mousse

Yield: 12 servings

8 ounces cooked fresh or
   canned salmon
¹/₂ ounce unflavored gelatin
3 tablespoons cold water
2 avocados
2 teaspoons anchovy paste

¹/₂ teaspoon salt
White pepper to taste
3 tablespoons half and half
Several drops of green food
   coloring
2 egg whites

Drain and flake salmon, reserving liquid; discard bones and skin. Soften gelatin in cold water in small saucepan. Heat until gelatin dissolves. Combine avocados, anchovy paste, reserved salmon liquid, salt and white pepper in blender container; process until smooth. Combine with gelatin in large bowl. Stir in half and half, salmon and food coloring. Whisk egg whites in bowl just until mixture holds its shape. Fold into salmon mixture with metal spoon. Spoon into fish or ring mold. Chill until set. Unmold onto serving plate. Garnish with stuffed olive slices and parsley.

Approx Per Serving: Cal 94; T Fat 7 g; 63% Calories from Fat;
       Prot 6 g; Carbo 3 g; Fiber 3 g; Chol 11 mg; Sod 208 mg.

*The lavendar-pink blossoms of chive are a delicious
addition to salads, eggs, potatoes or
cream cheese dishes.*

California Wine-Cheese Spread

Yield: 16 servings

This spread can also be used with apples, but the flavor of pears is especially good with it. The recipe won a prize in a contest sponsored by a pear distributor.

2 cups shredded Cheddar
  cheese
8 ounces cream cheese, softened
6 tablespoons rosé wine
1/2 cup finely chopped toasted
  almonds

1 1/2 teaspoons ginger
Tabasco sauce or cayenne
  pepper to taste
Salt to taste
5 fresh pears, sliced into wedges
2 tablespoons lemon juice

Combine Cheddar cheese, cream cheese, wine, almonds, ginger, Tabasco sauce and salt in bowl; mix well. Spoon into serving bowl. Brush pear wedges with lemon juice. Serve with spread.

Approx Per Serving: Cal 163; T Fat 12 g; 64% Calories from Fat;
  Prot 6 g; Carbo 10 g; Fiber 2 g; Chol 30 mg; Sod 131 mg.

Hot Seafood Mold

Yield: 20 servings

1 envelope unflavored gelatin
1/4 cup cold water
1 cup hot picante salsa
8 ounces cream cheese, softened
1/4 cup chopped onion
2 tablespoons chopped green
  bell pepper

1/2 cup chopped celery
1 6-ounce can crab meat
1 pound shrimp, cooked,
  chopped
4 drops of Tabasco sauce
1 cup mayonnaise

Soften gelatin in water in bowl. Bring picante salsa to a boil in saucepan. Stir in gelatin until dissolved. Beat in cream cheese. Cool to room temperature. Add onion, green pepper, celery, crab meat, shrimp and Tabasco sauce; mix well. Fold in mayonnaise. Chill until partially set. Spoon into greased mold. Chill overnight. Unmold onto serving plate. Serve with crackers.

Approx Per Serving: Cal 154; T Fat 13 g; 77% Calories from Fat;
  Prot 7 g; Carbo 2 g; Fiber <1 g; Chol 54 mg; Sod 218 mg.

Chive

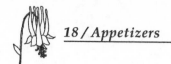

Gazpacho Mold

Yield: 30 servings

¼ cup chili sauce
1 cup catsup
2 cloves of garlic, crushed
1 green bell pepper, chopped
1 sweet onion, chopped
1 large tomato, peeled, seeded,
   chopped

1 cucumber, peeled, seeded
2 tablespoons white vinegar
2 drops of Tabasco sauce
1 tablespoon olive oil
1 teaspoon Worcestershire sauce
1 envelope unflavored gelatin
¼ cup cold water

Process first 11 ingredients in food processor until chopped. Soften gelatin in water in glass dish. Microwave on High for 10 seconds or until gelatin is dissolved. Add to vegetable mixture; mix well. Spoon into oiled mold. Chill until set. Unmold onto serving plate. Serve with tortilla chips.

Approx Per Serving: Cal 22; T Fat 1 g; 21% Calories from Fat;
    Prot 1 g; Carbo 4 g; Fiber 1 g; Chol 0 mg; Sod 128 mg.

Stuffed Lychee

Yield: 36 servings

8 ounces cream cheese, softened
2½ ounces crystallized ginger,
   finely chopped

2 20-ounce cans whole
   seedless lychee, drained

Combine cream cheese and ginger in mixer bowl; mix well. Spoon or pipe into lychee. Arrange on serving plate. Garnish with chopped macadamia nuts.

Approx Per Serving: Cal 43; T Fat 2 g; 44% Calories from Fat;
    Prot 1 g; Carbo 6 g; Fiber 1 g; Chol 7 mg; Sod 19 mg.
    Nutritional information does not include crystallized ginger.

Bacon Goodies

Yield: 30 servings

1 pound sliced bacon, cut into
   halves

½ cup sugar
30 Waverly wafer sections

Dip bacon into sugar, coating both sides. Wrap 1 slice bacon lengthwise around each wafer, tucking ends under. Place on paper towels in 2 glass dishes; cover with paper towels. Microwave ½ at a time on High for 4 minutes or until bacon is crisp.

Approx Per Serving: Cal 43; T Fat 2 g; 50% Calories from Fat;
    Prot 1 g; Carbo 4 g; Fiber 0 g; Chol 4 mg; Sod 82 mg.

Bacon Sticks

Yield: 16 servings

1 pound sliced bacon　　　　**2 cups grated Parmesan cheese**
16 breadsticks

Wrap 1 slice bacon diagonally around each breadstick, overlapping edges. Roll in cheese. Arrange on ridged microwave tray. Microwave for 7 to 8 minutes or until bacon is done to taste. Roll in cheese. Cool to room temperature.

Approx Per Serving: Cal 133; T Fat 8 g; 51% Calories from Fat;
　　Prot 8 g; Carbo 8 g; Fiber <1 g; Chol 15 mg; Sod 394 mg.

Brown Sugar and Nut-Glazed Brie　　*Yield: 16 servings*

1/4 cup packed brown sugar　　**1/4 cup chopped pecans**
1 tablespoon bourbon　　　　　**1　14-ounce round or wheel Brie**

Combine brown sugar, bourbon and pecans in glass dish. Microwave on High until brown sugar dissolves; mix well. Pour over Brie in glass dish. Microwave on High for 2 to 3 minutes or until heated through. Serve with crackers.

Approx Per Serving: Cal 114; T Fat 8 g; 65% Calories from Fat;
　　Prot 6 g; Carbo 5 g; Fiber <1 g; Chol 25 mg; Sod 158 mg.

Cheese Pinwheels

Yield: 48 servings

2¹/₂ cups flour　　　　　　　　**1 cup mixed dried herbs**
1 cup butter, softened　　　　 **3 cups shredded Cheddar**
1 cup sour cream　　　　　　　　**cheese**
Seasoned salt to taste　　　　 **Paprika to taste**

Combine flour, butter and sour cream in bowl; mix well to form dough. Divide into 4 parts; wrap in plastic wrap. Chill until firm. Roll into 6x12-inch rectangles on floured pastry cloth. Sprinkle with seasoned salt, herbs and cheese. Roll to enclose filling from long sides; seal edges. Chill in refrigerator. Cut into 1-inch slices; place slices on ungreased baking sheet. Sprinkle with paprika. Bake at 350 degrees for 25 to 30 minutes or until light brown. Serve warm.

Approx Per Serving: Cal 96; T Fat 7 g; 67% Calories from Fat;
　　Prot 3 g; Carbo 5 g; Fiber <1 g; Chol 20 mg; Sod 79 mg.

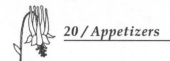

Hot Cheese Puffs

Yield: 32 servings

1 egg
1/2 cup mayonnaise
2 cups shredded Cheddar
   cheese, at room temperature

1/2 teaspoon cayenne pepper
1 loaf party rye bread

Beat egg in mixer bowl. Beat in mayonnaise. Stir in cheese and cayenne pepper. Cut bread into desired shapes. Spread with cheese mixture; place on baking sheet. Bake at 375 degrees for 20 minutes or until cheese is bubbly and begins to brown. May broil if preferred.

Approx Per Serving: Cal 92; T Fat 6 g; 56% Calories from Fat;
    Prot 3 g; Carbo 7 g; Fiber 1 g; Chol 16 mg; Sod 165 mg.

Lacy Cheese Crackers

Yield: 16 servings

2 cups shredded Cheddar
   cheese
1/2 cup butter, softened

1 teaspoon dill
1/2 cup whole wheat flour
Salt to taste

Combine cheese and butter in bowl; mix well. Add mixture of dill, flour and salt; mix well. Shape into 3 rolls 1 to 1 1/4 inches in diameter. Chill for 2 hours to overnight. Cut into 1/4-inch slices; place 2 inches apart on ungreased baking sheet. Bake at 350 degrees for 10 minutes. Cool slightly on baking sheet. Remove to wire rack to cool completely.

Approx Per Serving: Cal 120; T Fat 11 g; 77% Calories from Fat;
    Prot 4 g; Carbo 3 g; Fiber <1 g; Chol 30 mg; Sod 136 mg.

Roquefort Diablotins

Yield: 24 servings

1 cup crumbled Roquefort
   cheese
1/2 cup butter, softened

1/2 cup chopped pecans
1 loaf French bread, sliced

Combine cheese and butter in bowl; mix until smooth. Add pecans; mix well. Toast bread on 1 side. Spread untoasted side with cheese mixture; place on baking sheet. Broil until bubbly. Serve hot.

Approx Per Serving: Cal 122; T Fat 8 g; 57% Calories from Fat;
    Prot 3 g; Carbo 10 g; Fiber 1 g; Chol 15 mg; Sod 227 mg.

Prosciutto Roll-Ups

Yield: 24 servings

1 2-pastry package puff pastry, thawed
1 6-ounce jar honey mustard

8 ounces Parmesan cheese, finely grated
8 ounces prosciutto, thinly sliced

Spread pastries with mixture of honey mustard and cheese. Top with prosciutto. Fold long edges toward centers. Cut into 1/2-inch slices. Place on baking sheets lined with baking parchment. Bake at 325 degrees for 10 minutes or until golden.

Approx Per Serving: Cal 157; T Fat 9 g; 53% Calories from Fat; Prot 8 g; Carbo 10 g; Fiber <1 g; Chol 13 mg; Sod 452 mg.

Pupu Wings

Yield: 32 servings

Pupus are Hawaiian hors d'oeuvres.

1/2 cup soy sauce
6 tablespoons sugar
1 green onion, chopped
1 clove of garlic, chopped
4 pounds chicken drumettes

2 tablespoons garlic salt
MSG to taste
1 cup rice flour
1 cup cornstarch
Oil for deep frying

Combine soy sauce, sugar, green onion and garlic in bowl; mix well. Rinse chicken and pat dry. Sprinkle with garlic salt and MSG. Chill for 30 minutes. Coat with mixture of rice flour and cornstarch. Deep-fry in hot oil until brown; drain. Dip hot wings into soy sauce mixture. Serve hot or cold.

Approx Per Serving: Cal 113; T Fat 2 g; 20% Calories from Fat; Prot 13 g; Carbo 9 g; Fiber <1 g; Chol 40 mg; Sod 684 mg. Nutritional information does not include oil for deep frying.

Clams Casino

Yield: 24 servings

24 clams, opened
Rock salt

1/2 cup butter
8 slices bacon, cut into thirds

Arrange clams in baking pan lined with rock salt. Top each with butter and bacon. Bake at 400 degrees until bacon is crisp.

Approx Per Serving: Cal 53; T Fat 5 g; 84% Calories from Fat; Prot 2 g; Carbo <1 g; Fiber <1 g; Chol 15 mg; Sod 71 mg. Nutritional information does not include rock salt.

Empañadas

Yield: 80 servings

²/₃ cup finely chopped onion
1 cup finely chopped celery
1 pound ground beef
1   3-ounce jar mushrooms
1 cup finely chopped stuffed
   olives

1   8-ounce can tomato paste
½ teaspoon oregano
Salt and pepper to taste
3 packages pie crust mix
2 cups shredded Cheddar
   cheese

Sauté onion and celery in skillet sprayed with nonstick cooking spray for 8 minutes. Add ground beef. Cook until ground beef is brown and crumbly, stirring constantly; drain. Add mushrooms, olives, tomato paste, oregano, salt and pepper; mix well. Prepare pie crust mix using package directions. Roll dough very thin on floured surface. Cut into 2½ to 3-inch rounds. Spoon ground beef filling onto rounds; sprinkle with cheese. Moisten edges; fold dough over to enclose filling and seal with fork. Place on baking sheet. Bake at 400 degrees for 18 to 20 minutes or until light brown.

Approx Per Serving: Cal 60; T Fat 4 g; 60% Calories from Fat;
    Prot 2 g; Carbo 4 g; Fiber <1 g; Chol 7 mg; Sod 134 mg.

Ham Pick-Ups

Yield: 36 servings

3 packages party rolls
1 cup margarine, softened
3 tablespoons poppy seed
3 tablespoons dry mustard
1 medium onion, finely grated

1 tablespoon Worcestershire
   sauce
1 pound baked ham, thinly sliced
1 pound Swiss cheese, thinly
   sliced

Slice rolls horizontally into halves; do not separate rolls. Combine margarine, poppy seed, dry mustard, onion and Worcestershire sauce in bowl; mix well. Spread on cut sides of rolls. Layer ham and cheese on bottom half of rolls; replace top of rolls. Place in foil roll pan. Cut into individual rolls with sharp knife. Wrap in foil. Bake at 350 degrees for 25 minutes or until heated through.

Approx Per Serving: Cal 164; T Fat 11 g; 60% Calories from Fat;
    Prot 8 g; Carbo 8 g; Fiber <1 g; Chol 19 mg; Sod 341 mg.

*Blooms cut for horticulture entries in flower shows
will nearly always be more perfect if they are
cut in advanced bud and allowed to open indoors,
protected from wind, rain and insects.*

Krautberry Meatballs

Yield: 24 servings

2 pounds ground beef
1 envelope onion soup mix
1 cup fine bread crumbs
2 eggs
1 12-ounce bottle of chili sauce

1 16-ounce can whole
   cranberry sauce
1¹/₂ cups water
1 cup sauerkraut

Combine ground beef, soup mix, bread crumbs and eggs in bowl; mix well. Shape into small balls. Place in 9x13-inch baking pan. Combine chili sauce, cranberry sauce, water and sauerkraut in bowl; mix well. Spoon over meatballs. Bake at 350 degrees for 2 hours.

Approx Per Serving: Cal 146; T Fat 6 g; 37% Calories from Fat;
     Prot 9 g; Carbo 15 g; Fiber 1 g; Chol 43 mg; Sod 344 mg.

Black Olive Canapés

Yield: 40 servings

1¹/₂ cups minced black olives
2 tablespoons minced onion
¹/₂ cup mayonnaise
¹/₄ teaspoon curry powder

1 cup shredded sharp Cheddar
   cheese
5 English muffins, split, lightly
   toasted

Combine olives, onion, mayonnaise and curry powder in bowl; mix well. Stir in cheese. Spread on muffin halves; place on baking sheet. Broil 3 inches from heat source in preheated broiler for 3 to 4 minutes or until bubbly. Cut into quarters.

Approx Per Serving: Cal 59; T Fat 5 g; 68% Calories from Fat;
     Prot 1 g; Carbo 4 g; Fiber <1 g; Chol 5 mg; Sod 129 mg.

Olive Cheese Puffs

Yield: 42 servings

2 cups shredded sharp Cheddar
   cheese
1 cup flour

¹/₂ teaspoon paprika
¹/₂ cup butter, softened
42 small stuffed olives

Combine cheese, flour, paprika and butter in bowl; mix well. Roll by teaspoonfuls into balls. Press thumb into each ball. Insert olive into each ball; reshape dough to enclose olive. Place on baking sheet. Bake at 400 degrees for 15 minutes.

Approx Per Serving: Cal 56; T Fat 5 g; 72% Calories from Fat;
     Prot 2 g; Carbo 2 g; Fiber <1 g; Chol 12 mg; Sod 145 mg.

Onion Squares

Yield: 16 servings

Prepare in an 8-inch pie plate for a four-serving main dish.

1 cup fine cracker crumbs
1/2 cup melted butter
2 cups thinly sliced onions
2 teaspoons butter
3/4 cup milk
2 eggs, slightly beaten

3/4 teaspoon salt
Pepper to taste
1 cup shredded sharp Cheddar
  cheese
Paprika to taste

Mix cracker crumbs with 1/2 cup butter in 8x8-inch baking pan; press evenly over bottom and sides of pan. Sauté onions in 2 teaspoons butter in skillet until tender but not brown. Spoon into prepared pan. Combine milk, eggs, salt and pepper in bowl; mix well. Pour over onions. Sprinkle with cheese and paprika. Bake at 350 degrees for 30 minutes or until knife inserted in center comes out clean. Cut into squares.

Approx Per Serving: Cal 127; T Fat 10 g; 72% Calories from Fat;
    Prot 3 g; Carbo 6 g; Fiber <1 g; Chol 54 mg; Sod 278 mg.

Stuffed Green Pepper Slices

Yield: 24 servings

*Stuffed peppers may also be cut into rings and
served on shredded lettuce as a salad.*

1 cup cooked ground beef
3/4 cup finely chopped celery
18 stuffed green olives
2 teaspoons chopped parsley

6 ounces cream cheese, softened
Garlic salt and pepper to taste
3 medium green bell peppers

Combine ground beef with celery, olives, parsley, cream cheese, garlic salt and pepper in bowl; mix well. Cut off tops of green peppers; discard seed and membrane. Spoon filling into peppers. Chill until filling is firm. Cut crosswise into thin slices. Serve on relish or canapé tray.

Approx Per Serving: Cal 42; T Fat 4 g; 77% Calories from Fat;
    Prot 2 g; Carbo 1 g; Fiber <1 g; Chol 11 mg; Sod 98 mg.

Squash Blossom

Stuffed Banana Peppers

Yield: 20 servings

This recipe can also be prepared with canned sweet cherry peppers.

1 pound pork sausage
1 8-ounce can bean dip
3 ounces cream cheese, softened
1 clove of garlic, crushed

1 tablespoon prepared mustard
Tabasco sauce to taste
1 teaspoon Worcestershire sauce
20 banana peppers

Brown sausage in skillet, stirring until crumbly; drain. Combine with bean dip, cream cheese, garlic, mustard, Tabasco sauce and Worcestershire sauce in bowl; mix well. Cut off tops of peppers; discard seed and membrane. Spoon filling into peppers. Chill in refrigerator.

Approx Per Serving: Cal 73; T Fat 5 g; 68% Calories from Fat;
    Prot 3 g; Carbo 3 g; Fiber <1 g; Chol 14 mg; Sod 229 mg.

Cocktail Pizza

Yield: 32 servings

1 cup shredded sharp Cheddar
    cheese
1 cup mayonnaise

2 tablespoons chopped chives
1/2 teaspoon (or more) oregano
1 loaf party rye bread

Combine cheese, mayonnaise, chives and oregano in bowl; mix well. Spread on bread slices; arrange on baking sheet. Bake at 400 degrees for 5 minutes or until puffed and brown.

Approx Per Serving: Cal 100; T Fat 7 g; 64% Calories from Fat;
    Prot 2 g; Carbo 7 g; Fiber 1 g; Chol 8 mg; Sod 160 mg.

Vegetable Pizza

Yield: 24 servings

2 8-count cans crescent rolls
16 ounces cream cheese, softened
1/2 cup sour cream
1 envelope ranch salad dressing
    mix

3 tablespoons mayonnaise
2 cups chopped mixed vegetables
    such as broccoli, cauliflower,
    radishes and carrots
1 cup shredded Cheddar cheese

Line 10x15-inch baking pan with roll dough, pressing edges and perforations to seal. Bake at 350 degrees for 12 minutes. Cool to room temperature. Beat cream cheese until smooth. Add sour cream, salad dressing mix and mayonnaise; mix well. Spread over crust. Sprinkle with vegetables and Cheddar cheese.

Approx Per Serving: Cal 186; T Fat 14 g; 68% Calories from Fat;
    Prot 4 g; Carbo 11 g; Fiber 1 g; Chol 29 mg; Sod 337 mg.

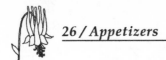
Polpette di Risotto

Yield: 14 servings

1 vegetable bouillon cube
2¹/₂ cups boiling water
1 tablespoon butter
1 cup long grain rice
¹/₂ cup grated Parmesan cheese
3 egg yolks, slightly beaten
¹/₂ teaspoon salt
¹/₄ teaspoon white pepper

2 tablespoons chopped
  mushrooms
1 tablespoon chopped onion
14 ¹/₄x1x1-inch squares of
  mozzarella cheese
3 egg whites, slightly beaten
1 cup fine dry bread crumbs
Oil for deep frying

Dissolve bouillon cube in boiling water in medium saucepan. Stir in butter and rice. Simmer, covered, for 15 minutes or until rice is tender; drain. Add Parmesan cheese, egg yolks, salt and white pepper; mix well. Stir in mushrooms and onion. Shape ¹/₄ cup mixture around each piece of cheese. Dip into egg whites; coat with bread crumbs. Deep-fry in oil heated to 375 degrees for 5 to 7 minutes or until golden brown.

Approx Per Serving: Cal 154; T Fat 6 g; 37% Calories from Fat;
    Prot 7 g; Carbo 17 g; Fiber <1 g; Chol 62 mg; Sod 338 mg.
    Nutritional information does not include oil for deep frying.

Salmon Pâté

Yield: 16 servings

1 16-ounce can salmon, flaked
8 ounces cream cheese, softened
1 tablespoon lemon juice
2 teaspoons grated onion

¹/₄ teaspoon liquid smoke
¹/₄ teaspoon salt
1 cup chopped pecans
3 tablespoons chopped parsley

Combine first 6 ingredients in bowl; mix well. Shape into ball or log. Roll in pecans; sprinkle with parsley.

Approx Per Serving: Cal 139; T Fat 12 g; 74% Calories from Fat;
    Prot 7 g; Carbo 2 g; Fiber 1 g; Chol 30 mg; Sod 216 mg.

Scallops with Bacon

Yield: 32 servings

32 scallops
16 slices bacon, cut into halves

Lemon pepper to taste

Wrap scallops with bacon; secure with wooden picks. Arrange in baking dish. Sprinkle with lemon pepper. Bake at 425 degrees for 25 minutes or until bacon is crisp; drain.

Approx Per Serving: Cal 25; T Fat 2 g; 59% Calories from Fat;
    Prot 2 g; Carbo <1 g; Fiber 0 g; Chol 5 mg; Sod 63 mg.

Hawaiian Sesame Shrimp   Yield: 24 servings

Purchase the sesame oil for this recipe at an Asian market; the sesame oil from the health food store is not the same.

1 tablespoon sesame seed	1/2 cup chopped green onions
2 tablespoons sesame oil	1 tablespoon brown sugar
2 tablespoons vegetable oil	1/2 teaspoon salt
1 pound medium shrimp,	1/4 teaspoon pepper
peeled, deveined	1 tablespoon soy sauce

Sprinkle sesame seed in baking pan. Toast in 300-degree oven until golden brown. Heat sesame oil and vegetable oil in wok or heavy saucepan over high heat. Add shrimp, green onions, brown sugar, salt and pepper. Stir-fry for 1 to 3 minutes or until shrimp is done to taste. Reduce heat to low. Stir in soy sauce; remove from heat. Sprinkle with sesame seed. Serve hot or at room temperature.

Approx Per Serving: Cal 40; T Fat 3 g; 59% Calories from Fat;
    Prot 3 g; Carbo 1 g; Fiber <1 g; Chol 30 mg; Sod 122 mg.

Pickled Shrimp   Yield: 50 servings

2 1/2 pounds shrimp	1 1/4 cups oil
1/2 cup chopped celery	1/4 cup white vinegar
1/4 cup mixed pickling spices	3 tablespoons capers with
Salt to taste	liquid
2 cups sliced onions	Tabasco sauce to taste
8 bay leaves	2 1/2 teaspoons (or less) salt

Add shrimp to boiling water to cover in saucepan. Add celery, pickling spices and salt to taste. Bring to a boil; remove from heat. Let stand, covered, for 2 minutes; drain. Rinse with cold water. Peel and devein shrimp. Alternate layers of shrimp and onions in shallow dish. Add bay leaves. Combine oil, vinegar, capers with liquid, Tabasco sauce and 2 1/2 teaspoons salt in bowl; mix well. Pour over layers. Chill, wrapped with plastic wrap, for 24 hours or longer. Discard bay leaves. Spoon shrimp and marinade mixture into serving dish. Serve with shrimp forks.

Approx Per Serving: Cal 68; T Fat 6 g; 75% Calories from Fat;
    Prot 4 g; Carbo <1 g; Fiber <1 g; Chol 35 mg; Sod 148 mg.
    Nutritional information does not include capers.

The white blossoms of the yucca plant are used in salads and soups in Latin America.

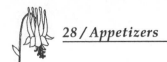

Shrimp Wheels

Yield: 40 servings

1 4-ounce can shrimp, drained, mashed
1/4 cup mayonnaise
2 tablespoons chili sauce
2 tablespoons chopped stuffed green olives
1 tablespoon minced celery
1 8-count can crescent rolls

Combine first 5 ingredients in bowl; mix well. Separate roll dough into 4 rectangles, pressing diagonal perforations to seal. Spread with shrimp mixture. Roll to enclose filling from narrow end. Cut each roll into 10 slices. Place cut side down on greased baking sheet. Bake at 375 degrees for 10 to 12 minutes or until golden brown. Serve hot.

Approx Per Serving: Cal 35; T Fat 2 g; 61% Calories from Fat; Prot 1 g; Carbo 2 g; Fiber <1 g; Chol 5 mg; Sod 148 mg

Spinach Balls

Yield: 24 servings

1 10-ounce package frozen chopped spinach, cooked
1½ cups stuffing mix
3 eggs
2 tablespoons chopped onion
1/4 cup melted butter
1/4 cup grated Parmesan cheese
1/8 teaspoon garlic powder
1/2 teaspoon pepper

Combine drained spinach and remaining ingredients in bowl; mix well. Shape into 1-inch balls; place on baking sheet. Bake at 350 degrees for 15 to 20 minutes or until brown.

Approx Per Serving: Cal 51; T Fat 3 g; 53% Calories from Fat; Prot 2 g; Carbo 4 g; Fiber <1 g; Chol 33 mg; Sod 109 mg.

Zucchini Hors d'Oeuvres

Yield: 48 servings

1¼ cups baking mix
1/2 cup finely chopped onion
1/2 cup grated Parmesan cheese
2 tablespoons chopped parsley
1/2 teaspoon baking powder
1/4 cup canola oil
4 eggs, slightly beaten
1/2 teaspoon garlic powder
1/2 teaspoon oregano
1/2 teaspoon seasoned salt
1/8 teaspoon pepper
3 cups grated zucchini

Mix first 11 ingredients in bowl. Fold in zucchini. Spread in lightly greased 9x13-inch baking pan. Bake at 350 degrees for 35 to 40 minutes or until set. Cut into 1½-inch squares. Serve warm.

Approx Per Serving: Cal 38; T Fat 2 g; 56% Calories from Fat; Prot 1 g; Carbo 3 g; Fiber <1 g; Chol 18 mg; Sod 80 mg.

Fruit Leather

Yield: 8 servings

2 cups drained crushed pineapple	2 cups crushed fresh strawberries
	2 cups sugar

Combine pineapple, strawberries and sugar in saucepan. Heat until sugar dissolves, stirring to mix well. Line 12x12-inch dehydrator pan with plastic wrap. Spread strawberry mixture in thin layer in prepared pan. Place in dehydrator. Set at high setting. Dry using manufacturer's directions until mixture is pliable but no longer sticky. Store, wrapped, in airtight container.

Approx Per Serving: Cal 248; T Fat <1 g; 1% Calories from Fat;
     Prot 1 g; Carbo 64 g; Fiber 3 g; Chol 0 mg; Sod 3 mg.

Chinese Oyster Crackers

Yield: 20 servings

¹/₂ cup oil	¹/₂ teaspoon garlic powder
1 16-ounce package oyster crackers	¹/₄ teaspoon curry powder
¹/₂ teaspoon Chinese 5-spice	¹/₂ envelope ranch salad dressing mix
1 teaspoon dillweed	

Combine oil and oyster crackers in bowl; mix well. Combine with 5-spice, dillweed, garlic powder, curry powder and salad dressing mix in paper bag. Shake bag every 10 minutes for 1 hour. Serve as hors d'oeuvre or with soup or salad.

Approx Per Serving: Cal 146; T Fat 8 g; 50% Calories from Fat;
     Prot 2 g; Carbo 16 g; Fiber 1 g; Chol 0 mg; Sod 333 mg.

Puppy Chow for People

Yield: 40 servings

1 cup milk chocolate chips	¹/₂ cup margarine
1 cup semisweet chocolate chips	1 12-ounce package Crispix
1 cup peanut butter	4 cups confectioners' sugar

Combine chocolate chips, peanut butter and margarine in saucepan. Heat over low heat until melted, stirring to mix well. Pour over cereal in large bowl; mix to coat well. Combine with confectioners' sugar in large paper bag. Shake until cereal is evenly coated.

Approx Per Serving: Cal 175; T Fat 8 g; 41% Calories from Fat;
     Prot 3 g; Carbo 25 g; Fiber 1 g; Chol 0 mg; Sod 124 mg.

Beverages

Mock Pink Champagne

Yield: 250 servings

12 cups sugar
6 quarts water
12 12-ounce cans frozen
   orange juice concentrate
12 12-ounce cans frozen
   grapefruit juice concentrate

24 28-ounce bottles of ginger
   ale, chilled
4 25-ounce bottles of
   grenadine syrup

Bring sugar and water to a boil in large saucepan. Cook for 5 minutes. Let stand until cool. Add juice concentrates. Chill in refrigerator. Pour into punch bowl. Add ginger ale and grenadine syrup. Serve at once. For 12 servings, use 1/2 cup sugar, 1 cup water, 6-ounce cans juice concentrates, 1 bottle of ginger ale and 1/2 cup grenadine syrup.

Approx Per Serving: Cal 155; T Fat <1 g; 1% Calories from Fat;
    Prot 1; Carbo 33 g; Fiber <1 g; Chol 0 mg; Sod 7 mg.

Mai Tai

Yield: 1 serving

1 cherry
1 slice pineapple
1 1/2 ounces light rum

1 1/2 ounces gold rum
1 ounce orgeat syrup
1/2 ounce 150-proof rum

Fill giant old-fashioned glasses with cracked ice. Place cherry and pineapple slice on toothpick. Add to glass. Pour remaining ingredients over ice. Garnish with vanda orchid and sprig of mint. Sip through straw.

Approx Per Serving: Cal 394; T Fat <1 g; 0% Calories from Fat;
    Prot <1; Carbo 21 g; Fiber 1 g; Chol 0 mg; Sod 3 mg.

Swedish Glogg

Yield: 30 servings

12 blanched almonds
6 whole cardamom seed
2 cinnamon sticks
3 whole cloves
¹/₄ cup raisins
¹/₄ cup currants

10 dried apricots
2 bottles of claret
1 pound lump sugar
1 bottle of vodka
1 cup brandy
2 bottles of port

Combine almonds, spices, fruit and claret in saucepan. Simmer for 1¹/₂ hours. Cool slightly. Strain, reserving fruit. Pour liquid into large punch bowl. Place wire rack over punch bowl. Arrange sugar on rack. Heat vodka and brandy in saucepan. Pour over sugar. Light sugar. Let flame for 10 minutes. Remove rack. Add heated port and reserved fruit.

Approx Per Serving: Cal 255; T Fat <1 g; 1% Calories from Fat;
    Prot <1; Carbo 28 g; Fiber <1 g; Chol 0 mg; Sod 8 mg.

Mint Julep

Yield: 1 serving

1 teaspoon sugar
1 tablespoon chopped mint
    leaves

1 tablespoon water
1 to 2 ounces Kentucky bourbon

Combine sugar and mint in bowl. Bruise leaves with muddler until smooth. Stir in water. Add bourbon. Pour into julep cup. Fill with crushed ice. Garnish with sprig of mint. Chill until frosted.

Approx Per Serving: Cal 145; T Fat 0 g; 0% Calories from Fat;
    Prot 0; Carbo 4 g; Fiber 0 g; Chol 0 mg; Sod <1 mg.

Company Mint Juleps

Yield: 12 servings

4 cups water
2 cups sugar
4 cups loosely packed mint
    leaves, chopped

4 cups bourbon
Crushed ice
12 mint leaves

Combine water and sugar in saucepan. Bring to a boil. Cook for 10 minutes. Add mint leaves. Simmer for 30 minutes. Let stand at room temperature overnight; strain. Add bourbon. Pour into crushed ice-filled julep cups. Garnish with mint leaves.

Approx Per Serving: Cal 298; T Fat 0 g; 0% Calories from Fat;
    Prot 0; Carbo 33 g; Fiber 0 g; Chol 0 mg; Sod 1 mg.

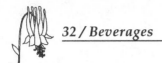

The Best Party Punch

Yield: 80 servings

1 ounce citric acid
4 pounds sugar
8 cups water
Juice of 6 lemons
2 46-ounce cans pineapple
    juice, chilled

1 46-ounce can grapefruit
    juice, chilled
1 2-quart bottle of ginger ale,
    chilled

Combine citric acid, sugar and water in large saucepan. Bring to a boil. Cook until sugar dissolves. Let stand until cool. Add juices. Pour over crushed ice in punch bowl. Add ginger ale. Punch may be frozen before adding ginger ale.

Approx Per Serving: Cal 122; T Fat <1 g; 0% Calories from Fat;
    Prot <1; Carbo 31 g; Fiber <1 g; Chol 0 mg; Sod 3 mg.

Flower Garden Punch

Yield: 24 servings

1 10-ounce jar mint jelly
1 cup hot water
1 cup fresh lemon juice

2 cups pineapple juice, chilled
2¹/₂ 18-ounce bottles of ginger
    ale

Dissolve mint jelly in water in pitcher. Let stand until cool. Add juices; mix well. Chill until serving time. Add ginger ale just before serving.

Approx Per Serving: Cal 63; T Fat <1 g; 1% Calories from Fat;
    Prot <1; Carbo 17 g; Fiber <1 g; Chol 0 mg; Sod 7 mg.

Golden Wedding Punch

Yield: 16 servings

2 6-ounce cans frozen orange
    juice concentrate
2 6-ounce cans frozen
    lemonade concentrate
2 5¹/₂-ounce cans apricot nectar

1 46-ounce can pineapple juice
6 cups water
1 cup sugar
2 18-ounce bottles of ginger
    ale, chilled

Combine thawed concentrates in pitcher. Add juices and water; mix well. Stir in sugar. Chill in refrigerator. Add ginger ale just before serving. May freeze before adding ginger ale.

Approx Per Serving: Cal 199; T Fat <1 g; 1% Calories from Fat;
    Prot 1; Carbo 50 g; Fiber 1 g; Chol 0 mg; Sod 8 mg.

Summer Juice

Yield: 9 servings

Freeze in ice cube trays for popsicles.

3 medium bananas
3 cups water
1 6-ounce can frozen orange
   juice concentrate

1 6-ounce can frozen guava
   juice concentrate
1 28-ounce can pineapple juice

Combine all ingredients in blender container. Process until blended. Chill until serving time.

Approx Per Serving: Cal 148; T Fat <1 g; 2% Calories from Fat;
    Prot 1; Carbo 37 g; Fiber <1 g; Chol 0 mg; Sod 2 mg.

Hot Wine Punch

Yield: 50 servings

Great after carolling at Christmas time.

2 32-ounce bottles of
   cranberry juice cocktail
4 cups water
4 cups sugar
4 cinnamon sticks

24 whole cloves
Peel of 1 lemon
1 gallon plus 1 fifth hearty
   Burgundy
1 cup lemon juice

Bring first 6 ingredients to a boil in saucepan. Cook until sugar is dissolved, stirring constantly. Simmer for 15 minutes. Add wine and lemon juice; strain.

Approx Per Serving: Cal 148; T Fat <1 g; 0% Calories from Fat;
    Prot <1; Carbo 23 g; Fiber <1 g; Chol 0 mg; Sod 6 mg.

Hot Buttered Rum Mix

Yield: enough mix for 48 servings

1 pint vanilla ice cream
1½ cups confectioners' sugar
1¼ cups packed dark brown
   sugar

1 cup butter, softened
1½ teaspoons nutmeg
1 teaspoon cinnamon

Combine all ingredients in blender container. Process until smooth. Spoon into airtight freezer container. Store in freezer. Combine 1 heaping tablespoon mix with 1 cup boiling water and 1 jigger dark rum in mug. Stir with cinnamon stick.

Approx Per Serving: Cal 86; T Fat 4 g; 45% Calories from Fat;
    Prot <1 g; Carbo 12 g; Fiber 0 g; Chol 13 mg; Sod 40 mg.

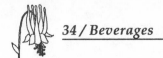

Wassail

Yield: 20 servings

An ideal warm-up after skating, skiing or snow shovelling.

4 cups hot tea
Juice of 5 lemons
1½ pounds brown sugar
1 gallon sweet cider
3 cinnamon sticks

1 tablespoon whole allspice
1 tablespoon whole cloves
½ teaspoon salt
5 oranges, sliced

Combine tea, lemon juice, brown sugar, cider, spices and salt in kettle. Bring to a boil. Simmer for 15 minutes, stirring frequently. Float orange slices on top. Serve hot.

Approx Per Serving: Cal 237; T Fat <1 g; 1% Calories from Fat;
    Prot <1; Carbo 61 g; Fiber 1 g; Chol 0 mg; Sod 74 mg.

Fireside Coffee

Yield: 96 servings

Fill small decorated jars with coffee mix for good gifts.

2 cups instant hot chocolate mix
2 cups non-dairy powdered
  creamer
1 cup instant coffee

1½ cups sugar
1 teaspoon cinnamon
½ teaspoon nutmeg

Combine all ingredients in bowl; mix well. Store in airtight container. Mix 3 to 4 teaspoons with 1 cup hot water for each serving.

Approx Per Serving: Cal 31; T Fat 1 g; 26% Calories from Fat;
    Prot 1; Carbo 6 g; Fiber <1 g; Chol 0 mg; Sod 13 mg.

Russian Tea

Yield: 120 servings

2 cups Tang
1 to 2 cups sugar
1 cup instant tea powder

1 3-ounce package lemonade mix
1 teaspoon cinnamon
1 teaspoon ground cloves

Combine Tang, sugar, tea powder, lemonade mix and spices in jar; mix well. Store, tightly covered, until serving time. Use 2 teaspoons to 1 cup hot water for each serving.

Approx Per Serving: Cal 28; T Fat <1 g; 0% Calories from Fat;
    Prot <1; Carbo 7 g; Fiber <1 g; Chol 0 mg; Sod 3 mg.

Soups & Salads

Atlantic Seaboard

Central Atlantic

Delaware • Maryland • National Capital Area
New Jersey • New York • Ohio • Pennsylvania

*T*he Region was the birthplace of National Council and for many years the home of the National Council of State Garden Clubs, Inc. was in New York City. Many National Council activities had their beginning in this Region including the first Garden Center, the first Flower Show School, the first mile of Blue Star Memorial Highway, The Friendship Garden at the United States National Arboretum, Washington, D.C. and now AmeriFlora '92 in celebration of Columbus' voyage to our New World.

Dinner from the Chesapeake

Clams Casino*   Cream of Crab Soup
Spinach Salad
Soft Shell Crabs   Crab Cakes*
Scalloped Oysters   Crab Meat Maryland*
Baked Stuffed Rockfish*   Vegetables of Choice
Sweet Potato Biscuits*
Lemon Meringue Pie

Pennsylvania Dutch Dinner

Pennsylvania Dutch cooking is known for being "hearty" and filling. Usually meals include "seven sweets and seven sours."

Chicken Potpie*
Salad of Endive, Escarole and Dandelion Greens
Hot Bacon Dressing*
Red Eggs and Pickled Beets*
Mashed Potato Casserole*
Apple Pie or Rice Pudding

*See index for recipes.

Soups

Cold Cantaloupe Soup

Yield: 4 servings

1 large ripe cantaloupe
2¼ cups orange juice

½ teaspoon cinnamon
2 tablespoons lime juice

Peel and chop cantaloupe coarsely. Purée with remaining ingredients in food processor. Chill until serving time. Garnish with mint sprigs.

Approx Per Serving: Cal 121; T Fat 1 g; 5% Calories from Fat;
    Prot 2 g; Carbo 29 g; Fiber 2 g; Chol 0 mg; Sod 15 mg.

Daniel Boone Hotel Cheese Soup

Yield: 8 servings

1 cup melted butter
6½ tablespoons flour
½ cup minced celery
½ cup minced carrot
½ cup minced onion
4½ cups milk

1 teaspoon white pepper
2 chicken bouillon cubes,
    crushed
2 cups wine
2¾ cups shredded sharp
    Cheddar cheese

Blend butter and flour in large heavy soup pot. Add minced vegetables. Stir in milk gradually. Cook until thickened, stirring constantly. Add remaining ingredients. Simmer for 15 minutes, stirring frequently.

Approx Per Serving: Cal 313; T Fat 18 g; 51% Calories from Fat;
    Prot 15 g; Carbo 14 g; Fiber 1 g; Chol 60 mg; Sod 598 mg.

Thirteen-Bean Soup

Yield: 10 servings

At Christmas, keep 2-cup jars of mixed dried beans—red, white, black, pinto, garbanzo, etc.—with your recipe attached in a basket by the front door for visitors.

2 cups mixed dried beans
7 cups water
1 pound ham, cubed
1 12-ounce can beer
2 cups chopped onions
2 cups chopped celery and leaves
4 to 6 cloves of garlic, chopped
2 16-ounce cans stewed
   tomatoes

1 green bell pepper, chopped
1 pound smoked sausage,
   thinly sliced
1½ pounds boned chicken,
   chopped
¾ cup chopped green onions
   and parsley
Seasoned salt and cayenne
   pepper to taste

Rinse and drain beans. Combine with water, ham and beer in 8-quart soup pot. Bring to a simmer. Add onions, celery, garlic, tomatoes, green pepper and sausage. Simmer, covered, for 2 hours, stirring occasionally. Add chicken, green onions and parsley, seasoned salt and cayenne pepper. Simmer until chicken is cooked, adding broth if necessary.

Approx Per Serving: Cal 439; T Fat 14 g; 29% Calories from Fat;
    Prot 41 g; Carbo 36 g; Fiber 8 g; Chol 88 mg; Sod 1245 mg.

New Mexico Chili Bean Soup

Yield: 6 servings

2 cups dried pinto beans
1 pound ham, cubed
4 cups water
1 22-ounce can tomato juice
2 cups chicken stock
3 onions, chopped
3 cloves of garlic, minced
¼ cup chopped green bell
   pepper
2 tablespoons brown sugar

1 teaspoon each salt, chili
   powder, crushed bay leaves,
   MSG and oregano
¼ teaspoon each crushed
   rosemary leaves, celery seed,
   thyme, marjoram and sweet
   basil
1 4-ounce can chopped green
   chilies
1 cup sherry

Rinse beans. Soak in water to cover overnight. Drain and rinse. Combine with ham, 4 cups water, tomato juice, chicken stock, onions, garlic, green pepper, brown sugar, seasonings and green chilies in soup pot. Simmer, covered, for 3 hours or until beans are tender. Stir in sherry. Ladle into soup bowls. Garnish with chopped green onions.

Approx Per Serving: Cal 453; T Fat 5 g; 11% Calories from Fat;
    Prot 37 g; Carbo 54 g; Fiber 16 g; Chol 42 mg; Sod 2149 mg.

Jerusalem Artichoke Soup

Yield: 4 servings

More than 200 varieties of Jerusalem artichokes are grown in Europe.
This is a French recipe from 1890.

1 pound Jerusalem artichokes
1 small red onion, chopped
1/4 cup butter
3 cups chicken stock

6 tablespoons whipping cream
1/2 teaspoon cinnamon
1/4 teaspoon nutmeg
Salt and pepper to taste

Cook unpeeled artichokes in water to cover in saucepan until skins can be removed. Drain, peel and chop artichokes. Sauté onion in butter in saucepan until tender. Add artichokes. Sauté for 5 minutes. Add chicken stock. Simmer for 35 minutes. Mash with potato masher. Simmer for 10 minutes longer. Stir in 6 tablespoons whipping cream. Simmer until thickened, stirring frequently. Stir in seasonings. Ladle into soup bowls. Garnish with drizzle of additional cream and pinch of additional cinnamon and nutmeg.

Approx Per Serving: Cal 268; T Fat 21 g; 68% Calories from Fat; Prot 7 g; Carbo 15 g; Fiber 10 g; Chol 62 mg; Sod 762 mg.

Apple-Butternut Bisque

Yield: 8 servings

1/4 cup margarine
1 cup coarsely chopped onion
2 cups chopped peeled apples
4 cups cubed peeled butternut
   squash
1 cup chopped celery
4 cups chicken stock

1 tablespoon molasses
2 tablespoons honey
2 teaspoons salt
1/4 teaspoon pepper
1/4 teaspoon nutmeg
1 cup whipping cream
1/2 cup coarsely chopped pecans

Heat margarine in large heavy saucepan until foamy. Add onion. Sauté until tender. Add apples, squash, celery and chicken stock. Simmer, covered, for 15 to 20 minutes or until squash is tender. Let stand until cool. Purée in blender or food processor; return to saucepan. Bring to a simmer. Stir in molasses, honey, salt, pepper, nutmeg and 1/2 cup cream. Heat to serving temperature; do not boil. Whip remaining 1/2 cup cream in bowl. Ladle soup into bowls. Top each serving with 2 tablespoons whipped cream and 1 tablespoon pecans.

Approx Per Serving: Cal 313; T Fat 23 g; 62% Calories from Fat; Prot 5 g; Carbo 26 g; Fiber 5 g; Chol 41 mg; Sod 1017 mg.

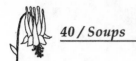

Cheesy Vegetable-Chicken Chowder Yield: 8 servings

1/2 cup chopped onion
1 clove of garlic
Celery salt or powder to taste
3/4 cup sliced carrots
2 cups chopped peeled potatoes
3 1/2 cups chicken broth
1 17-ounce can whole kernel
   corn, drained

1/4 cup melted margarine
1/4 cup flour
2 cups warm milk
Salt and pepper to taste
1/8 teaspoon paprika
1 2-ounce jar pimento strips
8 ounces Velveeta cheese
2 cups chopped cooked chicken

Combine onion, garlic, celery salt, carrots, potatoes and chicken broth in large soup pot. Simmer, covered, for 15 to 20 minutes or until potatoes are tender. Stir in corn; remove from heat. Blend margarine and flour in medium saucepan. Cook for 1 to 2 minutes, stirring constantly. Stir in warm milk gradually. Cook over medium heat until thickened, stirring constantly. Add salt, pepper, paprika, pimento, cheese and chicken. Cook until cheese melts, stirring constantly. Stir into vegetable mixture. Heat to serving temperature over low heat.

Approx Per Serving: Cal 378; T Fat 21 g; 48% Calories from Fat;
    Prot 24 g; Carbo 27 g; Fiber 2 g; Chol 67 mg; Sod 1011 mg.

Tortilla Soup Yield: 10 servings

*Double this "Mexican" French onion soup recipe for
a party—everyone wants seconds.*

1 medium onion, chopped
2 cloves of garlic, minced
2 tablespoons vegetable oil
3 beef bouillon cubes
3 cups water
2 cups chicken broth
1 teaspoon salt

1 teaspoon Worcestershire sauce
12 corn tortillas, cut into strips
Oil for frying
1 cup chopped cooked chicken
1/2 cup tomato juice
2 10-ounce cans tomatoes with
   jalapeño peppers

Sauté onion and garlic in 2 tablespoons oil in 5-quart saucepan. Add next 5 ingredients. Simmer for 1 hour. Deep-fry tortillas in hot oil until crisp; drain on paper towels. Add chicken, tomato juice and tomatoes with jalapeño peppers. Simmer for 5 minutes. Place several tortilla chips in each soup bowl. Ladle soup into bowls. Garnish with shredded Monterey Jack cheese or grated Parmesan cheese. Serve with remaining tortilla chips.

Approx Per Serving: Cal 158; T Fat 5 g; 30% Calories from Fat;
    Prot 8 g; Carbo 20 g; Fiber 4 g; Chol 13 mg; Sod 782 mg.
    Nutritional information does not include oil for frying.

Tortilla Dumpling Soup
Yield: 6 servings

May add or substitute half a can of pinto beans for corn if you wish.

½ cup chopped onion
2 cloves of garlic, crushed
1 28-ounce can tomatoes
4 cups chicken broth
1 cup shredded cooked chicken
  breast

½ cup medium picante sauce
1 16-ounce can whole kernel
  corn, drained
6 soft corn tortillas
1 cup shredded Monterey Jack
  cheese

Sauté onion and garlic in soup pot. Purée tomatoes in blender. Add tomatoes, broth, chicken, picante sauce and corn to soup pot. Simmer for 30 minutes. Cut tortillas into strips. Add to soup. Simmer for 10 minutes. Ladle into soup bowls. Sprinkle with cheese.

Approx Per Serving: Cal 294; T Fat 10 g; 28% Calories from Fat;
    Prot 19 g; Carbo 37 g; Fiber 5 g; Chol 34 mg; Sod 1131 mg.

Cream of Cauliflower Soup
Yield: 6 servings

2 to 3 cups chicken stock
2 cups water
Flowerets of 1 head cauliflower
¼ cup butter, melted

⅓ cup flour
½ cup sour cream
1 teaspoon salt
¼ teaspoon lemon juice

Bring stock and water to a boil in saucepan. Add cauliflowerets. Simmer, covered, until tender. Remove cauliflower with slotted spoon. Blend butter and flour in soup pot. Cook for 1 minute, stirring constantly. Blend in sour cream, salt and lemon juice. Add cooking liquid gradually. Add cauliflower. Simmer for 30 minutes, stirring occasionally.

Approx Per Serving: Cal 169; T Fat 13 g; 65% Calories from Fat;
    Prot 5 g; Carbo 10 g; Fiber 2 g; Chol 30 mg; Sod 828 mg.

Cold Crab Soup à la Baltimore
Yield: 6 servings

1 6-ounce can crab meat, drained
1 tablespoon curry powder

2 10-ounce cans cream of
  vichyssoise soup

Combine crab meat, curry powder and soup in bowl. Chill until serving time. Serve in chilled soup bowls or mugs.

Approx Per Serving: Cal 86; T Fat 3 g; 30% Calories from Fat;
    Prot 8 g; Carbo 7 g; Fiber 0 g; Chol 34 mg; Sod 512 mg.

No-Clam Chowder

Yield: 5 servings

1 medium onion, thinly sliced
3 tablespoons bacon drippings
1½ cups chopped peeled
   potatoes
½ cup water

1 17-ounce can cream-style corn
2 cups milk
1 teaspoon salt
Pepper to taste
5 slices crisp-fried bacon

Sauté onion in bacon drippings in saucepan until lightly browned. Add potatoes and water. Cook, covered, over medium heat for 10 to 15 minutes or until tender. Add corn, milk, salt and pepper. Heat to serving temperature over low heat, stirring frequently; do not boil. Ladle into soup bowls. Top with crumbled bacon.

Approx Per Serving: Cal 288; T Fat 15 g; 46% Calories from Fat;
    Prot 8 g; Carbo 33 g; Fiber 3 g; Chol 69 mg; Sod 930 mg.

Clam Chowder

Yield: 10 servings

4 slices bacon
3 medium onions, chopped
1 stalk celery
4 7-ounce cans clams
4 medium potatoes, peeled,
   chopped, cooked

2 carrots, chopped, cooked
4 cups milk
1 cup light cream
Salt and pepper to taste
1 8-ounce bottle of clam juice
2 tablespoons butter

Fry bacon in 3-quart saucepan until crisp; drain, reserving drippings. Sauté onions and celery in bacon drippings in saucepan. Add undrained clams and drained vegetables. Stir in milk, cream, salt and pepper. Bring to a simmer, stirring constantly. Add clam juice and butter. Simmer for 10 minutes.

Approx Per Serving: Cal 276; T Fat 24 g; 67% Calories from Fat;
    Prot 12 g; Carbo 15 g; Fiber 2 g; Chol 122 mg; Sod 242 mg.

Forsythia

Clam Bisque Elegante

Yield: 6 servings

½ cup chopped onion
6 tablespoons butter
6 tablespoons flour
1 8-ounce bottle of clam juice

3 6-ounce cans minced clams
3 cups light cream
3 tablespoons lemon juice
3 tablespoons tomato paste

Sauté onion in butter in 3-quart saucepan until golden brown. Add flour. Cook until bubbly, stirring constantly. Add clam juice and undrained clams. Cook until thickened and bubbly, stirring constantly. Cook for 1 minute. Simmer, covered, for 15 minutes. Stir in mixture of cream, lemon juice and tomato paste. Heat to serving temperature over low heat, stirring frequently.

Approx Per Serving: Cal 538; T Fat 55 g; 83% Calories from Fat; Prot 11 g; Carbo 15 g; Fiber 1 g; Chol 217 mg; Sod 261 mg.

Chesapeake House Fish Stew

Yield: 8 servings

*The Chesapeake House in Myrtle Beach will let you
sample this house specialty.*

8 ounces bacon, chopped
1 cup chopped onion
3 cups water
3 pounds flounder filets, cut up
1 tablespoon Tabasco sauce

2 tablespoons Worcestershire
  sauce
Salt and pepper to taste
1 6-ounce can tomato paste
1 16-ounce bottle of catsup

Fry bacon in skillet until crisp; drain, reserving bacon drippings. Sauté onion in drippings until brown. Bring water to a boil in soup pot. Add sautéed onion with drippings, flounder, Tabasco sauce, Worcestershire sauce, salt and pepper. Cook, covered, over low heat until fish flakes easily. Add tomato paste and catsup. Simmer for 2 hours. Serve with crackers or over hot cooked rice.

Approx Per Serving: Cal 406; T Fat 19 g; 43% Calories from Fat; Prot 38 g; Carbo 21 g; Fiber 2 g; Chol 174 mg; Sod 1051 mg.

*Prune forsythia and honeysuckle, as well as other
spring-flowering shrubs, after they bloom; shrubs
that flower in summer should be pruned when
they are dormant.*

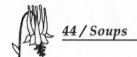

Garden Gazpacho

Yield: 8 servings

12 ripe red tomatoes
1 large green bell pepper
1 cucumber
1 medium onion
1 tablespoon sugar

1 tablespoon olive oil
2 tablespoons balsamic vinegar
Basil, parsley, salt and pepper
    to taste

Core tomatoes; seed green pepper and cucumber. Cut all vegetables into large chunks. Chop coarsely a small amount at a time in food processor using steel blade and adding sugar, olive oil, vinegar and seasonings. Combine in large bowl; mix well. Chill until serving time.

Approx Per Serving: Cal 71; T Fat 2 g; 25% Calories from Fat;
    Prot 2 g; Carbo 13 g; Fiber 4 g; Chol 0 mg; Sod 17 mg.

Portuguese Ham-Kidney Bean Soup

Yield: 8 servings

1 pound smoked ham, cubed
1½ cups dried red kidney beans
1 8-ounce can tomato sauce
4 stalks celery, chopped
1 cup chopped onion

6 cloves of garlic, chopped
Salt and pepper to taste
3 carrots, chopped
3 medium potatoes, peeled,
    chopped

Cook ham in water to cover by 1 inch in 2-quart saucepan for 30 minutes or until tender. Add beans. Cook, covered, until beans are half cooked. Add tomato sauce, celery, onion, garlic, salt and pepper. Simmer for 15 minutes. Add carrots and potatoes. Simmer for 20 minutes longer or until vegetables are tender.

Approx Per Serving: Cal 236; T Fat 2 g; 8% Calories from Fat;
    Prot 17 g; Carbo 39 g; Fiber 10 g; Chol 16 mg; Sod 586 mg.

Tea Rose

Vi's Kettle of Soup
Yield: 12 servings

1½ pounds ground beef
2 15-ounce cans tomato sauce
1 tomato sauce can water
3 cups coarsely chopped celery
4 large carrots, sliced
1 large onion, chopped

1 tomato, finely chopped
1 tablespoon seasoned pepper
1 packet Sweet 'N Low
Salt to taste
1 16-ounce package frozen
    oriental vegetables

Cook ground beef in large soup pot until brown and crumbly, stirring frequently; drain. Add tomato sauce, water, celery, carrots, onion, tomato, seasoned pepper, Sweet 'N Low and salt. Simmer, covered, until vegetables are tender-crisp. Add oriental vegetables. Simmer until tender, adding a small amount of water as necessary.

Approx Per Serving: Cal 180; T Fat 8 g; 40% Calories from Fat;
    Prot 13 g; Carbo 15 g; Fiber 4 g; Chol 37 mg; Sod 510 mg.

Mock Turtle Soup
Yield: 10 servings

1 pound ground beef
1 large onion, chopped
1 cup browned flour
2 tablespoons red wine vinegar
1 tablespoon A-1 sauce
1 12-ounce can beef gravy

1 12-ounce bottle of catsup
3 beef bouillon cubes
1 tablespoon whole allspice
10 cups water
1 lemon, thinly sliced
2 hard-boiled eggs, chopped

Brown ground beef with onion in 3-quart saucepan, stirring frequently; drain. Mix in flour. Add vinegar, A-1 sauce, gravy, catsup, bouillon cubes and allspice. Stir in water. Cook until thickened, stirring constantly. Cool. Let stand overnight for improved flavor. Reheat over low heat, stirring frequently. Ladle into soup bowls. Garnish with lemon slices and chopped hard-boiled egg.

Approx Per Serving: Cal 217; T Fat 9 g; 36% Calories from Fat;
    Prot 13 g; Carbo 22 g; Fiber 1 g; Chol 73 mg; Sod 670 mg.

Learning the technique of applying the proper amount of water is the most difficult aspect of gardening, whether one is cultivating a potted plant, seedlings or growing large or small plants out of doors. It requires knowledge and observation.

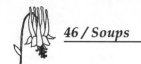

Mushroom Soup

Yield: 6 servings

*Serve as an appetizer or as a whole meal with homemade
bread on a snowy evening.*

8 ounces fresh mushrooms,
  sliced
2 tablespoons butter
1 medium onion, chopped
2 tablespoons butter
1/4 cup flour

1 teaspoon salt
1/4 teaspoon pepper
1 10-ounce can chicken broth
1 broth can water
1 cup half and half

Sauté mushrooms in 2 tablespoons butter in skillet until golden; remove with slotted spoon. Sauté onion in 2 tablespoons butter in skillet until tender. Stir in flour, salt and pepper. Cook for 1 to 2 minutes, stirring constantly. Add broth and water. Bring to a boil, stirring constantly. Add half and half and sautéed mushrooms. Heat to serving temperature; do not boil.

Approx Per Serving: Cal 165; T Fat 13 g; 68% Calories from Fat;
    Prot 4 g; Carbo 10 g; Fiber 1 g; Chol 36 mg; Sod 589 mg.

Golden Cream of Potato Soup

Yield: 4 servings

3 cups chopped peeled potatoes
1 cup water
1/2 cup sliced celery
1/2 cup sliced carrot
1/4 cup chopped onion
1 chicken bouillon cube
1 teaspoon parsley flakes

1/2 teaspoon salt
Pepper to taste
1 1/2 cups milk
2 tablespoons flour
4 ounces Mexican Velveeta
  cheese, chopped

Combine potatoes, water, celery, carrot, onion, bouillon cube, parsley flakes, salt and pepper in 1 1/2-quart saucepan. Simmer, covered, until vegetables are tender. Blend a small amount of milk with flour in bowl; mix in remaining milk. Stir into soup. Cook until thickened, stirring constantly. Add cheese. Cook until cheese melts, stirring constantly.

Approx Per Serving: Cal 275; T Fat 12 g; 39% Calories from Fat;
    Prot 12 g; Carbo 30 g; Fiber 2 g; Chol 40 mg; Sod 1020 mg.

Italian Sausage Soup with Tortellini *Yield: 8 servings*

1 pound Italian sausage
1 cup coarsely chopped onion
2 cloves of garlic, minced
5 cups beef broth
1/2 cup water
1 cup dry red wine
2 cups chopped peeled tomatoes

1 cup sliced carrots
1/2 teaspoon basil
1 teaspoon oregano
1   8-ounce can tomato sauce
3 tablespoons chopped parsley
1 medium green bell pepper
2 cups fresh or frozen tortellini

Remove casing from sausage. Brown in soup pot, stirring until crumbly; drain and set aside. Sauté onion and garlic in soup pot until tender. Add broth, water, wine, tomatoes, carrots, basil, oregano, tomato sauce and sausage. Simmer, covered, for 30 minutes. Skim soup. Stir in parsley, green pepper and tortellini. Simmer, covered, for 35 to 40 minutes or until tortellini is tender. Ladle into soup bowls. Garnish with sprinkle of Parmesan cheese.

Approx Per Serving: Cal 249; T Fat 11 g; 42% Calories from Fat;
    Prot 13 g; Carbo 21 g; Fiber 2 g; Chol 36 mg; Sod 1118 mg.

Cream of Peanut Soup *Yield: 8 servings*

1 cup thinly sliced celery
1 medium onion, finely
    chopped
1/4 cup butter

2 tablespoons flour
4   13-ounce cans chicken broth
1 cup creamy peanut butter
1 cup light cream

Sauté celery and onion in butter in soup pot over low heat until tender but not brown. Add flour; mix well. Stir in chicken broth gradually. Bring to a boil, stirring constantly. Add peanut butter; mix well. Simmer for 15 minutes. Add cream just before serving.

Approx Per Serving: Cal 375; T Fat 33 g; 75% Calories from Fat;
    Prot 14 g; Carbo 10 g; Fiber 3 g; Chol 49 mg; Sod 788 mg.

Honeysuckle

Cold Red Raspberry Soup

Yield: 8 servings

This beautiful, tasty soup welcomes the family to Christmas dinner.

2 10-ounce packages frozen red raspberries	**¹/₂ cup sour cream**
¹/₂ cup rosé	**1 cup raspberry sherbet**
	¹/₂ cup milk

Combine raspberries, wine, sour cream, sherbet and milk in blender container; process until well blended. Strain if desired. Pour into small bowls. Float lime slice on top. Add several drops of fresh lime juice.

Approx Per Serving: Cal 157; T Fat 4 g; 24% Calories from Fat; Prot 2 g; Carbo 27 g; Fiber 3 g; Chol 10 mg; Sod 27 mg.

Cold Squash Soup

Yield: 6 servings

1 pound yellow summer squash	**¹/₂ cup sour cream**
1 medium onion	**Salt and white pepper to taste**
1¹/₂ cups chicken stock	**Dillweed to taste**

Scrub squash. Chop squash and onion finely. Cook in 1 cup chicken stock in saucepan for 30 minutes or until tender. Purée in blender or food processor. Blend with remaining ¹/₂ cup chicken stock in bowl. Let stand until cool. Blend in sour cream, salt and pepper. Garnish with dillweed.

Approx Per Serving: Cal 75; T Fat 5 g; 53% Calories from Fat; Prot 3 g; Carbo 6 g; Fiber 2 g; Chol 9 mg; Sod 207 mg.

Tomato Bouillon

Yield: 4 servings

1 small onion, chopped	**¹/₂ small bay leaf**
3 cups strained tomato juice	**2 tablespoons chopped fennel**
¹/₄ cup chopped celery and leaves	**2 whole cloves**
	1 tablespoon fresh basil

Sauté onion in skillet until tender. Combine with remaining ingredients in saucepan. Simmer for 5 minutes. Strain; skim if necessary. Adjust seasonings. Discard bay leaf. Garnish with dollop of sour cream.

Approx Per Serving: Cal 42; T Fat <1 g; 4% Calories from Fat; Prot 2 g; Carbo 10 g; Fiber 2 g; Chol 0 mg; Sod 668 mg.

Cream of Zucchini Soup

Yield: 4 servings

Prepare and freeze the zucchini mixture to use that extra zucchini.
Make the white sauce and add zucchini anytime.

3 cups sliced zucchini
½ cup water
1 tablespoon instant minced
  onion
½ teaspoon seasoned salt
1 teaspoon parsley flakes
1 teaspoon instant chicken
  bouillon

2 tablespoons melted butter
2 tablespoons flour
⅓ teaspoon white pepper
1 teaspoon instant chicken
  bouillon
1 cup milk
½ cup half and half

Combine zucchini, water, onion, seasoned salt, parsley flakes and 1 teaspoon chicken bouillon in saucepan. Cook until zucchini is tender and a small amount of liquid remains. Process in blender or put through sieve; set aside. Blend butter and flour in large saucepan. Add pepper and 1 teaspoon chicken bouillon; mix well. Stir in milk and half and half. Cook until thickened, stirring constantly. Stir in zucchini mixture. Heat to serving temperature. Add additional milk if desired.

Approx Per Serving: Cal 163; T Fat 12 g; 64% Calories from Fat;
    Prot 5 g; Carbo 10 g; Fiber 1 g; Chol 35 mg; Sod 691 mg.

Beefy Vegetable Soup

Yield: 12 servings

1 14-ounce can tomatoes,
   mashed
1 15-ounce can tomato sauce
6 cups water
¼ cup chopped onion
1 medium carrot, sliced
2 stalks celery, sliced
2 medium potatoes, cubed
¼ cup chopped green bell
   pepper

1 small turnip, cubed
1 cup chopped cabbage
1 cup frozen corn
3 small bay leaves
Mrs. Dash herbs and spices to
   taste
1 pound beef cubes
Salt and pepper to taste
2 tablespoons oil

Combine tomatoes, tomato sauce and water in 5-quart soup pot. Add next 10 ingredients. Bring to a simmer. Cut beef into small pieces; season with salt and pepper. Sauté beef in oil in skillet until tender; do not brown. Add to soup mixture. Simmer, covered, for 1 hour or until vegetables are tender. Discard bay leaves.

Approx Per Serving: Cal 111; T Fat 5 g; 36% Calories from Fat;
    Prot 9 g; Carbo 10 g; Fiber 2 g; Chol 21 mg; Sod 296 mg.

Salads

Spicy Applesauce Mold

Yield: 6 servings

1/2 cup red hot cinnamon candies
1 cup water
1   6-ounce package raspberry
   gelatin

2   15-ounce cans applesauce
2 tablespoons vinegar

Melt candies in boiling water in saucepan. Pour over gelatin in large bowl; stir until gelatin dissolves. Stir in applesauce and vinegar. Pour into 6-cup mold. Chill until firm. Unmold onto serving plate. Garnish with endive and orange slices.

Approx Per Serving: Cal 297; T Fat <1 g; 1% Calories from Fat;
   Prot 3 g; Carbo 74 g; Fiber 2 g; Chol 0 mg; Sod 98 mg.

Artichoke Rice Salad

Yield: 8 servings

1   7-ounce package chicken-
   flavored Rice-A-Roni, cooked
2 green onions, chopped
1 green bell pepper, chopped
1/2 cup sliced black olives

1   6-ounce jar marinated
   artichoke hearts
1/2 teaspoon curry powder
1/3 cup reduced-calorie
   mayonnaise

Combine rice, green onions, green pepper and olives in bowl. Drain artichoke hearts, reserving marinade. Blend reserved marinade with curry powder and mayonnaise in small bowl. Add artichokes to rice mixture. Add dressing; mix gently. Chill until serving time.

Approx Per Serving: Cal 96; T Fat 6 g; 57% Calories from Fat;
   Prot 1 g; Carbo 10 g; Fiber 2 g; Chol 3 mg; Sod 344 mg.

Broccoli Salad

Yield: 12 servings

Flowerets of 1 bunch broccoli
1 cup chopped celery
1/2 cup chopped red onion
6 slices crisp-fried bacon,
    crumbled
1/2 cup raisins

1   11-ounce can mandarin
    oranges, drained
3/4 cup reduced-fat mayonnaise
2 tablespoons vinegar
1/4 cup sugar
1/2 cup sliced almonds, toasted

Combine broccoli, celery, onion, bacon, raisins and mandarin oranges in salad bowl. Blend mayonnaise, vinegar and sugar in small bowl. Add to broccoli mixture; mix until coated. Top with almonds. Chill until serving time.

Approx Per Serving: Cal 141; T Fat 7 g; 41% Calories from Fat;
    Prot 3 g; Carbo 19 g; Fiber 2 g; Chol 7 mg; Sod 145 mg.

Caesar Salad à la Swordfish

Yield: 4 servings

1 large clove of garlic
1/2 cup olive oil
1/4 cup fresh lemon juice
3 tablespoons sour cream
1 tablespoon Worcestershire
    sauce
1/2 teaspoon anchovy paste
1 teaspoon Dijon mustard
1/2 teaspoon salt

1/4 teaspoon freshly ground
    pepper
3   6-ounce swordfish steaks
3 small heads romaine lettuce
1 1/2 cups freshly grated
    Parmesan cheese
Salt and freshly ground pepper
    to taste

Process garlic, olive oil, lemon juice, sour cream, Worcestershire sauce, anchove paste, mustard, 1/2 teaspoon salt and 1/4 teaspoon pepper in blender or food processor; set aside. Rinse fish; pat dry. Brush 1 tablespoon olive oil mixture on both sides of each fish steak. Place fish in grilling basket over hot coals. Grill for 3 minutes on each side or until opaque in center. Place on warm plate; tent with foil. Rinse romaine lettuce; pat dry. Tear into bite-sized pieces; place in large salad bowl. Pour remaining dressing over romaine lettuce. Add 1 cup cheese, salt and pepper; toss to mix. Divide salad among 4 salad plates. Cut fish into bite-sized pieces; arrange in center of romaine lettuce. Sprinkle with remaining cheese. Serve immediately.

Approx Per Serving: Cal 589; T Fat 44 g; 67% Calories from Fat;
    Prot 41 g; Carbo 7 g; Fiber 2 g; Chol 79 mg; Sod 1019 mg.

Creamy Chicken Salad

Yield: 4 servings

1½ cups chopped cooked
  chicken
1 cup thinly sliced celery
1 tablespoon lemon juice
½ teaspoon grated lemon rind
2 green onions, finely chopped
½ teaspoon salt

⅛ teaspoon paprika
¼ cup white wine
1 medium avocado
½ cup coarsely chopped salted
  cashews
⅓ cup mayonnaise

Combine chicken, celery, lemon juice, lemon rind, green onions, salt, paprika and wine in bowl. Chill for several hours. Peel avocado; cut into small chunks or balls. Add avocado, cashews and mayonnaise to chicken mixture; toss lightly. Serve in crisp lettuce cups.

Approx Per Serving: Cal 414; T Fat 33 g; 72% Calories from Fat;
    Prot 19 g; Carbo 10 g; Fiber 6 g; Chol 58 mg; Sod 540 mg.

Curried Chicken Salad

Yield: 8 servings

3 cups chopped cooked chicken
½ cup finely chopped celery
1 8-ounce can sliced water
  chestnuts, drained
1 medium apple, chopped
¾ cup green grape halves
1 8-ounce can pineapple
  tidbits, drained
½ cup raisins

½ cup slivered almonds
1¼ cups reduced-calorie
  mayonnaise
¼ cup pineapple juice
1 tablespoon reduced-sodium
  soy sauce
1 tablespoon vinegar
¼ teaspoon lemon juice
1 to 3 teaspoons curry powder

Combine first 8 ingredients in salad bowl. Blend mayonnaise with pineapple juice, soy sauce, vinegar, lemon juice and curry powder in small bowl. Add to chicken mixture; toss to mix. Chill for several hours. Serve on lettuce-lined plates with breadsticks and melon wedges.

Approx Per Serving: Cal 329; T Fat 16 g; 43% Calories from Fat;
    Prot 18 g; Carbo 30 g; Fiber 3 g; Chol 57 mg; Sod 341 mg.

Chrysanthemum blooms range in taste from faintly peppery to a mild cauliflower flavor. Blanch petals and sprinkle them on a salad or try leaves in a vinaigrette.

Japanese Chicken Salad

Yield: 8 servings

3 chicken breasts, cooked,
   shredded
1 head lettuce, shredded
4 green onions, slivered
2 tablespoons sesame seed,
   toasted
3 tablespoons almonds, toasted,
   chopped

2 ounces bean thread
Oil for deep frying
1/4 cup sugar
2 teaspoons salt
1/2 teaspoon pepper
1 teaspoon MSG
1/4 cup vinegar
1/2 cup vegetable oil

Combine chicken, lettuce, green onions, sesame seed and almonds in salad bowl. Deep-fry bean thread in hot oil in skillet a small amount at a time until puffed and golden; drain on paper towels. Mix sugar, salt, pepper, MSG, vinegar and oil in covered container; shake vigorously. Add bean thread and dressing to salad; toss lightly. Serve immediately.

Approx Per Serving: Cal 237; T Fat 18 g; 67% Calories from Fat;
   Prot 12 g; Carbo 8 g; Fiber 1 g; Chol 27 mg; Sod 1097 mg.
   Nutritional information does not include bean thread and oil
   for deep frying.

Tropical Chicken Salad

Yield: 4 servings

1 pound chicken breast and
   thighs, boned, skinned
1 teaspoon oil
Salt and pepper to taste
1 apple, thinly sliced
1 small banana, sliced

1 8-ounce can pineapple
   tidbits, drained
1 teaspoon mango chutney
2 teaspoons sour cream
1 teaspoon mayonnaise
2 teaspoons curry powder

Rinse chicken; pat dry. Cut into slices. Cook in oil in skillet until brown. Season with salt and pepper. Combine in bowl with apple, banana and pineapple. Blend chutney and remaining ingredients in bowl. Add chicken mixture; mix well. Chill, covered, until serving time.

Approx Per Serving: Cal 234; T Fat 6 g; 22% Calories from Fat;
   Prot 27 g; Carbo 18 g; Fiber 2 g; Chol 74 mg; Sod 79 mg.

Raspberry

Pesto Chicken Salad

Yield: 6 servings

2 cups chopped cooked chicken
1 red bell pepper, chopped
1 green bell pepper, chopped
½ cup chopped pecans

½ cup chopped celery
1 Granny Smith apple, chopped
¼ cup (about) mayonnaise
2 tablespoons pesto

Combine chicken with remaining ingredients in salad bowl; toss lightly. Chill until serving time.

Approx Per Serving: Cal 265; T Fat 20 g; 67% Calories from Fat; Prot 15 g; Carbo 7 g; Fiber 2 g; Chol 48 mg; Sod 118 mg.

Shoe Peg Salad

Yield: 15 servings

1 16-ounce can Shoe Peg corn
1 16-ounce can French-style green beans
1 16-ounce can tiny peas
1 2-ounce jar chopped pimento
1 onion, sliced into rings
1 green bell pepper, chopped

1 cup chopped celery
1 8-ounce can sliced water chestnuts, drained
½ cup wine vinegar
1 cup sugar
½ cup oil
Salt to taste

Drain corn, beans, peas and pimento. Combine all vegetables in salad bowl. Mix vinegar, sugar, oil and salt in small bowl. Add to vegetable mixture; mix well. Marinate in refrigerator overnight.

Approx Per Serving: Cal 182; T Fat 8 g; 36% Calories from Fat; Prot 3 g; Carbo 28 g; Fiber 3 g; Chol 0 mg; Sod 221 mg.

Christmas Cranberry Salad

Yield: 14 servings

2 cups sugar
1 cup water
4 cups cranberries
2 cups miniature marshmallows

3 cups drained mandarin oranges
½ cup pecans
2 apples, chopped
3 bananas, sliced

Boil sugar and water in saucepan until syrupy. Add cranberries. Cook until cranberries burst. Remove from heat. Let stand, covered, for 10 minutes. Cook, uncovered, for 5 minutes. Pour into large bowl. Chill in refrigerator. Fold in remaining ingredients. Chill until serving time. Serve with whipped cream.

Approx Per Serving: Cal 244; T Fat 3 g; 11% Calories from Fat; Prot 1 g; Carbo 57 g; Fiber 2 g; Chol 0 mg; Sod 12 mg.

Crab Salad Delight

Yield: 12 servings

1 10-ounce can tomato soup
8 ounces cream cheese, softened
2 envelopes unflavored gelatin
1 cup cold water
1 cup mayonnaise
1 7-ounce can crab meat

1 cup mixed chopped celery,
　onion and green bell pepper
1 cup mayonnaise
1 large cucumber, chopped
2 tablespoons chili sauce

Bring soup to a boil in saucepan. Add cream cheese, stir until melted. Soften gelatin in cold water. Add to hot soup mixture; stir until dissolved. Cool. Stir in 1 cup mayonnaise, crab meat and celery, onion and green pepper. Pour into 10x10-inch dish. Chill until set. Process 1 cup mayonnaise, cucumber and chili sauce in blender or food processor. Serve over congealed layer.

Approx Per Serving: Cal 374; T Fat 36 g; 86% Calories from Fat;
　　Prot 7 g; Carbo 7 g; Fiber <1 g; Chol 57 mg; Sod 526 mg.

Springtime Fruit Salad

Yield: 16 servings

1 fresh pineapple
1 quart fresh strawberries
1/2 cup fresh blueberries
1/2 cup fresh raspberries
1 11-ounce can mandarin
　oranges, drained

2 cups orange juice
1 cup sugar
1/4 cup cream sherry
1/2 teaspoon almond extract
1/2 teaspoon vanilla extract

Peel pineapple; cut into chunks. Combine with remaining fruit in large bowl. Combine orange juice, sugar, sherry and extracts in bowl; mix until sugar dissolves. Pour over fruit; toss lightly. Chill for 2 to 3 hours.

Approx Per Serving: Cal 113; T Fat <1 g; 3% Calories from Fat;
　　Prot 1 g; Carbo 27 g; Fiber 2 g; Chol 0 mg; Sod 3 mg.

Use the orange, white or yellow petals of calendula blossoms to give a delicate saffron-like, mild pepper flavor to salads, egg dishes and cheese dishes.

Frozen Grape Salad

Yield: 8 servings

1 20-ounce can pineapple tidbits	2½ cups miniature marshmallows
6 ounces cream cheese, softened	1 cup whipping cream, whipped
2 tablespoons mayonnaise	2 cups Tokay grape halves

Drain pineapple, reserving 2 tablespoons juice. Blend reserved juice with cream cheese and mayonnaise in bowl. Add marshmallows and drained pineapple. Fold in whipped cream and grapes. Spoon into square 1-quart dish. Freeze until firm. Cut into squares.

Approx Per Serving: Cal 341; T Fat 21 g; 54% Calories from Fat; Prot 3 g; Carbo 37 g; Fiber 1 g; Chol 66 mg; Sod 111 mg.

Curried Pasta and Chicken Salad

Yield: 8 servings

1 pound boneless skinless chicken breasts	2½ tablespoons plain low-fat yogurt
¼ cup white wine	¾ cup low-fat mayonnaise-type salad dressing
½ teaspoon thyme	
1 carrot, quartered	1½ tablespoons honey
½ onion, quartered	1½ tablespoons lemon juice
¾ cup water	¼ teaspoon curry powder
¼ teaspoon salt	½ teaspoon salt
½ cup uncooked pasta	⅛ teaspoon pepper
¼ cup thinly sliced celery	2 cups seedless grapes
¼ cup thinly sliced green onions	⅓ cup slivered almonds, toasted

Combine chicken, wine, thyme, carrot, onion, water and ¼ teaspoon salt in saucepan. Simmer, covered, for 45 minutes or until chicken is tender. Drain and cool chicken. Cut into 1-inch cubes. Cook pasta using package directions; drain, rinse and cool. Combine chicken, pasta, celery and green onions in bowl. Blend yogurt, mayonnaise, honey, lemon juice, curry powder, ½ teaspoon salt and pepper in small bowl. Add to chicken mixture; toss lightly. Chill until serving time. Add grapes; toss lightly. Spoon onto lettuce-lined plate. Sprinkle with almonds.

Approx Per Serving: Cal 226; T Fat 9 g; 36% Calories from Fat; Prot 16 g; Carbo 20 g; Fiber 2 g; Chol 42 mg; Sod 355 mg.

Gazpacho Macaroni Salad

Yield: 6 servings

4 cups cooked macaroni
1 10-ounce package frozen
   peas, thawed
3 medium tomatoes, peeled,
   chopped
1 cup chopped celery
1 medium cucumber, chopped
1 green bell pepper, chopped
5 green onions, thinly sliced

6 ounces salami, cubed
1/4 cup chopped parsley
1/3 cup olive oil
1/4 cup wine vinegar
1 teaspoon salt
1/2 teaspoon Worcestershire
   sauce
1 clove of garlic, pressed
Hot pepper sauce to taste

Combine macaroni, vegetables, salami and parsley in salad bowl. Blend olive oil, vinegar, salt, Worcestershire sauce, garlic and hot pepper sauce in small bowl. Add to macaroni mixture; toss lightly. Serve immediately or chill for no more than 1 hour. Spoon into lettuce cups on salad plates. Garnish with black olives.

Approx Per Serving: Cal 320; T Fat 18 g; 50% Calories from Fat;
    Prot 11 g; Carbo 30 g; Fiber 6 g; Chol 17 mg; Sod 767 mg.

Pasta Seafood Salad

Yield: 4 servings

2 cups uncooked rotini
1 teaspoon onion powder
1 teaspoon garlic powder
1 tablespoon olive oil
1/2 cup cholesterol-free
   mayonnaise
1/4 cup olive oil Italian salad
   dressing

1/2 cup grated skim milk
   Parmesan cheese
8 ounces imitation lobster
1 cup broccoli flowerets,
   partially cooked
1/2 cup green bell pepper
1 tablespoon instant minced
   onion

Cook rotini using package directions and adding onion powder, garlic powder and olive oil to cooking water; drain and cool. Combine mayonnaise, salad dressing and Parmesan cheese in bowl; mix well. Combine rotini, lobster, broccoli, green pepper, onion and mayonnaise mixture in salad bowl; toss lightly. Chill until serving time.

Approx Per Serving: Cal 461; T Fat 30 g; 56% Calories from Fat;
    Prot 18 g; Carbo 36 g; Fiber 2 g; Chol 18 mg; Sod 976 mg.
    Nutritional information includes entire amount of olive oil.

Crunchy Pea Salad

Yield: 8 servings

1/2 cup mayonnaise-type salad
   dressing
1/4 cup Italian salad dressing
1   10-ounce package frozen
   peas, thawed, drained
1 cup chopped celery

1 cup peanuts
6 slices crisp-fried bacon,
   crumbled
1/4 cup chopped red onion
8 tomatoes

Blend salad dressings in medium bowl. Add peas, celery, peanuts, bacon
and onion; mix lightly. Chill until serving time. Core tomatoes; cut into
wedges to but not through bottom. Place tomatoes on salad plates;
separate wedges gently. Spoon salad into tomatoes.

Approx Per Serving: Cal 279; T Fat 21 g; 63% Calories from Fat;
   Prot 10 g; Carbo 19 g; Fiber 6 g; Chol 8 mg; Sod 282 mg.

Pear and Swiss Cheese Salad

Yield: 4 servings

1/4 cup sour cream
1/4 cup plain yogurt
Cardamom and cinnamon to taste

2 fresh pears, cored, sliced
4 ounces Swiss cheese, shredded
1/2 cup chopped roasted cashews

Blend first 4 ingredients in bowl. Add pears, cheese and cashews; toss
lightly. Serve on lettuce-lined salad plates.

Approx Per Serving: Cal 281; T Fat 19 g; 57% Calories from Fat;
   Prot 12 g; Carbo 19 g; Fiber 3 g; Chol 33 mg; Sod 95 mg.

Fruited Pork Salad

Yield: 4 servings

1/4 cup grapefruit juice
1 tablespoon vegetable oil
2 teaspoons honey
2 tablespoons red wine vinegar
1 teaspoon poppy seed
1/2 teaspoon Dijon mustard

1 pound boneless pork loin,
   thinly sliced
1 head green leaf lettuce
Sections of 2 red grapefruit
1 1/2 cups seedless green grapes
1 cup fresh strawberries

Combine first 6 ingredients in jar with tight fitting lid; shake vigorously.
Stir-fry pork in preheated nonstick skillet over medium-high heat for 4
minutes or until cooked through. Place on lettuce-lined plates. Top with
fruit. Drizzle dressing over top.

Approx Per Serving: Cal 313; T Fat 12 g; 33% Calories from Fat;
   Prot 25 g; Carbo 29 g; Fiber 4 g; Chol 69 mg; Sod 71 mg.

Layered Egg and Potato Salad

Yield: 8 servings

This is a special recipe of the Basque people in Oregon.

1/2 cup thinly sliced green
  onions
2/3 cup olive oil
2 tablespoons red wine vinegar
1 clove of garlic, minced
1/2 teaspoon each sugar, paprika
  and pepper

1 1/2 teaspoons salt
2 pounds white new potatoes
1/2 cup chopped parsley
8 hard-boiled eggs, sliced
2 tablespoons chopped
  pimento, drained

Combine green onions, olive oil, vinegar, garlic, sugar, paprika, pepper and salt in small bowl; mix well. Cook potatoes in boiling salted water for 30 minutes or just until tender; drain and cool slightly. Peel and slice thinly; place in bowl. Pour dressing over warm potatoes; mix gently to coat. Chill, covered, for 4 hours to overnight, mixing gently several times. Drain potatoes, reserving dressing. Layer potato slices, parsley, eggs and reserved dressing 1/2 at a time in shallow serving bowl. Garnish with pimento. Chill, covered, until serving time.

Approx Per Serving: Cal 332; T Fat 24 g; 63% Calories from Fat;
    Prot 10 g; Carbo 21 g; Fiber 5 g; Chol 213 mg; Sod 483 mg.

Southern Potato Salad

Yield: 12 servings

12 medium potatoes
1 large onion
1/2 cup chopped pickles
1/2 cup chopped celery
5 hard-boiled eggs, chopped

2 cups mayonnaise
2 tablespoons sugar
2 tablespoons mustard
Salt and pepper to taste

Cook potatoes as desired; peel and cube. Combine with onion, pickles, celery and eggs in bowl. Blend mayonnaise, sugar, mustard, salt and pepper in small bowl. Add to potato mixture; mix well.

Approx Per Serving: Cal 339; T Fat 32 g; 83% Calories from Fat;
    Prot 4 g; Carbo 11 g; Fiber 2 g; Chol 110 mg; Sod 385 mg.

Marjoram

Texas Potato Salad

Yield: 75 servings

20 pounds white potatoes
1/2 cup salt
2 tablespoons coarsely ground pepper
1/4 cup sugar
1 cup white vinegar
16 hard-boiled eggs, chopped
1 pound white onions, thinly sliced

8 ounces green bell pepper, finely chopped
2 bunches celery, finely chopped
1 7-ounce jar minced pimento, drained
1/2 cup minced fresh parsley
2 to 3 quarts mayonnaise

Cook unpeeled potatoes in boiling salted water to cover for 30 minutes or until tender. Drain and cool slightly. Peel potatoes; cut into 1/4-inch slices. Place in large container. Pour mixture of salt, pepper, sugar and vinegar over warm potatoes. Add eggs, onions, green pepper, celery, pimento, parsley and desired amount of mayonnaise; mix well. Chill for several hours.

Approx Per Serving: Cal 373; T Fat 29 g; 69% Calories from Fat; Prot 5 g; Carbo 24 g; Fiber 5 g; Chol 66 mg; Sod 920 mg.

Pumpkin Aspic

Yield: 6 servings

1 6-ounce package orange gelatin
1 1/2 cups boiling water
1/4 teaspoon ginger

2 tablespoons sugar
1 cup canned pumpkin
2 tablespoons apple butter

Dissolve gelatin in boiling water in bowl. Add ginger, sugar, pumpkin and apple butter; mix well. Pour into 8x8-inch dish. Chill until partially set, stirring occasionally. Chill until firm. May substitute 1 tablespoon brown sugar for sugar for less sweet aspic or add 1/4 teaspoon grated orange rind for more zing.

Approx Per Serving: Cal 146; T Fat <1 g; 1% Calories from Fat; Prot 3 g; Carbo 35 g; Fiber 1 g; Chol 0 mg; Sod 92 mg.

 The faint wintergreen taste of Johnny jump-ups is mild and pleasant as an edible garnish. The blossoms can be crystallized in the same manner as violets.

Raspberry and Rice Salad

Yield: 6 servings

1¹/₂ cups minute rice
3 cups milk
¹/₂ cup sugar
1 teaspoon salt
2 teaspoons vanilla extract

1 cup whipping cream, whipped
1   10-ounce package frozen
    raspberries, thawed
2 tablespoons cornstarch

Combine rice, milk, sugar and salt in saucepan. Bring to a simmer, stirring constantly. Simmer for 10 minutes or until thickened, stirring frequently. Stir in vanilla. Chill, covered, in refrigerator. Fold in whipped cream. Mix raspberries and cornstarch in saucepan. Cook until thickened, stirring constantly. Cool. Spoon rice mixture into pretty bowl; make well in center. Spoon raspberry mixture into well.

Approx Per Serving: Cal 423; T Fat 19 g; 40% Calories from Fat;
    Prot 7 g; Carbo 58 g; Fiber 3 g; Chol 71 mg; Sod 422 mg.

Seafood-Bread Salad

Yield: 15 servings

1   24-ounce loaf sandwich
    bread, frozen
1¹/₂ cups butter, softened
1   8-ounce can crab meat,
    drained
2   8-ounce cans tiny shrimp,
    drained

1 cup finely chopped onion
1 cup finely chopped celery
8 hard-boiled eggs, chopped
3³/₄ cups mayonnaise
Salt, pepper, garlic salt and
    chives to taste

Trim crusts from bread; spread bread with butter. Stack 4 slices at a time and make 3 cuts in each direction to cut into cubes. Combine bread, crab meat, shrimp, onion, celery, eggs and mayonnaise in bowl. Add seasonings; mix well. Chill for 3 hours. Serve on lettuce-lined salad plates. Garnish with cherry tomatoes and olives.

Approx Per Serving: Cal 775; T Fat 68 g; 78% Calories from Fat;
    Prot 18 g; Carbo 25 g; Fiber 1 g; Chol 262 mg; Sod 841 mg.

Sweet Woodruff

Asian Coleslaw

Yield: 12 servings

1/2 head cabbage, shredded
3 tablespoons sesame seed,
   toasted
3 green onions, slivered
1/2 cup slivered almonds,
   toasted
2 tablespoons sesame oil
3 tablespoons vinegar

1 teaspoon pepper
1/4 cup vegetable oil
3 tablespoons sugar
1/4 teaspoon MSG
1 teaspoon seasoned salt
1 package ramen noodles,
   crushed

Combine cabbage, sesame seed, green onions and almonds in salad bowl. Chill until serving time. Combine sesame oil, vinegar, pepper, vegetable oil, sugar, MSG and seasoned salt in tightly covered jar; shake vigorously. Add dressing and noodles to cabbage mixture just before serving; toss lightly.

Approx Per Serving: Cal 150; T Fat 12 g; 69% Calories from Fat;
   Prot 3 g; Carbo 9 g; Fiber 1 g; Chol 0 mg; Sod 306 mg.

Pepper Slaw

Yield: 8 servings

1 each red, orange, green,
   purple and yellow bell
   peppers
1 red onion, thinly sliced
1 jalapeño pepper, minced
2 tablespoons wine vinegar
1 tablespoon Dijon mustard
2 teaspoons sugar

1 teaspoon salt
1/4 teaspoon Tabasco sauce
1/2 teaspoon freshly ground
   pepper
1/4 cup vegetable oil
2 tablespoons peanut oil
1 tablespoon caraway seed
2 teaspoons grated lime zest

Cut bell peppers into julienne strips. Combine with onion in salad bowl. Mix jalapeño pepper, vinegar, mustard, sugar, salt, Tabasco sauce and pepper in small bowl. Whisk in oils until smooth and thickened. Add to pepper mixture. Add caraway seed and lime zest; toss to mix. Chill, covered, for several hours.

Approx Per Serving: Cal 115; T Fat 11 g; 79% Calories from Fat;
   Prot 1 g; Carbo 6 g; Fiber 1 g; Chol 0 mg; Sod 293 mg.

 Cherries, small-fruited flowering crabapple, dogwoods, mulberry, mountain-ash, hawthorn, fringetree, viburnum and pyracantha provide food for birds.

Red Slaw

Yield: 12 servings

6 cups shredded cabbage
1/4 cup sugar
1 teaspoon salt

1/2 teaspoon pepper
1 cup catsup
1/4 teaspoon vinegar

Combine cabbage and remaining ingredients in bowl; mix well. Chill for 1 hour or longer.

Approx Per Serving: Cal 48; T Fat <1 g; 3% Calories from Fat;
Prot 1 g; Carbo 12 g; Fiber 1 g; Chol 0 mg; Sod 421 mg.

Spinach Salad Supreme

Yield: 6 servings

1/2 cup mayonnaise
1 teaspoon vinegar
1/4 teaspoon Tabasco sauce
1/4 teaspoon salt
2 tablespoons prepared
    horseradish

1/4 cup finely chopped celery
1/4 cup finely chopped onion
2 hard-boiled eggs, chopped
1/3 cup 1/8-inch Old English
    cheese cubes
2 cups chopped fresh spinach

Combine first 5 ingredients in bowl; mix well. Add celery, onion, eggs, cheese and spinach; mix well. Chill for several hours.

Approx Per Serving: Cal 192; T Fat 19 g; 86% Calories from Fat;
Prot 5 g; Carbo 3 g; Fiber 1 g; Chol 89 mg; Sod 278 mg.

Spinach and Sprouts Salad

Yield: 8 servings

1 bunch fresh spinach, torn
1 cup alfalfa sprouts
1 8-ounce can sliced water
    chestnuts, drained
4 hard-boiled eggs, chopped
4 ounces bacon, crisp-fried,
    crumbled

1/2 cup oil
1/4 cup sugar
2 teaspoons Worcestershire
    sauce
1 teaspoon onion salt
1/2 cup catsup
2 tablespoons vinegar

Combine first 5 ingredients in salad bowl. Mix oil, sugar, Worcestershire sauce, onion salt, catsup and vinegar in small bowl. Add to spinach mixture just before serving; toss lightly.

Approx Per Serving: Cal 250; T Fat 19 g; 66% Calories from Fat;
Prot 6 g; Carbo 16 g; Fiber 2 g; Chol 110 mg; Sod 571 mg.

Spinach and Tomato Salad

Yield: 6 servings

Make the dressing with your favorite herbs—parsley, basil, oregano, chives or tarragon.

3 tablespoons olive oil
3 tablespoons cider or wine
  vinegar
2 tablespoons water
1 to 2 teaspoons stone-ground
  mustard
1 tablespoon finely chopped or
  1/2 teaspoon dried herbs

1 1/2 pounds fresh spinach
Whites of 2 hard-boiled eggs,
  chopped
12 cherry tomatoes, cut into
  quarters
1 small red onion, cut into thin
  rings
1/2 teaspoon lemon pepper

Combine olive oil, vinegar, water, mustard and herbs in small bowl; mix well. Chill in refrigerator. Rinse spinach with cold water; drain well. Tear spinach into bite-sized pieces; discard stems. Place in salad bowl. Add eggs, tomatoes and onion. Add dressing and lemon pepper; toss lightly. Serve immediately.

Approx Per Serving: Cal 107; T Fat 7 g; 56% Calories from Fat;
    Prot 5 g; Carbo 8 g; Fiber 5 g; Chol 0 mg; Sod 131 mg.

Strawberry Pretzel Salad

Yield: 15 servings

4 cups coarsely crushed pretzels
3 tablespoons sugar
3/4 cup melted margarine
8 ounces cream cheese, softened
1 cup sugar
8 ounces whipped topping

1 6-ounce package strawberry
  gelatin
2 cups boiling water
1 16-ounce package frozen
  strawberries, thawed

Combine pretzels, 3 tablespoons sugar and margarine in bowl; mix well. Press into 9x13-inch baking dish. Bake at 350 degrees for 10 minutes. Cool completely. Blend cream cheese, 1 cup sugar and whipped topping in bowl. Spread over pretzel crust. Dissolve gelatin in boiling water in bowl. Stir in strawberries. Pour over cream cheese layer. Chill until firm. Garnish with additional whipped topping.

Approx Per Serving: Cal 388; T Fat 19 g; 44% Calories from Fat;
    Prot 5 g; Carbo 51 g; Fiber 1 g; Chol 17 mg; Sod 558 mg.

The mild taste of arugula blossoms is delicious in salads and sandwiches.

Fire and Ice Tomatoes

Yield: 10 servings

6 medium tomatoes, peeled
1 medium onion, sliced into
    rings
1 medium green bell pepper,
    cut into strips
1 large cucumber, peeled, sliced
3/4 cup cider vinegar

1/4 cup water
5 teaspoons sugar
1 1/2 teaspoons celery salt
1 1/2 teaspoons mustard seed
1/2 teaspoon red pepper
Salt and black pepper to taste

Cut tomatoes into quarters. Combine with onion, green pepper and cucumber in bowl. Combine vinegar, water, sugar, celery salt, mustard seed, red pepper, salt and black pepper in saucepan. Bring to a boil. Boil for 1 minute. Let stand until cool. Pour over vegetables. Chill for 8 hours. May substitute zucchini for cucumbers or Tabasco sauce to taste for red pepper.

Approx Per Serving: Cal 36; T Fat <1 g; 6% Calories from Fat;
    Prot 1 g; Carbo 9 g; Fiber 2 g; Chol 0 mg; Sod 315 mg.

Hearty Turkey and Fruit Salad

Yield: 4 servings

1 cup chopped cooked turkey
2 tablespoons French salad
    dressing
1 8-ounce can pineapple
    chunks, drained
1 8-ounce can mandarin
    oranges, drained

1 cup seedless green grape
    halves
3 stalks celery, chopped
1/4 cup nonfat mayonnaise-type
    salad dressing

Toss turkey with French dressing in bowl. Marinate in refrigerator overnight. Add fruit, celery and mayonnaise-type salad dressing; toss lightly. Chill until serving time. Spoon into lettuce cups. Garnish with toasted almonds.

Approx Per Serving: Cal 218; T Fat 7 g; 26% Calories from Fat;
    Prot 11 g; Carbo 31 g; Fiber 2 g; Chol 27 mg; Sod 358 mg.

Rosemary

Main-Dish Turkey Salad
Yield: 8 servings

2/3 cup low-fat mayonnaise
1/3 cup milk
2 tablespoons lemon juice
3 cups cubed cooked turkey breast
1 1/2 cups cooked wild rice
1 1/2 cups cooked long grain rice
1/3 cup finely chopped green onions

1/2 cup finely chopped celery
1 8-ounce can sliced water chestnuts, drained
1/2 teaspoon salt
1/8 teaspoon pepper
1 cup seedless green grape halves
1 cup cashews

Blend mayonnaise, milk and lemon juice in small bowl. Combine turkey, rices, green onions, celery, water chestnuts, salt and pepper in large bowl. Add mayonnaise mixture; toss to mix. Chill, covered, for 2 to 3 hours. Add grapes and cashews just before serving. Garnish with small clusters of grapes and sprinkle of paprika.

Approx Per Serving: Cal 343; T Fat 15 g; 39% Calories from Fat;
Prot 21 g; Carbo 32 g; Fiber 3 g; Chol 47 mg; Sod 287 mg.

Confetti Yam Salad
Yield: 20 servings

Serve this colorful salad in a glass salad bowl. It is good for summer potlucks since there is nothing to spoil if not refrigerated.

4 pounds fresh yams
1/2 cup sliced green onions
1/2 cup chopped red bell pepper
1/2 cup chopped green bell pepper
1/2 cup chopped celery
1/3 cup chopped cilantro

1/4 cup lemon juice
1 teaspoon salt
1/4 teaspoon pepper
1/3 cup vegetable oil
1/2 teaspoon grated lemon zest
1/2 cup coarsely chopped dry-roasted peanuts

Cook yams in boiling salted water to cover in large saucepan for 30 minutes or just until tender. Cool slightly. Peel and cut into large cubes. Combine with green onions, red pepper, green pepper, celery and cilantro in salad bowl. Mix lemon juice, salt, pepper, oil and lemon zest in small bowl. Pour over vegetables; toss to mix. Chill until serving time. Sprinkle with peanuts just before serving.

Approx Per Serving: Cal 145; T Fat 5 g; 31% Calories from Fat;
Prot 2 g; Carbo 23 g; Fiber 3 g; Chol 0 mg; Sod 120 mg.

Zucchini and Artichoke Salad
Yield: 14 servings

1 8-ounce bottle of Italian
   salad dressing
2 4-ounce envelopes ranch-
   style salad dressing mix
4 medium zucchini, sliced
2 14-ounce cans artichoke
   hearts, drained, cut into halves

1 8-ounce can whole
   mushrooms, drained
1 6-ounce can pitted black
   olives
1 8-ounce can bamboo shoots,
   drained

Blend Italian salad dressing and ranch dressing mix in bowl. Combine zucchini, artichokes, mushrooms, olives and bamboo shoots in lettuce-lined salad bowl. Add dressing. Chill, covered, for 8 hours.

Approx Per Serving: Cal 166; T Fat 13 g; 61% Calories from Fat;
   Prot 2 g; Carbo 17 g; Fiber 2 g; Chol 0 mg; Sod 1495 mg.

Celery Seed Salad Dressing
Yield: 32 servings

1 cup oil, chilled
1/2 cup vinegar, chilled
3/4 cup sugar
1 teaspoon dry mustard

1 tablespoon grated onion
1 teaspoon celery seed
1 teaspoon salt

Combine all ingredients in blender container. Process for 2 to 3 minutes. Store in jar in refrigerator for up to 3 weeks. Serve on tossed salad or coleslaw.

Approx Per Serving: Cal 79; T Fat 7 g; 76% Calories from Fat;
   Prot <1 g; Carbo 5 g; Fiber 0 g; Chol 0 mg; Sod 67 mg.

Honey French Salad Dressing
Yield: 16 servings

1/4 cup canola oil
1/4 cup honey
1/4 cup catsup

1/4 cup vinegar
Salt, pepper, celery salt and
   garlic powder to taste

Combine all ingredients in blender container. Process for several seconds. Store in jar in refrigerator. Dressing will thicken with chilling. May add crumbled bleu cheese if desired.

Approx Per Serving: Cal 51; T Fat 3 g; 57% Calories from Fat;
   Prot <1 g; Carbo 6 g; Fiber <1 g; Chol 0 mg; Sod 45 mg.

Hot Bacon Dressing

Yield: 16 servings

3 slices bacon
1 tablespoon flour
5 tablespoons sugar
1 egg, beaten

1/2 cup milk
1/4 cup vinegar
Salt and pepper to taste

Fry bacon in skillet until crisp; drain and crumble. Blend flour and sugar with bacon drippings in skillet. Beat egg with milk and vinegar in bowl. Stir into bacon drippings. Cook until thickened, stirring constantly. Add a small amount of water or additional milk to make of desired consistency. Serve warm dressing over assorted greens such as endive, escarole, dandelion or lettuce. Crumble bacon over top. Garnish with sliced hard-boiled egg.

Approx Per Serving: Cal 51; T Fat 3 g; 54% Calories from Fat; Prot 1 g; Carbo 5 g; Fiber <1 g; Chol 27 mg; Sod 45 mg.

Papaya Seed Dressing

Yield: 64 servings

3 to 4 teaspoons papaya seed
1 cup sugar
1 tablespoon salt
1 tablespoon dry mustard

1 cup white wine vinegar
1 cup vegetable oil
1 small onion, chopped

Process papaya seed in blender to consistency of coarse pepper; reserve. Combine remaining ingredients in blender container. Process for several seconds. Add papaya seed. Store in refrigerator.

Approx Per Serving: Cal 44; T Fat 3 g; 68% Calories from Fat; Prot <1 g; Carbo 4 g; Fiber <1 g; Chol 0 mg; Sod 100 mg. Nutritional information does not include papaya seed.

Poppy Seed Dressing

Yield: 24 servings

1/2 cup sugar
1 teaspoon dry mustard
1 teaspoon salt
51/2 tablespoons vinegar

1 cup vegetable oil
11/2 teaspoons grated onion
21/2 teaspoons poppy seed

Combine first 4 ingredients in mixer bowl; beat until well mixed. Add oil gradually, beating constantly. Stir in onion and poppy seed. Serve on fresh fruit or spinach salad.

Approx Per Serving: Cal 99; T Fat 9 g; 82% Calories from Fat; Prot <1 g; Carbo 4 g; Fiber <1 g; Chol 0 mg; Sod 89 mg.

Meat Entrées

Run for the Roses

South Atlantic

*S*tretching from the Tidewater of the Atlantic westward to touch the Mississippi, the Region traces much of the westward migration of early settlers. While reaching out for tomorrow, there is the challenging responsibility for members to protect and preserve our heritage be it the buildings and gardens of colonial times, the streams and mountains to the west or the bluegrass meadows of Kentucky.

West Virginia Country Ham Bake

Country Ham*   Sweet Potato Casserole*
Mustard Greens with Ham Hock*   Corn Bread*
Shortcake*

North Carolina Barbecue Festival

When October arrives the cooks get out the aprons and heat up the grills, and barbecue pits begin to smoke. There may be chicken, ribs, roast and sausage, but the barbecue hams and pork shoulders are the favorite for the smoked flavor. Six restaurants participate in preparing 10,000 pounds of pork, 2500 pounds of cabbage for the red slaw, and 200 gallons of sauce for the meat. The secret is in the sauce. We share it now in this menu for a family. Kings, queens and presidents have enjoyed this treat from North Carolina.

Barbecued Ribs, Ham and Sausage*
Red Slaw   Dill Pickles
Barbecued Pinto Beans*
Southern Potato Salad*   Hush Puppies*
Fried Apple Pies*

*See index for recipes.

Meat Entrées

Lone Star Brisket

Yield: 12 servings

1 5-pound beef brisket
2 teaspoons meat tenderizer
1 4-ounce bottle of liquid
    smoke
1 teaspoon celery salt

1 teaspoon paprika
1/4 teaspoon nutmeg
1/4 teaspoon garlic powder
1 teaspoon onion salt
1 tablespoon brown sugar

Sprinkle brisket with tenderizer. Place in shallow baking dish. Add liquid smoke. Chill, covered, overnight. Mix remaining ingredients in bowl. Sprinkle over brisket. Bake, tightly covered, at 300 degrees for 2 hours; reduce temperature to 200 degrees. Bake, loosely covered, for 5 hours. Let stand for 1 hour. Chill pan juices in freezer; skim. Slice brisket thinly cross grain. Serve in heated pan juices or barbecue sauce of choice.

Approx Per Serving: Cal 253; T Fat 11 g; 40% Calories from Fat;
    Prot 35; Carbo 1 g; Fiber 0 g; Chol 106 mg; Sod 400 mg.
    Nutritional information does not include liquid smoke.

Barbecued Flank Steak

Yield: 6 servings

1 2-pound flank steak
3/4 cup oil
1/2 cup soy sauce
2 tablespoons vinegar

2 tablespoons honey
1 1/2 teaspoons ginger
1 teaspoon onion flakes

Score flank steak on both sides. Place in shallow glass dish. Combine remaining ingredients in small bowl; mix well. Pour over flank steak. Marinate in refrigerator for 8 hours or longer, turning occasionally. Grill steak over hot coals until done to taste. Slice very thinly.

Approx Per Serving: Cal 473; T Fat 36 g; 68% Calories from Fat;
    Prot 30; Carbo 8 g; Fiber 0 g; Chol 85 mg; Sod 1419 mg.

Buloggi

Yield: 4 servings

1¹/2 pounds flank steak
¹/3 cup soy sauce
2 green onions, thinly sliced
1 clove of garlic, crushed
2 tablespoons sugar

2 tablespoons sake or dry sherry
1 tablespoon sesame seed,
 toasted, crushed
1 tablespoon sesame oil
Pepper to taste

Chill flank steak in freezer until partially frozen. Slice very thinly diagonally cross grain. Place in large shallow glass dish. Combine soy sauce, green onions, garlic, sugar, sake, sesame seed, sesame oil and pepper in bowl; mix well. Pour over steak. Let stand at room temperature for 15 minutes. Drain, reserving marinade. Pat steak dry with paper towel. Grill over hot coals for 1¹/2 minutes on each side. Serve over hot rice with reserved marinade.

Approx Per Serving: Cal 301; T Fat 13 g; 41% Calories from Fat;
 Prot 33; Carbo 9 g; Fiber <1 g; Chol 96 mg; Sod 1411 mg.

Italian Beef

Yield: 16 servings

1 7-pound rolled beef rump
 roast
3 cloves of garlic, cut into
 halves
2 cups water
1 bouillon cube
1 teaspoon marjoram
1 teaspoon thyme

1 teaspoon oregano
Several drops of hot pepper
 sauce
1 tablespoon Worcestershire
 sauce
¹/2 cup chopped green bell
 pepper
1 12-ounce can beer

Cut 6 slits in roast. Insert 1 piece garlic in each slit. Place in roasting pan. Roast at 325 degrees until juices on bottom are browned. Add water and bouillon cube. Roast for 1 hour longer. Add herbs, hot pepper sauce, Worcestershire sauce, green pepper and beer. Roast to 150 degrees on meat thermometer, 2 to 2¹/2 hours in all. Let cool in pan juices. Slice roast thinly. Marinate in pan juices in refrigerator. Reheat in marinade. Serve on Italian or Vienna bread.

Approx Per Serving: Cal 270; T Fat 11 g; 40% Calories from Fat;
 Prot 37; Carbo 1 g; Fiber <1 g; Chol 112 mg; Sod 125 mg.

Colorado Columbine

Korean Beef

Yield: 6 servings

2 pounds sirloin tip, very
    thinly sliced
2 pounds onions, sliced into
    thin rings

1 6-ounce bottle of soy sauce
1/4 cup sugar
1 teaspoon red pepper
2 tablespoons oil

Place sirloin in shallow glass dish. Combine onions, soy sauce, sugar and red pepper in bowl; mix well. Pour over beef. Marinate for 30 minutes or longer. Stir-fry in hot oil in wok or skillet just until beef is no longer pink. Serve over rice or rice noodles.

Approx Per Serving: Cal 336; T Fat 14 g; 36% Calories from Fat;
    Prot 32; Carbo 22 g; Fiber 2 g; Chol 85 mg; Sod 1670 mg.

Lemon Pot Roast

Yield: 8 servings

3 tablespoons oil
1 small onion, chopped
2 cloves of garlic, minced
1 boneless 4-pound beef chuck
    shoulder roast
1 teaspoon salt

1 teaspoon marjoram
1 teaspoon freshly ground
    pepper
Grated rind and juice of 1
    lemon
1/2 cup hot water

Heat oil in heavy saucepan. Add onion and garlic. Sauté until tender. Add roast. Brown on both sides, spooning onion over roast. Sprinkle with salt, marjoram, pepper and lemon rind. Add lemon juice and water. Cook, covered, over low heat for 3 hours or until roast is tender, basting occasionally and adding additional water if necessary. Cut roast into diagonal slices; arrange on serving plate. Spoon pan juices over top.

Approx Per Serving: Cal 351; T Fat 18 g; 48% Calories from Fat;
    Prot 43; Carbo 2 g; Fiber <1 g; Chol 128 mg; Sod 336 mg.

After Oriental poppies bloom, the foliage turns brown and dies away. It will resume growth in late August. Annuals should not be planted over these dormant plants. Faded flowers should be removed to prevent the formation of unwanted seed. These poppies like a well drained soil and can be killed by "wet feet."

Pasties

Yield: 10 servings

1½ cups shortening
4 cups flour
1 teaspoon salt
1 cup plus 2 tablespoons ice water
1 pound round steak, cubed
1 pound pork steak, cubed
6 medium potatoes, thinly sliced

½ medium onion, thinly sliced
¾ cup thinly sliced rutabaga
Salt and pepper to taste
5 teaspoons butter
¼ cup milk
1 tablespoon melted butter
½ cup boiling water

Cut shortening into mixture of flour and salt in bowl until crumbly. Add 1 cup ice water gradually, mixing well after each addition. Add enough remaining ice water to make of pie crust consistency. Shape into ball. Let rest for several minutes. Combine round steak, pork steak, vegetables, salt and pepper in bowl; mix well. Divide pastry into 5 portions. Roll each portion into 10-inch circle. Spoon ⅕ of the filling onto bottom half of each circle. Top each with 1 teaspoon butter. Fold over to enclose filling, leaving ¾-inch edge. Fold 1 edge over the other; seal. Cut 1-inch slit in each. Place on lightly floured baking sheet. Brush with milk. Bake at 350 degrees for 45 minutes to 1 hour. Spoon mixture of 1 tablespoon melted butter and boiling water into slit of each pasty. Bake for 5 minutes longer. Cut pasties into halves.

Approx Per Serving: Cal 748; T Fat 40 g; 48% Calories from Fat;
Prot 26; Carbo 71 g; Fiber 5 g; Chol 63 mg; Sod 290 mg.

Shepherd's Pie

Yield: 6 servings

*This recipe can be prepared with ground beef or
finely chopped lamb or pork.*

1 pound finely chopped beef
1 medium onion, finely
  chopped
1 cup beef stock
Salt and pepper to taste

3 tablespoons cornstarch
1 pound potatoes, cooked
2 tablespoons butter
½ cup (about) milk

Sauté beef with onion in saucepan until tender. Stir in beef stock. Simmer for 30 minutes, skimming fat as needed. Season with salt and pepper. Stir in mixture of cornstarch and a small amount of water. Cook for 3 minutes or until thickened, stirring constantly. Spoon into baking dish. Mash potatoes with butter and milk in bowl. Spoon carefully over top of pie; mark top with form. Bake at 350 degrees for 30 minutes or until brown. May add 1 tablespoon tomato purée or top with shredded Cheddar cheese if desired.

Approx Per Serving: Cal 286; T Fat 15 g; 48% Calories from Fat;
Prot 18; Carbo 19 g; Fiber 3 g; Chol 63 mg; Sod 226 mg.

Steak and Kidney Pie

Yield: 4 servings

2 cups flour
1/2 teaspoon salt
2 teaspoons baking powder
4 ounces suet, chopped
1/2 cup cold water
1 large onion, chopped
1/4 cup butter

1 pound trimmed rump steak,
   cut into 1 1/2-inch cubes
2 tablespoons seasoned flour
1 8-ounce lamb kidney, sliced
1 cup beef stock
Salt and pepper to taste
8 ounces mushrooms, sliced

Sift flour, salt and baking powder into bowl. Cut in suet until crumbly. Add water; mix well. Knead gently on floured surface. Roll into 1/4-inch thick circle; set aside. Sauté onion in butter in skillet. Remove onion with slotted spoon. Coat steak with seasoned flour. Add to skillet. Cook until browned. Coat kidney with remaining seasoned flour. Add to skillet. Cook until browned. Add beef stock. Season with salt and pepper. Spoon into pie plate. Bake in preheated 300-degree oven for 1 3/4 hours. Add mushrooms. Bake for 30 minutes longer. Top with pie pastry. Bake for 20 minutes or until golden brown.

Approx Per Serving: Cal 832; T Fat 48 g; 52% Calories from Fat;
   Prot 42; Carbo 57 g; Fiber 4 g; Chol 279 mg; Sod 819 mg.

Mushroom Beef Birds

Yield: 4 servings

1 1/2 pounds round steak
2 tablespoons flour
1 teaspoon salt
1/8 teaspoon pepper
1/2 cup chopped onion
1 4-ounce can mushrooms,
   drained

1/2 cup chopped celery
1/2 teaspoon poultry seasoning
3 tablespoons butter
1 beef bouillon cube
1 cup water
2 tablespoons melted butter
2 tablespoons flour

Cut round steak into 4 portions. Pound with meat mallet until flat and thin. Sprinkle with mixture of 2 tablespoons flour, salt and pepper. Pound into steak. Layer onion, mushrooms and celery on each piece. Season with poultry seasoning. Roll to enclose filling; fasten with wooden picks. Brown in 3 tablespoons butter in skillet. Place steak rolls in casserole. Add mixture of bouillon and water. Cook, covered, at 350 degrees for 1 1/2 hours or until tender. Place on serving plate; remove picks. Blend remaining 2 tablespoons butter and flour in saucepan. Add pan juices. Cook until thickened, stirring constantly. Serve over steak rolls.

Approx Per Serving: Cal 396; T Fat 24 g; 56% Calories from Fat;
   Prot 34; Carbo 10 g; Fiber 1 g; Chol 134 mg; Sod 1056 mg.

Rouladen

Yield: 4 servings

4 1/4-inch thick 4-ounce round
   steaks
2 tablespoons Dijon mustard
1 dill pickle, sliced into thin
   strips
4 slices bacon, cut into halves
1/4 cup chopped onion

1/4 cup oil
2 cups boiling water
4 bouillon cubes
1/2 teaspoon tomato paste
3 tablespoons cornstarch
1 cup sour cream

Spread steak with mustard. Place 1 pickle strip at narrow end of each
steak. Place 2 pieces bacon on each steak. Sprinkle with onion. Roll to
enclose filling; tuck in sides and secure with wooden picks. Brown in oil
in skillet. Add water, bouillon cubes and tomato paste. Simmer, covered,
for 1 1/2 to 2 hours or until tender. Remove steak rolls to serving platter;
remove picks. Add mixture of cornstarch and sour cream; mix well.
Cook just until thickened, stirring constantly; do not boil. Pour over
steak rolls.

Approx Per Serving: Cal 468; T Fat 36 g; 69% Calories from Fat;
   Prot 26; Carbo 10 g; Fiber <1 g; Chol 95 mg; Sod 1314 mg.

Rancher's Steak

Yield: 2 servings

1 teaspoon salt
1 teaspoon pepper
1 teaspoon MSG

Hickory-smoked salt to taste
1 1-inch thick 16-ounce sirloin
   steak

Combine salt, pepper, MSG and hickory-smoked salt in bowl; mix well.
Press mixture onto both sides of steak. Preheat cast-iron skillet over
medium-high heat. Render small piece of steak fat to grease skillet. Place
steak in skillet. Cook for 1 1/2 to 2 minutes or until browned on under-
side; turn steak over. Place in preheated 450-degree oven. Cook for 4
minutes for rare, 6 minutes for medium or 8 minutes for well done.
Serve immediately.

Approx Per Serving: Cal 298; T Fat 13 g; 41% Calories from Fat;
   Prot 42; Carbo 0 g; Fiber 0 g; Chol 128 mg; Sod 3278 mg.

*Even though you may have read that Christmas
roses and allied species of Helleborus should not
be disturbed once they are growing well, these plants
divide easily after blooming and should bloom the
next spring. They prefer a woodsy soil with
abundant humus in a shady spot.*

Savory Roast Beef

Yield: 15 servings

1 6-pound rump roast
1 10-ounce can cream of
    mushroom soup
1/2 cup tomato sauce
1/2 cup hot water
Salt and pepper to taste
1/4 teaspoon rosemary
1/4 teaspoon crushed garlic

2 teaspoons Worcestershire
    sauce
2 teaspoons Kitchen Bouquet
1/4 cup dried onion flakes
4 teaspoons chopped parsley
1/4 cup flour
1/2 cup water

Tenderize 1 side of roast with meat mallet. Brown on all sides in electric skillet. Turn tenderized side down. Combine soup, tomato sauce, hot water, seasonings, Kitchen Bouquet, onion flakes and parsley in bowl; mix well. Pour over roast. Cook, covered, at 250 degrees for 2 1/2 hours. Remove roast to serving platter. Stir mixture of flour and water into pan juices. Cook until thickened, stirring constantly. Serve with roast. Roast may be sealed in foil with sauce after browning and cooked in electric skillet or oven.

Approx Per Serving: Cal 271; T Fat 12 g; 40% Calories from Fat;
    Prot 35; Carbo 4 g; Fiber <1 g; Chol 102 mg; Sod 265 mg.

Marinated Beef Tenderloin

Yield: 12 servings

This is a nice change from turkey or ham during the holidays.

1 cup catsup
2 teaspoons prepared mustard
1/2 teaspoon Worcestershire
    sauce

1 1/2 cups water
2 envelopes Italian salad
    dressing mix
1 6-pound beef tenderloin

Combine catsup, mustard, Worcestershire sauce, water and salad dressing mix in bowl; mix well. Pierce tenderloin in several places with meat fork. Place in heavy plastic bag. Add catsup mixture; seal tightly. Place in shallow dish. Marinate in refrigerator for 8 hours, turning occasionally. Drain, reserving marinade. Place tenderloin on rack in roasting pan. Roast at 425 degrees for 30 to 45 minutes or to 140 degrees on meat thermometer for rare, 150 degrees for medium-rare or 160 degrees for medium. Brush occasionally with reserved marinade. Serve with heated remaining marinade.

Approx Per Serving: Cal 325; T Fat 13 g; 37% Calories from Fat;
    Prot 43; Carbo 7 g; Fiber <1 g; Chol 128 mg; Sod 479 mg.

Oven Beef Burgundy

Yield: 6 servings

2 pounds beef chuck, trimmed,
    cut into 1½-inch cubes
1 tablespoon Kitchen Bouquet
¼ cup cream of rice cereal
4 carrots, cut into thin strips
2 cups thinly sliced onions
1 cup thinly sliced celery
1 clove of garlic, minced

¼ to ½ teaspoon pepper
¼ to ½ teaspoon marjoram
¼ to ½ teaspoon thyme
1 cup (or more) Burgundy
1   6-ounce can browned-in-
    butter mushrooms
2 teaspoons salt

Place beef cubes in 3-quart casserole. Sprinkle with Kitchen Bouquet and cream of rice cereal; mix well. Add carrots, onions, celery and garlic; mix gently. Season with pepper, marjoram and thyme. Add wine, mushrooms and salt; mix gently. Bake, covered, at 325 degrees for 2½ hours or until beef and vegetables are tender, stirring every 30 minutes. Serve with new potatoes, rice or noodles.

Approx Per Serving: Cal 309; T Fat 9 g; 27% Calories from Fat;
    Prot 31; Carbo 18 g; Fiber 3 g; Chol 85 mg; Sod 915 mg.

Sauerbraten

Yield: 8 servings

1   4-pound beef chuck roast
1½ teaspoons salt
1 large onion, sliced
1½ cups vinegar
½ cup packed brown sugar
3 bay leaves
3 cloves

10 peppercorns
2 teaspoons oil
2 tablespoons flour
2 teaspoons sugar
5 or 6 gingersnaps, crushed
Salt and pepper to taste
½ cup red wine

Wipe roast with damp cloth; rub with 1½ teaspoons salt. Place in earthenware bowl. Combine onion, vinegar, brown sugar, bay leaves, cloves and peppercorns in bowl. Pour over roast. Add enough water to cover. Marinate in refrigerator for 48 hours, turning twice each day. Drain, reserving marinade. Brown roast on all sides in oil in skillet. Place in roasting pan. Stir flour into drippings in skillet. Cook until brown, stirring constantly. Add sugar, cookie crumbs, salt and pepper to taste and reserved marinade. Cook until smooth, stirring frequently. Pour over roast. Roast, covered, at 400 degrees for 1½ hours, basting frequently. Add red wine. Roast for 30 minutes longer. Discard bay leaves.

Approx Per Serving: Cal 428; T Fat 15 g; 32% Calories from Fat;
    Prot 43 g; Carbo 28 g; Fiber <1 g; Chol 128 mg; Sod 508 mg.

Mountain Stew

Yield: 6 servings

2 pounds beef chuck, cut into
   1½-inch cubes
⅓ cup flour
½ teaspoon seasoned salt
½ teaspoon onion salt
¼ cup oil
4 cups boiling water
1 teaspoon lemon juice
1 teaspoon Worcestershire sauce

2 cloves of garlic, chopped
2 bay leaves
½ teaspoon pepper
½ teaspoon paprika
¼ teaspoon allspice
1 teaspoon sugar
1 16-ounce package frozen
   mixed vegetables
8 ounces fresh mushrooms, sliced

Coat beef with mixture of flour, seasoned salt and onion salt. Cook in oil in skillet over medium-high heat for 20 minutes or until brown and crusty, turning constantly. Add water, lemon juice, Worcestershire sauce, garlic, bay leaves, seasonings and sugar. Bring to a boil; reduce heat. Simmer for 2 hours or until beef is tender, stirring frequently and adding additional water if necessary. Add vegetables and mushrooms. Cook until vegetables are tender. Remove bay leaves. Serve over hot buttered noodles sprinkled with poppy seed.

Approx Per Serving: Cal 363; T Fat 18 g; 45% Calories from Fat;
   Prot 32; Carbo 18 g; Fiber 4 g; Chol 85 mg; Sod 362 mg.

Secret Beef Stew

Yield: 6 servings

No one ever guesses the secret ingredient.

2 cups grapefruit juice
1½ pounds stew beef
1¼ teaspoons Worcestershire
   sauce
2 cloves of garlic, chopped
1 large onion, chopped
2 small bay leaves

½ teaspoon salt
½ teaspoon pepper
½ teaspoon paprika
¼ teaspoon cloves
5 carrots, cut into quarters
4 potatoes, cut into quarters
6 onions, cut into halves

Place grapefruit juice in saucepan. Place over medium heat. Add beef cubes; mix well. Add Worcestershire sauce, garlic, onion, bay leaves and seasonings; mix well. Reduce heat to low. Simmer for 2 hours. Add vegetables. Bring to a boil; reduce heat. Simmer for 20 to 25 minutes. Remove bay leaves. May be stored in freezer. Thaw in refrigerator and reheat with a small amount of additional water.

Approx Per Serving: Cal 292; T Fat 7 g; 22% Calories from Fat;
   Prot 25; Carbo 32 g; Fiber 6 g; Chol 64 mg; Sod 251 mg.

Texas Stew

Yield: 10 servings

1½ pounds stew beef
1 10-ounce can beef broth
1 broth can water
⅛ teaspoon pepper
½ teaspoon thyme
2 tablespoons flour
2 tablespoons oil
1 teaspoon salt
1 clove of garlic

1 teaspoon horseradish
1 bay leaf, crumbled
1 16-ounce package frozen
   soup vegetables
2 tablespoons flour
½ teaspoon salt
½ teaspoon pepper
½ cup picante sauce

Combine beef, broth, water, ⅛ teaspoon pepper, thyme, flour, oil, 1 teaspoon salt, garlic, horseradish and bay leaf in large saucepan. Cook over low heat until beef is tender. Add vegetables. Simmer for 30 minutes. Add mixture of remaining 2 tablespoons flour, ½ teaspoon salt and pepper and picante sauce. Simmer, covered, until thickened, stirring occasionally. Serve with biscuits and salad.

Approx Per Serving: Cal 159; T Fat 7 g; 39% Calories from Fat;
    Prot 15; Carbo 9 g; Fiber 2 g; Chol 39 mg; Sod 513 mg.

New England Boiled Dinner

Yield: 10 servings

1 4-pound corned beef brisket
6 medium potatoes, peeled
6 medium carrots, peeled

6 medium whole white turnips
1 medium head cabbage, cut
   into quarters

Wipe corned beef with damp paper towel. Place in saucepan with enough water to cover. Bring to a boil. Cook for 5 minutes; skim surface. Simmer, covered, for 3¼ hours; skim excess fat. Add vegetables. Cook, covered, for 15 minutes. Place cabbage on top. Cook for 30 minutes or until vegetables are tender. Serve brisket on large platter surrounded by vegetables.

Approx Per Serving: Cal 300; T Fat 11 g; 32% Calories from Fat;
    Prot 36; Carbo 14 g; Fiber 4 g; Chol 102 mg; Sod 131 mg.

When watering gardens, allow enough time to completely saturate the soil. This is much more beneficial than many light sprinklings with a hand-held hose. Such sprinkling will only moisten the top of the soil and the plant's foliage.

Bean Burrito Bake

Yield: 8 servings

1 pound ground beef
1 16-ounce can refried beans
1 cup baking mix
1/4 cup water
1 avocado, sliced

1 cup thick salsa
1 1/2 cups shredded Cheddar
  cheese
1/2 cup sour cream

Brown ground beef in skillet, stirring until crumbly; drain. Combine beans, baking mix and water in bowl; mix well. Spread over bottom and halfway up side of greased 10-inch pie plate. Layer ground beef, avocado, salsa and cheese in prepared pie plate. Bake at 375 degrees for 30 minutes. Cut into wedges; top with sour cream.

Approx Per Serving: Cal 412; T Fat 26 g; 55% Calories from Fat;
    Prot 22; Carbo 25 g; Fiber 8 g; Chol 66 mg; Sod 641 mg.

Burritos with Green Chili Sauce

Yield: 6 servings

1 tablespoon shortening
1/2 cup chopped onion
2 tablespoons flour
2 4-ounce cans chopped green
  chilies
1 cup chicken broth
1/4 teaspoon garlic powder
3/4 teaspoon salt
1 pound ground beef

Salt and garlic powder to taste
1/4 teaspoon cumin
1/4 teaspoon oregano
6 flour tortillas
2 green onions, finely chopped
1/2 cup shredded Monterey Jack
  cheese
3 cups coarsely chopped
  Romaine lettuce

Melt shortening in 250-degree electric skillet. Add onion. Sauté until tender. Stir in flour. Add chilies and chicken broth; mix well. Season with 1/4 teaspoon garlic powder and 3/4 teaspoon salt. Simmer for 20 minutes, stirring frequently; set aside. Brown ground beef in skillet, stirring until crumbly; drain. Season with salt and garlic powder to taste, cumin and oregano. Warm tortillas in foil in 350-degree oven using package directions. Spoon ground beef mixture onto tortillas. Sprinkle with green onions and cheese. Roll tortillas up. Place seam side down in 12x14-inch baking dish. Bake at 350 degrees for 10 minutes or until cheese melts. Sprinkle lettuce around tortillas. Serve with green chili sauce. May substitute 2 cups canned tomatoes for chicken broth for red chili sauce.

Approx Per Serving: Cal 348; T Fat 19 g; 47% Calories from Fat;
    Prot 21; Carbo 26 g; Fiber 2 g; Chol 58 mg; Sod 895 mg.

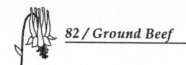

Easy Cheesy Beef Burritos

Yield: 12 servings

3 pounds ground beef
1 onion, finely chopped
1 green bell pepper, finely
  chopped
1 tablespoon oil
1/2 cup mild picante sauce
1 12-ounce can enchilada sauce
Salt and pepper to taste

12 flour tortillas
1 1/2 pounds process cheese,
  chopped
1 10-ounce can cream of
  mushroom soup
1 soup can milk
1 4-ounce can chopped green
  chilies, drained

Brown ground beef in skillet, stirring until crumbly; drain and set aside. Sauté onion and green pepper in oil in skillet for 5 minutes. Add ground beef. Stir in picante sauce and enchilada sauce. Simmer for 20 minutes. Season with salt and pepper. Soften tortillas 5 or 6 at a time in microwave using package directions. Spoon ground beef onto tortillas; roll up. Place seam side down in 9x13-inch casserole. Combine cheese, soup, milk and green chilies in saucepan. Cook over low heat until cheese melts, stirring occasionally. Pour over burritos. Bake at 350 degrees for 20 minutes. Serve immediately.

Approx Per Serving: Cal 644; T Fat 41 g; 57% Calories from Fat;
    Prot 38; Carbo 32 g; Fiber 2 g; Chol 131 mg; Sod 1686 mg.

Tailgater's Chili

Yield: 8 servings

2 pounds ground chuck
1 20-ounce can kidney beans,
  drained
3 tablespoons chopped green
  chilies
1 envelope onion soup mix
1 8-ounce can tomato sauce

1 12-ounce can beer
1 1/2 tablespoons chili powder
1 10-ounce package corn bread
  mix
1 cup shredded sharp Cheddar
  cheese

Brown ground chuck in skillet, stirring until crumbly; drain. Add kidney beans and chilies. Stir in onion soup mix, tomato sauce, beer and chili powder. Pour into 3-quart casserole. Bake, covered, at 350 degrees for 1 hour. Prepare corn bread mix using package directions. Stir in cheese. Spoon evenly over casserole. Bake, uncovered, for 25 minutes or until golden brown.

Approx Per Serving: Cal 474; T Fat 22 g; 43% Calories from Fat;
    Prot 33; Carbo 33 g; Fiber 7 g; Chol 89 mg; Sod 583 mg.

Lasagna

Yield: 8 servings

1 pound ground chuck
2 tablespoons oil
1/2 cup minced onion
1 1/2 teaspoons garlic powder
1 teaspoon salt
1/2 teaspoon pepper
1 teaspoon oregano
3 tablespoons chopped parsley
1 20-ounce can tomatoes

1 8-ounce can tomato sauce
8 tablespoons grated Parmesan cheese
1 8-ounce package lasagna noodles, cooked
12 ounces mozzarella cheese, thinly sliced
16 ounces ricotta cheese

Brown ground chuck in skillet, stirring until crumbly. Add onion. Sauté until onion is tender; drain. Add seasonings, parsley, tomatoes, tomato sauce and 2 tablespoons Parmesan cheese; mix well. Simmer for 30 minutes. Add enough cold water to noodles to cover. Spread thin layer of meat sauce in 9x13-inch baking dish. Drain lasagna noodles. Layer 1/3 of the noodles, half the mozzarella and ricotta cheeses, 2 tablespoons Parmesan cheese and 1/3 of the remaining sauce in prepared dish. Repeat layers. Top with remaining noodles, sauce and Parmesan cheese. Bake at 350 degrees for 30 minutes. Let stand for 10 minutes before serving.

Approx Per Serving: Cal 518; T Fat 30 g; 52% Calories from Fat;
    Prot 32; Carbo 30 g; Fiber 3 g; Chol 102 mg; Sod 888 mg.

Special Microwave Meatballs

Yield: 5 servings

1 16-ounce can pineapple chunks
1 pound ground beef
2 slices bread, crumbled
1 egg, slightly beaten

1/4 teaspoon allspice
1/4 teaspoon ground cloves
1 tablespoon onion flakes
1/2 cup (about) catsup
1/2 cup packed brown sugar

Drain pineapple, reserving juice. Combine ground beef, 2 tablespoons reserved pineapple juice, bread crumbs, egg, spices and onion flakes in bowl; mix well. Shape into bite-sized meatballs. Place in 9x13-inch glass baking dish. Cover with waxed paper. Microwave on High for 3 to 5 minutes or until brown; drain. Combine remaining pineapple juice with enough catsup to measure 1 cup. Mix with brown sugar in bowl. Pour over meatballs. Add pineapple chunks. Microwave for 3 to 5 minutes longer or until sauce is thickened. Serve over rice for main dish or may serve as appetizer.

Approx Per Serving: Cal 434; T Fat 15 g; 30% Calories from Fat;
    Prot 20; Carbo 58 g; Fiber 2 g; Chol 102 mg; Sod 421 mg.

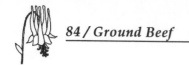

Louisiana Meat Pies

Yield: 12 servings

1¹/₂ pounds ground beef
1¹/₂ pounds ground pork
1 cup chopped green onions
1 tablespoon salt
1 teaspoon pepper
¹/₂ teaspoon cayenne pepper

¹/₃ cup all-purpose flour
2 cups self-rising flour
¹/₃ cup shortening
1 egg, beaten
³/₄ cup milk
Oil for deep frying

Brown ground beef and ground pork with green onions and seasonings in skillet, stirring until crumbly; drain. Sift all-purpose flour over meat mixture; mix well. Remove from heat. Let stand until cool. Drain in large colander. Sift self-rising flour into bowl. Cut in shortening until crumbly. Stir in mixture of egg and milk. Roll ¹/₃ at a time on floured pastry cloth. Cut into 5-inch circles. Stack circles between sheets of waxed paper. Place heaping tablespoon filling on 1 half of each circle. Fold circles over to enclose filling. Seal with fork dipped in water. Prick tops. Deep-fry in 350-degree hot oil until golden brown.

Approx Per Serving: Cal 320; T Fat 19 g; 52% Calories from Fat;
Prot 18; Carbo 19 g; Fiber 1 g; Chol 72 mg; Sod 812 mg.
Nutritional information does not include oil for deep frying.

Lebanese Meat Pies (Fatiar)

Yield: 16 servings

2 envelopes dry yeast
2¹/₂ cups warm water
7 cups (about) flour
1 tablespoon sugar
1 tablespoon salt
2 pounds lean ground beef

2 small onions, chopped
Juice of 3 lemons
2 teaspoons salt
¹/₂ teaspoon pepper
¹/₂ teaspoon allspice
¹/₂ cup oil

Dissolve yeast in 1 cup warm water in large bowl. Add remaining 1¹/₂ cups water, 6 cups flour, sugar and salt; mix well. Add enough remaining 1 cup flour to make moderately stiff dough. Knead on floured surface for 10 minutes or until smooth and elastic. Place in greased bowl, turning to coat surface. Let rise, covered, until doubled in bulk. Brown ground beef with onions in skillet, stirring frequently; drain and cool. Stir in lemon juice and seasonings. Punch dough down. Shape into small balls. Roll each ball into 5-inch circle. Spoon ¹/₄ cup ground beef mixture into center of each circle. Fold dough to center; pinch to seal and make 3-cornered tart. Pour oil into deep baking sheet. Place meat pies on baking sheet. Bake at 350 degrees for 25 minutes or until brown.

Approx Per Serving: Cal 387; T Fat 15 g; 36% Calories from Fat;
Prot 17; Carbo 45 g; Fiber 2 g; Chol 37 mg; Sod 701 mg.

Picadillo

Yield: 6 servings

This recipe is a flower arranger's delight because it looks beautiful, tastes delightful and can be prepared easily.

1½ pounds lean ground beef
1 16-ounce can tomatoes
1 green onion, chopped
1 green bell pepper, chopped
¼ cup pitted black olives
¼ cup pitted green olives
2 tablespoons capers

1 tablespoon (heaping) raisins
1 teaspoon chopped parsley
½ teaspoon oregano
1 bay leaf
⅛ teaspoon garlic powder
Salt and pepper to taste

Sauté ground beef with tomatoes, green onion and green pepper in large skillet, stirring frequently. Add olives, capers, raisins, herbs and seasonings; mix well. Simmer, covered, over medium heat for 30 minutes, stirring occasionally. Serve over rice.

Approx Per Serving: Cal 264; T Fat 18 g; 59% Calories from Fat;
Prot 22; Carbo 6 g; Fiber 1 g; Chol 74 mg; Sod 300 mg.
Nutritional information does not include capers.

Pizza Burgers

Yield: 10 servings

1 pound ground beef
1 10-ounce can tomato soup
¼ soup can oil
3 medium onions, chopped
1 teaspoon garlic salt
1 pound sharp Cheddar cheese,
   shredded

1 4-ounce can black olives,
   drained, chopped
½ teaspoon oregano
1 loaf French bread, sliced
   diagonally

Brown ground beef in skillet, stirring until crumbly; drain. Let stand until cool. Combine soup, oil, onions, garlic salt, cheese, olives, oregano and ground beef in bowl; mix well. Spread on French bread slices; place on baking sheet. Broil until brown and bubbly.

Approx Per Serving: Cal 522; T Fat 33 g; 57% Calories from Fat;
Prot 25; Carbo 31 g; Fiber 2 g; Chol 77 mg; Sod 1059 mg.

Fallen leaves have many uses in the well managed garden. They can be used in thin layers to keep the winter soil frozen; this prevents the freezing and thawing which uproots perennials and can kill them. Add shredded leaves to compost piles or incorporate directly into the soil.

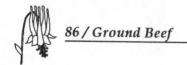

Ravioli Casserole

Yield: 8 servings

1 pound lean ground beef
1 medium onion, chopped
1 clove of garlic, minced
2 tablespoons oil
1   10-ounce package frozen
    chopped spinach
1   16-ounce can spaghetti sauce
    with mushrooms
1   8-ounce can tomato sauce

1   6-ounce can tomato paste
1/2 teaspoon salt
1   7-ounce package shell
    macaroni, cooked
1 cup shredded sharp American
    cheese
1/2 cup soft bread crumbs
2 eggs, well beaten
1/4 cup oil

Brown ground beef with onion and garlic in 2 tablespoons oil in skillet, stirring frequently; drain. Cook spinach using package directions; drain, reserving liquid. Add enough water to reserved liquid to measure 1 cup. Combine spinach liquid, spaghetti sauce, tomato sauce, tomato paste and salt in bowl; mix well. Stir into ground beef mixture. Combine spinach, macaroni, cheese, bread crumbs, eggs and remaining 1/4 cup oil in bowl; mix well. Spread in 9x13-inch baking dish. Spoon ground beef mixture over top. Bake at 350 degrees for 30 minutes. Let stand for 5 to 10 minutes before serving.

Approx Per Serving: Cal 483; T Fat 28 g; 50% Calories from Fat;
    Prot 22; Carbo 39 g; Fiber 4 g; Chol 104 mg; Sod 898 mg.

Beef Tacos

Yield: 12 servings

1 pound ground beef
1 onion, chopped
1 clove of garlic, chopped
1   8-ounce can taco sauce
1/4 cup green chili salsa
12 taco shells

2 cups chopped lettuce
2 tomatoes, chopped
2 cups shredded Cheddar
    cheese
1 cup guacamole
1 cup sour cream

Brown ground beef with onion and garlic in skillet, stirring frequently. Add taco sauce and salsa; mix well. Simmer for 10 minutes. Spoon into taco shells. Top each taco with lettuce, tomato, cheese, guacamole and sour cream. May substitute 2 cups chopped cooked chicken for ground beef if preferred.

Approx Per Serving: Cal 307; T Fat 21 g; 60% Calories from Fat;
    Prot 15; Carbo 17 g; Fiber 2 g; Chol 53 mg; Sod 483 mg.

Stuffed Cabbage Rolls

Yield: 6 servings

¼ cup uncooked rice
⅔ cup milk
1 pound ground beef
1 teaspoon salt
1 teaspoon minced onion
1 egg
1 tablespoon tomato paste
1   3-pound head cabbage

2 cups beef broth
1 small onion
6 whole cloves
½ cup sour cream
2 tablespoons tomato purée
2 tablespoons flour
1 cup beef broth

Combine rice and milk in saucepan. Bring to a boil; reduce heat. Simmer, covered, until rice is tender; drain. Add ground beef, salt, minced onion, egg and tomato paste; mix well. Parboil cabbage until outer leaves are easily removed. Repeat process until 12 leaves have been removed. Let stand until cool. Remove middle vein of each leaf. Place 2 tablespoons ground beef mixture on each leaf. Roll leaves to enclose filling. Place seam side down in 9x13-inch baking dish. Pour 2 cups beef broth over cabbage rolls. Add onion studded with cloves. Bake at 375 degrees for 1 hour, turning once. Combine sour cream, tomato purée, flour and remaining 1 cup beef broth in saucepan. Cook over low heat until smooth and thick, stirring constantly. Serve with cabbage rolls.

Approx Per Serving: Cal 333; T Fat 17 g; 45% Calories from Fat;
   Prot 22; Carbo 25 g; Fiber 6 g; Chol 97 mg; Sod 865 mg.

Country Ham

Yield: 40 servings

This recipe has been used since the 1700s.

1   20-pound country ham
20 whole cloves

1 cup packed brown sugar

Scrub country ham under cold running water with stiff brush. Soak in cold water to cover in crock for 24 hours, changing water 3 times. Place ham in deep stockpot. Add water to cover. Simmer for 3 hours. Remove ham. Let stand until cool. Remove skin from ham. Score ham diagonally. Stud with cloves. Place in roasting pan. Sprinkle with brown sugar. Bake at 250 degrees for 6 hours or until tender.

Approx Per Serving: Cal 239; T Fat 17 g; 65% Calories from Fat;
   Prot 13; Carbo 7 g; Fiber 0 g; Chol 53 mg; Sod 1022 mg.

Ham and Asparagus Casserole

Yield: 6 servings

1   10-ounce package frozen
   asparagus
2 cups chopped cooked ham
3 hard-boiled eggs, chopped
2 tablespoons tapioca
1/2 cup shredded Cheddar
   cheese
1/2 cup chopped red bell pepper
1/2 cup chopped green bell
   pepper

1/4 cup chopped onion
1 tablespoon chopped fresh
   parsley
1 tablespoon lemon juice
1/2 cup evaporated milk
1   10-ounce can cream of
   mushroom soup
1 cup soft bread crumbs
2 tablespoons melted butter

Blanch asparagus in boiling water in saucepan for 3 minutes; drain and chop. Combine asparagus, ham and eggs in 3-quart baking dish. Sprinkle with tapioca, cheese, peppers, onion and parsley; mix gently. Add mixture of lemon juice, evaporated milk and soup; mix gently. Combine bread crumbs and butter in small bowl; mix well. Sprinkle over casserole. Bake at 375 degrees for 25 to 30 minutes or until browned.

Approx Per Serving: Cal 314; T Fat 18 g; 51% Calories from Fat;
   Prot 22; Carbo 17 g; Fiber 1 g; Chol 158 mg; Sod 1268 mg.

Glazed Ham and Raisin Balls

Yield: 5 servings

8 ounces ground ham
8 ounces ground pork
1 cup raisin bran flakes
2/3 cup evaporated milk
1 egg
1 tablespoon chopped onion

Salt and pepper to taste
Dried thyme to taste
1/4 cup packed brown sugar
1/4 cup corn syrup
1 tablespoon vinegar
1/2 teaspoon dry mustard

Combine ground ham, ground pork, cereal, evaporated milk, egg, onion, salt, pepper and thyme in bowl; mix well. Shape into 10 balls. Place in 7x11-inch baking pan. Bake at 350 degrees for 30 minutes. Combine brown sugar, corn syrup, vinegar and mustard in saucepan. Bring to a boil. Pour over ham balls. Bake for 20 minutes longer, basting several times.

Approx Per Serving: Cal 389; T Fat 19 g; 42% Calories from Fat;
   Prot 19; Carbo 38 g; Fiber 1 g; Chol 110 mg; Sod 568 mg.

Southwest Skillet Supper

Yield: 4 servings

1 large onion, chopped
1 cup chopped celery
2 tablespoons canola oil
1/2 teaspoon garlic powder
1 cup uncooked rice
1/2 teaspoon salt
2 cups water

1 16-ounce can black beans, drained
8 ounces very lean ham, chopped
White pepper to taste
1 4-ounce can chopped green chilies

Sauté onion and celery in oil in skillet for 1 minute, stirring constantly.; reduce heat. Cook, covered, for 3 minutes or until celery is tender. Add garlic powder, rice and salt. Stir in water. Bring to a boil; reduce heat. Simmer, covered, for 10 minutes. Add black beans and ham; mix well. Add white pepper to taste. Stir in chilies. Serve hot.

Approx Per Serving: Cal 430; T Fat 11 g; 22% Calories from Fat;
Prot 23; Carbo 60 g; Fiber 2 g; Chol 31 mg; Sod 1721 mg.

Upside-Down Ham Loaf

Yield: 10 servings

3 tablespoons butter
5 tablespoons brown sugar
3 slices pineapple, cut into halves
1 pound lean smoked ham, ground

8 ounces lean fresh pork, ground
1/2 cup bread crumbs
1/4 teaspoon pepper
2 eggs, beaten
1/4 cup milk

Melt butter in 5x9-inch loaf pan. Add brown sugar. Cook until sugar dissolves, stirring constantly. Arrange pineapple in pan. Cook over low heat for 5 minutes. Combine ham, pork, bread crumbs, pepper, eggs and milk in bowl; mix well. Spread over pineapple; press down. Bake at 350 degrees for 1 hour. Invert onto serving plate. Serve with whipped cream flavored with horseradish to taste.

Approx Per Serving: Cal 216; T Fat 9 g; 39% Calories from Fat;
Prot 19; Carbo 13 g; Fiber <1 g; Chol 95 mg; Sod 701 mg.

Evergreen

Basque Lamb Chops

Yield: 6 servings

2 cups Burgundy
3 tablespoons olive oil
2 tablespoons minced garlic
1 small onion, chopped

1 bay leaf
1/2 teaspoon salt
1/4 teaspoon pepper
6 lamb chops

Combine wine, olive oil, garlic, onion, bay leaf, salt and pepper in shallow dish; mix well. Add lamb chops, turning to coat with marinade. Marinate, covered, in refrigerator for 6 hours, turning chops several times; drain. Grill lamb chops until done to taste.

Approx Per Serving: Cal 283; T Fat 14 g; 43% Calories from Fat;
Prot 22; Carbo 4 g; Fiber <1 g; Chol 66 mg; Sod 243 mg.

Sweet and Sour Lamb Meatballs

Yield: 10 servings

2 pounds lean ground lamb
1 egg, beaten
1 egg white
2 teaspoons garlic powder
2/3 cup dry bread crumbs
2 20-ounce cans pineapple
   chunks
1 cup green bell pepper strips

3/4 cup sugar
1 teaspoon salt
1/4 cup cornstarch
1 cup water
1/2 cup vinegar
1/4 cup soy sauce
6 chicken bouillon cubes

Combine lamb, egg, egg white, garlic powder and bread crumbs in bowl; mix well. Shape into 20 meatballs. Place on rack in baking pan. Bake at 275 degrees for 20 to 25 minutes or until cooked through. Drain pineapple, reserving juice. Combine pineapple, green pepper and meatballs in slow cooker. Combine sugar, salt and cornstarch with reserved pineapple juice in saucepan; mix well. Add water, vinegar, soy sauce and bouillon cubes. Cook over medium heat until thickened, stirring constantly. Pour over meatballs. Cook on High for 1½ hours. Serve with rice. May be baked in casserole at 300 degrees for 1½ hours.

Approx Per Serving: Cal 356; T Fat 7 g; 19% Calories from Fat;
Prot 23; Carbo 48 g; Fiber 1 g; Chol 86 mg; Sod 1436 mg.

*The flowers and leaves of the colorful nasturtium
give a peppery, radish-like taste to dishes.*

Moussaka

Yield: 4 servings

1 pound eggplant, thinly sliced
2 tablespoons olive oil
2 large onions, thinly sliced
1 clove of garlic, chopped
1 pound lamb, coarsely chopped
1   14-ounce can tomatoes
2 tablespoons tomato purée

Several drops of Tabasco sauce
Salt and pepper to taste
2 eggs
1 cup cream
1 cup shredded Cheddar cheese
2 ounces Parmesan cheese,
   grated

Sauté eggplant ⅓ at a time in olive oil in skillet, turning once. Remove eggplant; drain on paper towel. Add onions and garlic. Sauté until golden brown. Add lamb. Cook for 15 minutes, stirring frequently. Add tomatoes, tomato purée and Tabasco sauce; mix well. Simmer for 20 minutes. Season with salt and pepper. Layer eggplant and lamb sauce alternately in 7x11-inch baking dish. Beat eggs and cream in bowl. Add cheeses; mix well. Pour over layers. Bake at 350 degrees for 35 to 40 minutes or until topping is set.

Approx Per Serving: Cal 740; T Fat 53 g; 64% Calories from Fat;
   Prot 45; Carbo 21 g; Fiber 6 g; Chol 307 mg; Sod 703 mg.

Lamb with Herb Butter Sauce

Yield: 2 servings

This is a no-fail method for cooking rack of lamb—always perfect.

1¼ pounds Frenched rack of
   lamb, trimmed
Salt and freshly ground pepper
   to taste
¼ cup unsalted butter, softened
1 tablespoon minced scallion

1 tablespoon minced fresh basil
   leaves
1 tablespoon lemon juice
1 tablespoon minced fresh
   sorrel

Preheat oven-proof skillet over medium-high heat. Season lamb with salt and pepper. Brown in preheated skillet for 5 minutes, turning frequently. Drain excess drippings. Place lamb fat side up. Bake at 500 degrees for 10 minutes for rare. Combine butter, scallion, basil, salt, pepper, lemon juice and sorrel in bowl; mix well. Remove lamb to cutting board. Let stand for 10 minutes. Add butter mixture to hot skillet, stirring to deglaze skillet. Cut lamb between ribs. Place on serving plates. Pour butter around lamb. Serve remaining butter with lamb.

Approx Per Serving: Cal 598; T Fat 44 g; 68% Calories from Fat;
   Prot 45; Carbo 2 g; Fiber <1 g; Chol 211 mg; Sod 146 mg.

Leg of Lamb with Prosciutto

Yield: 8 servings

1 7-pound leg of lamb, boned, trimmed	10 slices prosciutto
5 cloves of garlic, minced	1/2 teaspoon pepper
10 basil leaves, cut lengthwise into strips	2 sprigs of thyme
	2 bay leaves, crushed
	2 sprigs of rosemary

Unroll leg of lamb. Rub inside with garlic. Sprinkle with basil. Arrange prosciutto over top to cover. Roll into cylinder. Rub outside with pepper, thyme, bay leaves and rosemary. Tie with butcher's string. Chill, covered, overnight. Place on rack in roasting pan. Let stand until warmed to room temperature. Roast at 425 degrees to 140 degrees on meat thermometer for rare. Let rest for 15 minutes. Remove string; slice.

Approx Per Serving: Cal 515; T Fat 22 g; 39% Calories from Fat; Prot 74; Carbo 1 g; Fiber <1 g; Chol 232 mg; Sod 633 mg.

Braised Lamb Shanks

Yield: 4 servings

2 lamb shanks or 1 pound lamb stew meat	1 tablespoon Worcestershire sauce
1 tablespoon oil	1/4 cup cider vinegar
1/2 cup catsup	2 tablespoons brown sugar
1/2 cup water	1 teaspoon dry mustard
1/2 teaspoon garlic salt	1/2 cup chopped onion

Brown lamb in hot oil in skillet. Place in slow cooker. Combine catsup, water, garlic salt, Worcestershire sauce, vinegar, brown sugar and dry mustard in bowl; mix well. Pour over lamb. Sprinkle onion on top. Cook on High for 5 to 6 hours or until lamb is tender. May bake in casserole at 350 degrees for 2 hours. Serve over noodles or rice.

Approx Per Serving: Cal 130; T Fat 4 g; 28% Calories from Fat; Prot 3; Carbo 22 g; Fiber 2 g; Chol 0 mg; Sod 652 mg.

Tulips and daffodils can be fertilized with recommended bulb food as soon as they emerge in the spring and again when they have finished flowering. Do not allow seed pods to form but allow the foliage to remain until it yellows and can easily be pulled from the underground bulb.

Swedish Lamb Stew

Yield: 4 servings

2¹/₂ pounds lamb shoulder,
  trimmed, cut into cubes
4¹/₂ cups water
4 whole allspice
¹/₈ teaspoon salt
4 large carrots, peeled, sliced
¹/₄ cup flour

¹/₂ cup water
¹/₄ cup vinegar
2 tablespoons sugar
1 egg yolk, beaten
2 tablespoons chopped fresh
  dill

Rinse lamb. Place in large saucepan. Add 4¹/₂ cups water or enough to cover. Bring to a boil; skim surface. Add allspice and salt. Simmer for 1 hour. Add carrots. Simmer for 45 minutes or until lamb is tender. Remove lamb and carrots with slotted spoon. Combine flour and remaining ¹/₂ cup water in bowl; mix until smooth. Add vinegar, sugar and egg yolk; mix well. Whisk into cooking liquid. Add dill. Simmer until thickened, stirring constantly. Add lamb and carrots. Heat to serving temperature. Serve with boiled red potatoes and coleslaw.

Approx Per Serving: Cal 579; T Fat 26 g; 42% Calories from Fat; Prot 63; Carbo 20 g; Fiber 3 g; Chol 261 mg; Sod 222 mg.

Alsatian Pork Chop Casserole

Yield: 4 servings

6 slices bacon
4 lean 6-ounce pork chops
4 large potatoes, peeled, thinly
  sliced
2 medium onions, thinly sliced
1 teaspoon salt

¹/₄ teaspoon pepper
1 teaspoon caraway seed
2 cloves of garlic, crushed
1 tablespoon minced parsley
³/₄ cup dry white wine

Fry bacon in skillet until crisp. Remove bacon, reserving drippings. Brown pork chops in reserved bacon drippings; drain. Layer half the potatoes and onions in deep baking dish. Arrange pork chops in single layer on top. Layer remaining potatoes and onions over pork chops. Sprinkle salt, pepper, caraway seed, garlic, parsley and crumbled bacon over onions. Pour wine over layers. Cover with double thickness of foil. Bake at 300 degrees for 2¹/₂ hours.

Approx Per Serving: Cal 502; T Fat 16 g; 31% Calories from Fat; Prot 41; Carbo 40 g; Fiber 4 g; Chol 112 mg; Sod 778 mg.

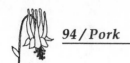

Pork Steaks with Apple

Yield: 6 servings

6 ¹/₂-inch thick pork steaks
1 tablespoon oil
Salt and pepper to taste
3 cups toasted bread cubes
1¹/₂ cups chopped unpeeled
   apples
¹/₂ cup chopped celery

¹/₂ cup chopped onion
¹/₂ cup chicken broth
1 teaspoon poultry seasoning
1 teaspoon salt
3 tart unpeeled red apples, cut
   into halves, cored
2 teaspoons sugar

Brown pork steaks on both sides in hot oil in skillet. Remove to shallow baking dish; season with salt and pepper. Combine bread cubes, chopped apples, celery, onion, chicken broth, poultry seasoning and salt in bowl; mix lightly. Spoon onto pork steaks. Top each steak with ¹/₂ apple; sprinkle lightly with sugar. Cover tightly with foil. Bake at 350 degrees for 1 hour.

Approx Per Serving: Cal 406; T Fat 14 g; 31% Calories from Fat;
   Prot 35 g; Carbo 37 g; Fiber 4 g; Chol 98 mg; Sod 707 mg.

Pork Chops with Red Cabbage

Yield: 4 servings

1 small Granny Smith apple
1 small onion
4 ounces red cabbage
2 tablespoons cornstarch
¹/₄ teaspoon salt
¹/₄ teaspoon pepper
4 lean center-cut pork chops,
   cut ¹/₄ inch thick

1 tablespoon oil
1 cup apple juice
¹/₂ teaspoon caraway seed
¹/₂ teaspoon sugar
¹/₄ teaspoon salt
¹/₄ teaspoon pepper
1 to 2 tablespoons vinegar

Shred apple, onion and cabbage in food processor fitted with shredding blade. Combine cornstarch and ¹/₄ teaspoon each salt and pepper. Coat pork chops with cornstarch mixture, reserving any leftover mixture. Brown pork chops in oil in skillet for 5 minutes on each side. Add apple juice. Bring to a boil; reduce heat. Simmer, covered, for 5 minutes or until pork chops are tender. Remove pork chops; keep warm. Add cabbage mixture to skillet. Bring to a boil. Add caraway seed, sugar, remaining ¹/₄ teaspoon salt and pepper and mixture of any remaining cornstarch mixture and vinegar. Simmer until cabbage is tender. Arrange pork chops on platter with cabbage mixture around edges.

Approx Per Serving: Cal 345; T Fat 14 g; 37% Calories from Fat;
   Prot 33; Carbo 21 g; Fiber 2 g; Chol 98 mg; Sod 351 mg.

Pork Chop and Potato Bake

Yield: 6 servings

6 pork chops
Seasoned salt and pepper to
   taste
1 10-ounce can cream of celery
   soup
1/2 cup milk
1/2 cup sour cream
1/2 teaspoon salt

1/4 teaspoon pepper
1 32-ounce package frozen
   hashed brown potatoes,
   thawed
1 3-ounce can French-fried
   onions
1 cup shredded Cheddar cheese

Brown pork chops on both sides in skillet. Sprinkle with seasoned salt and pepper to taste; set aside. Combine soup, milk, sour cream, 1/2 teaspoon salt, 1/4 teaspoon pepper, potatoes, half the onions and half the cheese in bowl; mix well. Spoon into greased 9x13-inch baking dish. Arrange pork chops over potatoes. Bake, covered, at 350 degrees for 40 minutes. Sprinkle remaining onions and cheese over top. Bake, uncovered, for 5 minutes longer.

Approx Per Serving: Cal 838; T Fat 50 g; 53% Calories from Fat;
    Prot 45; Carbo 55 g; Fiber 3 g; Chol 134 mg; Sod 923 mg.

Bratwurst and Onions in Beer

Yield: 8 servings

2 12-ounce packages bratwurst
3 medium onions, sliced
2 tablespoons oil
1 teaspoon caraway seed

1/2 teaspoon salt
1 12-ounce can beer
8 frankfurter rolls, split, toasted

Grill bratwurst over hot coals for 10 minutes. Sauté onions in oil in large saucepan on grill for 2 to 3 minutes. Stir in caraway seed, salt and beer. Bring to a boil. Add bratwurst. Heat, covered, for 10 minutes or longer. Serve on toasted rolls.

Approx Per Serving: Cal 265; T Fat 13 g; 45% Calories from Fat;
    Prot 8; Carbo 27 g; Fiber 2 g; Chol 16 mg; Sod 661 mg.

Dandelion

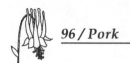

Kahlua Pig Mainland-Style

Yield: 16 servings

The Hawaiians cook the whole suckling pig in a pit lined with hot rocks. This version seems more practical for those of us who don't have such facilities.

1 8-pound boned fresh ham or pork butt
1½ tablespoons coarse salt
¼ cup liquid smoke

Ti leaves, corn husks or banana leaves
8 sweet potatoes

Make slits in pork roast. Sprinkle with salt; rub with liquid smoke. Wrap in leaves; tie with butcher's string. Wrap roast in heavy duty foil. Place on rack in roasting pan. Roast at 500 degrees for 30 minutes. Reduce oven temperature to 375 degrees. Roast for 4 hours. Arrange sweet potatoes around roast. Roast for 30 minutes to 1 hour or until roast and sweet potatoes are tender. Remove foil, string and leaves. Shred or cut meat into small pieces. Slice sweet potatoes. Serve with wasabi sauce and rice.

Approx Per Serving: Cal 386; T Fat 15 g; 36% Calories from Fat;
     Prot 46; Carbo 14 g; Fiber 2 g; Chol 140 mg; Sod 716 mg.
     Nutritional information does not include liquid smoke.

Pancit

Yield: 4 servings

This recipe can also be prepared with shrimp or chicken.

2 3-ounce packages ramen noodles
2 cups hot water
1 clove of garlic, crushed
1 onion, chopped
2 carrots, sliced
2 cups green beans

2 tablespoons soy sauce
1 green, red or yellow bell pepper, chopped
1 tomato, cut into wedges
2 hard-boiled eggs, sliced
2 cups chopped cooked pork

Soften noodles in hot water in saucepan. Add flavor packets; mix well. Add garlic, onion, carrots, green beans, soy sauce, pepper and tomato. Cook for 5 minutes or until vegetables are tender-crisp. Add eggs and pork. Heat to serving temperature.

Approx Per Serving: Cal 390; T Fat 16 g; 35% Calories from Fat;
     Prot 28; Carbo 37 g; Fiber 5 g; Chol 162 mg; Sod 1240 mg.

Hawaiian Roast Loin of Pork

Yield: 10 servings

1 5-pound boned pork loin	1/2 cup chopped onion
1 clove of garlic, minced	1/4 cup butter
1 teaspoon salt	4 cups cooked rice
1/4 teaspoon freshly ground pepper	1 13-ounce can pineapple tidbits, drained
2 tablespoons honey	1/2 cup golden raisins
1/4 cup soy sauce	1 teaspoon salt
1 cup beef broth	1 teaspoon curry powder
2 tablespoons dry sherry	1 teaspoon oregano

Rub pork with mixture of garlic, 1 teaspoon salt, pepper, honey, soy sauce, broth and sherry. Let stand for 2 hours, rubbing marinade into pork and turning frequently. Place in roasting pan. Roast at 325 degrees for 2 1/2 to 3 hours or until tender, basting frequently with marinade and pan drippings. Sauté onion in butter in skillet. Add rice, pineapple, raisins and seasonings; mix well. Spoon into greased 6-cup baking dish. Bake at 325 degrees for 30 minutes. Serve with roast.

Approx Per Serving: Cal 523; T Fat 20 g; 34% Calories from Fat; Prot 48; Carbo 36 g; Fiber 1 g; Chol 151 mg; Sod 1066 mg.

Posole

Yield: 5 servings

8 ounces posole, rinsed	1/2 teaspoon oregano
3 cups cold water	1 teaspoon salt
2 onions, chopped	1/4 teaspoon pepper
2 cloves of garlic, chopped	1 cup chicken broth
2 tablespoons oil	1 4-ounce can green chilies
1 1/2 pounds pork, cut into cubes	1 jalapeño pepper, minced

Combine posole and water in large heavy saucepan. Simmer, covered, for 3 to 4 hours or until kernels burst and are almost tender. Sauté onions and garlic in 2 tablespoons oil in skillet. Remove with slotted spoon. Add pork. Cook until brown. Add onions, garlic and pork to posole. Add remaining ingredients. Simmer for 3 hours.

Approx Per Serving: Cal 358; T Fat 15 g; 38% Calories from Fat; Prot 31; Carbo 24 g; Fiber 1 g; Chol 83 mg; Sod 1230 mg.

Easy Posole

Yield: 6 servings

2 16-ounce cans white hominy
2 pounds cooked pork, chopped
1 green bell pepper, chopped
Pork broth to taste
1 clove of garlic, chopped

Tabasco sauce to taste
Salt and pepper to taste
1 cup enchilada sauce
8 ounces Velveeta cheese,
    chopped

Combine hominy, pork, green pepper and enough broth to make of desired consistency in saucepan. Cook for 10 minutes. Add garlic, seasonings and enchilada sauce. Cook until tender. Add cheese. Cook until cheese melts.

Approx Per Serving: Cal 458; T Fat 23 g; 45% Calories from Fat;
    Prot 41; Carbo 22 g; Fiber <1 g; Chol 128 mg; Sod 1218 mg.

Barbecued Ribs, Ham and Sausage

Yield: 24 servings

15 pounds ham or pork shoulder
Barbecue Sauce (below)

12 pounds pork spareribs
6 pounds link sausage

Build fire of hickory or oak wood slabs. Let burn for several hours to prepare bed of coals. Cover ham with thick pieces of cardboard to prevent ashes from hot coals settling on meat. Place ham on rack over coals. Cook for 8 hours or to 180 degrees on meat thermometer. Chop or slice ham. Mix with Barbecue Sauce. Simmer ribs in water in saucepan over medium heat for 30 minutes; drain. Place on grill rack. Grill until tender, basting every 10 minutes with Barbecue Sauce. Place sausage on grill toward end of cooking time. Grill until done to taste. You may need several recipes of Barbecue Sauce to prepare this amount of meat.

Nutritional information for this recipe is not available.

Barbecue Sauce

Yield: 64 tablespoons

1/2 cup sugar
1 1/2 cups margarine
1 14-ounce bottle of catsup
1/2 8-ounce bottle of
    Worcestershire sauce

Salt, black pepper and red
    pepper to taste
2 lemons, sliced
2 cups vinegar

Combine sugar, margarine, catsup, Worcestershire sauce, seasonings, lemons and vinegar in saucepan. Cook over medium heat for 30 minutes.

Approx Per Tablespoon: Cal 13; T Fat 1 g; 69% Calories from Fat;
    Prot <1; Carbo 1 g; Fiber <1 g; Chol 0 mg; Sod 33 mg.

Hot and Sour Spareribs

Yield: 4 servings

1/4 cup minced green onions
2 cloves of garlic, minced
1 large piece fresh ginger, 1/2 inch thick, chopped
1/4 cup peanut oil
2 pounds country-style spareribs, cut into 1 1/2-inch pieces
1 teaspoon salt
3 tablespoons sugar

3 tablespoons dry sherry
2 tablespoons reduced-sodium soy sauce
2 tablespoons hoisen sauce
2 tablespoons chili pepper oil
2 tablespoons red wine vinegar
1/2 teaspoon pepper
1 cup chicken broth
2 tablespoons chopped fresh cilantro

Sauté green onions, garlic and ginger in peanut oil in Dutch oven for 3 minutes. Rub ribs with salt. Add to skillet. Cook for 8 minutes or until brown on all sides. Add mixture of sugar, sherry, soy sauce, hoisen sauce, chili pepper oil, vinegar and pepper. Cook for 5 minutes. Add chicken broth. Simmer, covered, for 20 minutes. Simmer, uncovered, for 10 minutes longer. Bake at 375 degrees for 1 hour. Transfer to serving plate. Garnish with cilantro.

Approx Per Serving: Cal 537; T Fat 40 g; 69% Calories from Fat; Prot 28; Carbo 13 g; Fiber <1 g; Chol 104 mg; Sod 1196 mg. Nutritional information does not include hoisen sauce and chili pepper oil.

Hungarian Goulash

Yield: 6 servings

3 pounds boneless veal, cut into 1 1/2-inch cubes
4 cups onion wedges
2 teaspoons salt
2 teaspoons pepper

2 tablespoons Hungarian paprika
1 cup (about) water
1 cup sour cream
4 cups buttered noodles

Combine veal, onions, salt, pepper and paprika in heavy kettle; do not add water. Cook, covered, over medium heat for 20 minutes, stirring frequently. Simmer, covered, for 2 hours or until tender. Add enough water to make gravy of desired consistency. Serve with sour cream, buttered noodles and German rye bread.

Approx Per Serving: Cal 504; T Fat 16 g; 29% Calories from Fat; Prot 52; Carbo 36 g; Fiber 5 g; Chol 237 mg; Sod 852 mg.

Osso Buco

Yield: 2 servings

4 veal shins
1/4 cup flour
3 tablespoons oil
1/4 cup margarine
3/4 cup white wine

1/4 cup chopped fresh parsley
3 cloves of garlic, chopped
1 tablespoon chopped rosemary
2 cups chicken broth
Salt and pepper to taste

Rinse veal shins; coat with flour. Fry in oil and margarine in skillet until golden brown on both sides. Add wine. Cook until wine evaporates. Add parsley, garlic and rosemary. Add chicken broth, salt and pepper. Cook, covered, over medium-low heat for 2 hours or until veal is tender.

Approx Per Serving: Cal 805; T Fat 51 g; 57% Calories from Fat;
    Prot 54; Carbo 16 g; Fiber 1 g; Chol 195 mg; Sod 1172 mg.

Veal Scallopini

Yield: 4 servings

1/2 cup flour
1 teaspoon salt
1/4 teaspoon pepper
1/4 teaspoon oregano
1/4 teaspoon garlic powder
1 pound thinly sliced veal
1/4 cup vegetable oil
2 tablespoons butter

1 medium onion, chopped
2 cloves of garlic, minced
1 cup sliced mushrooms
2 teaspoons chopped parsley
1 teaspoon salt
1/4 teaspoon pepper
1/4 teaspoon oregano
3 tomatoes

Combine flour, 1 teaspoon salt, 1/4 teaspoon pepper, 1/4 teaspoon oregano and garlic powder in small bowl. Cut veal into 2-inch pieces. Coat well with flour mixture. Sauté veal in mixture of oil and butter in large skillet until golden brown on both sides. Remove to platter. Add onion and garlic to skillet. Sauté until transparent. Add mushrooms, parsley, 1 teaspoon salt, 1/4 teaspoon pepper and 1/4 teaspoon oregano; mix well. Squeeze tomatoes into mushroom mixture. Add veal. Cook over medium heat until veal is tender, stirring frequently.

Approx Per Serving: Cal 390; T Fat 23 g; 53% Calories from Fat;
    Prot 26; Carbo 20 g; Fiber 3 g; Chol 109 mg; Sod 1182 mg.

Elk or Moose Steak Parmigiana   *Yield: 3 servings*

½ cup dry bread crumbs
⅓ cup grated Parmesan cheese
¼ cup flour
1 egg
2 tablespoons water
1¼ pounds elk or moose round
  steak
⅓ cup oil

1 medium onion, chopped
1 6-ounce can tomato paste
2 cups hot water
½ teaspoon marjoram
1 teaspoon salt
¼ teaspoon pepper
8 ounces part-skim mozzarella
  cheese, shredded

Combine bread crumbs, Parmesan cheese and flour in dish. Blend egg and water in bowl. Dip steak in egg mixture; coat with crumbs. Brown on both sides in oil in skillet. Place in casserole. Top with onion, tomato paste, water, marjoram, salt, pepper and mozzarella cheese. Bake at 350 degrees for 30 minutes.

Approx Per Serving: Cal 789; T Fat 43 g; 51% Calories from Fat;
    Prot 56; Carbo 37 g; Fiber 4 g; Chol 203 mg; Sod 1412 mg.

Elk Steak Teriyaki   *Yield: 4 servings*

2 pounds elk steaks
¼ cup soy sauce
3 tablespoons honey
½ cup oil
1½ teaspoons ginger

1½ tablespoons finely chopped
  garlic
2 tablespoons wine vinegar
2 onions, chopped

Pierce steak slightly with fork. Place in shallow dish. Cover with mixture of soy sauce, honey, oil, ginger, garlic, vinegar and onions. Marinate in refrigerator for 12 to 24 hours. Grill over hot coals until done to taste.

Approx Per Serving: Cal 517; T Fat 28 g; 49% Calories from Fat;
    Prot 33; Carbo 23 g; Fiber 1 g; Chol 99 mg; Sod 1033 mg.

*"Damp Off" is a danger when starting seedlings.
It is often blamed on fungus in the soil, but it
is only a problem when the planting medium sup-
porting the seeds is excessively damp.*

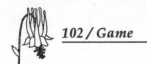

Old Settler's Venison Beans

Yield: 18 servings

2 pounds ground venison
1 onion, chopped
2/3 cup packed brown sugar
2/3 cup sugar
1/2 cup catsup
1/2 cup barbecue sauce
1/4 cup molasses
1/4 cup mustard
1 teaspoon chili powder

2 teaspoons salt
1 teaspoon pepper
1   31-ounce can pork and beans
1   17-ounce can green lima
    beans
1   17-ounce can red kidney
    beans
1 pound bacon, crisp-fried,
    drained

Sauté ground venison with onion in skillet until browned. Add brown sugar, sugar, catsup, barbecue sauce, molasses, mustard and seasonings; mix well. Drain beans. Add to venison mixture. Crumble bacon; stir into beans. Pour mixture into 10x14-inch baking pan. Bake, covered, at 350 degrees for 30 minutes. Bake, uncovered, for 30 minutes longer.

Approx Per Serving: Cal 290; T Fat 6 g; 18% Calories from Fat;
    Prot 19; Carbo 41 g; Fiber 7 g; Chol 34 mg; Sod 917 mg.

Venison Curry

Yield: 4 servings

1 large onion, chopped
1 tart green apple, peeled,
    chopped
2 tablespoons butter
2 tablespoons flour
1 tablespoon curry powder

1 cup warm beef stock
1/2 cup pale dry sherry
1 tablespoon lemon juice
1/4 teaspoon nutmeg
Salt and pepper to taste
2 cups chopped, cooked venison

Sauté onion and apple in butter in skillet for 5 minutes or until onion is transparent. Remove onion and apple; set aside. Stir in flour and curry powder. Cook over low heat for 4 to 5 minutes; do not brown. Add stock and sherry, stirring constantly. Add lemon juice, nutmeg, salt and pepper. Cook over low heat until sauce thickens, stirring constantly. Stir in sautéed onion, apple and venison. Simmer for 3 to 4 minutes. Serve hot over rice with chutney and condiments such as raisins or dried currants, fresh pineapple and roasted peanuts.

Approx Per Serving: Cal 245; T Fat 8 g; 29% Calories from Fat;
    Prot 23; Carbo 12 g; Fiber 2 g; Chol 62 mg; Sod 298 mg.

Poultry & Seafood

Peaches & Cream

Deep South

Alabama • Florida • Georgia • Louisiana
Mississippi • Tennessee

*S*uccessfully combining the traditions of the Old South with the varied expertise of transplanted "snowbirds" makes this a dynamic region. The personal response of countless members to the challenge of beautification and conservation adds new dimensions to the Region, the nation and the world. The members are the strength as surely as the memories are the pride of the Region.

Florida's Sea Treasures

Hot Crab Salad*
Carrots à l'Orange*
Tossed Salad
Corny Corn Bread*
Ambrosia

Eating Georgia Style

These recipes feature peanuts and chicken—two Georgia products which are exported worldwide.

Cream of Peanut Soup*
Georgia-Style Country Captain*
Buttered Asparagus Delight
Broiled Peach Halves with Chutney
Angel Biscuits*
Georgia Peach Cobbler or
Dried Peach Custard Pie*

*See index for recipes.

Poultry

Fricassee and Lemon Dumplings

Yield: 2 servings

4 chicken legs
1 cup water
1   10-ounce package frozen
    mixed vegetables
1/4 cup chopped celery
1 tablespoon chopped onion
1 teaspoon chicken-flavored
    gravy base
1/2 teaspoon salt
Pepper to taste

3 tablespoons flour
1/2 cup cold water
1/3 cup flour
1/2 teaspoon baking powder
1/4 teaspoon salt
1/4 cup milk
1/2 teaspoon chopped parsley
1/4 teaspoon grated lemon rind
1/2 teaspoon lemon juice

Rinse chicken well. Combine with 1 cup water, frozen mixed vegetables, celery, onion, gravy base, 1/2 teaspoon salt and pepper in 2-quart saucepan. Simmer for 20 minutes or until chicken is tender. Stir in mixture of 3 tablespoons flour and 1/2 cup cold water. Cook over medium heat until thickened, stirring constantly. Mix 1/3 cup flour, baking powder and 1/4 teaspoon salt in bowl. Combine milk, parsley, lemon rind and lemon juice in small bowl; mix well. Add to dry ingredients; mix just until moistened. Drop into hot chicken mixture. Simmer, covered, for 20 minutes.

Approx Per Serving: Cal 528; T Fat 11 g; 20% Calories from Fat;
    Prot 57 g; Carbo 47 g; Fiber 7 g; Chol 163 mg; Sod 1242 mg.

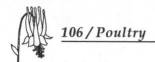

Cherry-Sauced Chicken Breasts

Yield: 6 servings

6 large chicken breasts
3 tablespoons butter
Salt and pepper to taste
1 16-ounce can light or dark
   sweet cherries

1 tablespoon cornstarch
2 tablespoons lemon juice
1/4 teaspoon cinnamon

Rinse chicken and pat dry. Cook in butter in skillet until golden brown. Season with salt and pepper. Place in shallow baking dish. Bake, covered, at 350 degrees for 30 minutes. Drain cherries, reserving juice. Heat juice in skillet. Stir in mixture of cornstarch, lemon juice and cinnamon gradually. Cook until thickened, stirring constantly. Stir in cherries. Pour over chicken. Bake, covered, for 15 minutes. Serve with steamed rice.

Approx Per Serving: Cal 400; T Fat 12 g; 27% Calories from Fat;
     Prot 53 g; Carbo 18 g; Fiber <1 g; Chol 160 mg; Sod 177 mg.

Chicken Breasts Tarragon

Yield: 8 servings

8 8-ounce chicken breasts
2 tablespoons oil
2 tablespoons margarine
6 shallots, chopped
2 carrots, sliced 1/4 inch thick
1/4 cup brandy or Cognac
1 cup dry white wine
1 1/2 tablespoons chopped fresh
   chervil or 1/2 teaspoon dried
   chervil

1/4 cup chopped fresh tarragon
   or 2 teaspoons dried tarragon
1/2 teaspoon salt
1/8 teaspoon pepper
1 cup half and half
1 egg yolk
1 tablespoon flour
4 ounces mushrooms, thinly
   sliced
2 tablespoons margarine

Rinse chicken and pat dry. Cook in oil and 2 tablespoons margarine in heavy saucepan, removing to platter when brown on both sides. Add shallots and carrots to drippings in saucepan. Sauté for 5 minutes. Return chicken to saucepan. Cook until heated through. Heat brandy in small saucepan over medium heat. Ignite brandy; pour over chicken. Add wine, chervil, tarragon, salt and pepper. Simmer, covered, for 30 minutes. Remove chicken to heated platter; keep warm. Strain pan drippings, discarding vegetables. Return drippings to saucepan. Whisk half and half, egg yolk and flour in bowl until smooth. Stir into drippings. Bring to a boil, stirring constantly. Sauté mushrooms in 2 tablespoons margarine in skillet for 5 minutes. Spoon sauce over chicken; spoon mushrooms over top. Garnish with sprigs of fresh tarragon.

Approx Per Serving: Cal 482; T Fat 19 g; 36% Calories from Fat;
     Prot 56 g; Carbo 12 g; Fiber 2 g; Chol 182 mg; Sod 351 mg.

Guava Jelly Barbecued Chicken

Yield: 8 servings

5 pounds chicken thighs
Salt to taste
½ cup water
¼ cup soy sauce
2 tablespoons sugar
Juice of 1 lime

½ teaspoon allspice
½ teaspoon pepper
1 cup guava jelly
1 tablespoon cornstarch
1 tablespoon water

Rinse chicken, removing skin and fat. Cut skin into ½-inch strips. Arrange chicken bone side up in foil-lined 9x13-inch baking pan; sprinkle with salt. Place strips of fat between pieces of chicken. Bake at 400 degrees for 30 minutes. Turn chicken over. Bring ½ cup water and next 5 ingredients to a boil in saucepan. Stir in jelly until melted. Blend cornstarch with 1 tablespoon water in small bowl. Add to saucepan. Cook until thickened, stirring constantly. Pour over chicken. Reduce oven temperature to 375 degrees. Bake for 30 minutes or until chicken is tender. Discard strips of fat. Skim fat from sauce. Serve sauce with chicken.

Approx Per Serving: Cal 405; T Fat 16 g; 35% Calories from Fat;
Prot 37 g; Carbo 28 g; Fiber <1 g; Chol 134 mg; Sod 648 mg.

Georgia-Style Country Captain

Yield: 6 servings

1 green bell pepper, chopped
1 medium onion, chopped
1 small clove of garlic, minced
1 tablespoon oil
2 28-ounce cans tomatoes,
    crushed
1 teaspoon curry powder
1 tablespoon chopped parsley
1 tablespoon thyme
1 teaspoon salt

½ teaspoon pepper
6 chicken breasts
Salt and pepper to taste
1 cup buttermilk
¾ cup flour
1 cup oil for frying
¼ cup currants
4 ounces almonds, toasted
3 cups cooked rice

Sauté green pepper, onion and garlic in 1 tablespoon oil in skillet for 4 minutes or until tender. Add next 6 ingredients; mix well. Cook for 10 minutes; set aside. Rinse chicken and pat dry. Season with salt and pepper to taste. Dip in buttermilk. Sprinkle with flour, coating well. Fry in 1 cup oil in skillet over medium heat until golden brown on both sides; drain on paper towel. Place chicken in baking dish. Stir currants into prepared sauce. Spoon over chicken. Bake, covered, at 350 degrees for 45 minutes. Place chicken on serving platter. Spoon rice around chicken; sprinkle with almonds. Serve with sauce.

Approx Per Serving: Cal 524; T Fat 17 g; 28% Calories from Fat;
Prot 38 g; Carbo 57 g; Fiber 7 g; Chol 74 mg; Sod 895 mg.
Nutritional information does not include oil for frying.

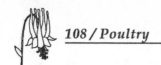

Ginger Chicken

Yield: 4 servings

1 teaspoon grated fresh ginger	4 chicken breasts, skinned
1/3 cup honey	1 tablespoon cornstarch
1/3 cup chili sauce	2 tablespoons water
1/3 cup soy sauce	

Combine ginger, honey, chili sauce and soy sauce in 7x11-inch glass dish; mix well. Rinse chicken and pat dry. Place in prepared dish, turning to coat well. Microwave, covered, on Medium-High for 20 minutes. Pour mixture of cornstarch and water over chicken. Microwave for 2 minutes longer. Serve on rice.

Approx Per Serving: Cal 275; T Fat 3 g; 10% Calories from Fat;
      Prot 29 g; Carbo 34 g; Fiber <1 g; Chol 72 mg; Sod 1874 mg.

Hawaiian Chicken

Yield: 6 servings

2 10-ounce packages frozen chopped spinach, thawed	1 12-ounce can coconut milk
2 pounds chicken pieces	1 teaspoon onion flakes
1 10-ounce can cream of chicken soup	1 teaspoon sugar
	Salt to taste

Spread spinach in baking dish. Rinse chicken and pat dry. Arrange over spinach. Combine soup, coconut milk, onion flakes, sugar and salt in bowl; mix well. Spoon over chicken; do not mix. Bake at 375 degrees for 1 1/2 hours. May thicken with cornstarch if desired.

Approx Per Serving: Cal 328; T Fat 21 g; 55% Calories from Fat;
      Prot 27 g; Carbo 11 g; Fiber 3 g; Chol 71 mg; Sod 525 mg.

Honey-Mustard Grilled Chicken

Yield: 4 servings

4 chicken breasts, skinned	1/2 cup honey
1/4 cup brown mustard	1 teaspoon curry powder

Rinse chicken and pat dry. Arrange in shallow baking dish. Combine mustard, honey and curry powder in small saucepan; mix well. Cook just until heated through. Pour over chicken. Marinate for 1 hour. Drain, reserving marinade. Grill chicken over hot coals until tender, brushing occasionally with reserved marinade.

Approx Per Serving: Cal 281; T Fat 4 g; 12% Calories from Fat;
      Prot 27 g; Carbo 36 g; Fiber <1 g; Chol 72 mg; Sod 261 mg.

Chicken Vermouth

Yield: 8 servings

8 large pieces chicken, boned,
   skinned
¾ cup dry vermouth
¼ cup soy sauce
¼ cup oil

2 tablespoons water
1 tablespoon brown sugar
1 teaspoon ginger
¼ teaspoon oregano

Rinse chicken and pat dry. Arrange in baking dish. Combine vermouth, soy sauce, oil, water, brown sugar, ginger and oregano in bowl; mix well. Spoon over chicken. Bake, covered, at 375 degrees for 1½ hours.

Approx Per Serving: Cal 260; T Fat 13 g; 46% Calories from Fat;
   Prot 25 g; Carbo 4 g; Fiber 0 g; Chol 76 mg; Sod 592 mg.

Yorkshire Chicken

Yield: 4 servings

The topping on this chicken puffs like Yorkshire pudding as it bakes.

1   3-pound chicken, cut up
⅓ cup flour
1½ teaspoons sage
2 teaspoons salt
¼ teaspoon pepper
¼ cup shortening
1 cup flour

1 teaspoon baking powder
1 teaspoon salt
3 eggs, beaten
1½ cups milk
¼ cup melted margarine
¼ cup chopped parsley

Rinse chicken well. Coat with mixture of ⅓ cup flour, sage, 2 teaspoons salt and pepper. Brown on all sides in shortening in skillet; drain. Place in 2-quart baking dish. Sift 1 cup flour, baking powder and 1 teaspoon salt in bowl. Combine eggs, milk, margarine and parsley in bowl; mix well. Add to dry ingredients; mix well. Spoon over chicken. Bake at 350 degrees for 1 hour.

Approx Per Serving: Cal 808; T Fat 45 g; 50% Calories from Fat;
   Prot 61 g; Carbo 37 g; Fiber 1 g; Chol 324 mg; Sod 2053 mg.

Branches for forcing can be cut when the ground is free of snow and plants are easier to reach. They need not all be taken indoors at the same time but can be left lying on the ground outdoors until time to begin the forcing process inside.

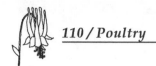

Cheese-Stuffed Chicken Breasts
Yield: 4 servings

4 chicken breast filets
4 1-ounce sticks mozzarella
   cheese
2 tablespoons flour
1 tablespoon grated Parmesan
   cheese

1 teaspoon chopped parsley
1/4 teaspoon paprika
Pepper to taste
1 egg white, beaten

Rinse chicken and pat dry. Cut a small pocket in thickest part of chicken with sharp knife. Insert 1 stick mozzarella cheese into each slit. Mix flour, Parmesan cheese, parsley, paprika and pepper in bowl. Dip chicken into egg white; coat with flour mixture. Arrange in 6x10-inch baking dish coated with nonstick cooking spray. Bake at 375 degrees for 20 to 25 minutes or until chicken is tender.

Approx Per Serving: Cal 244; T Fat 9 g; 35% Calories from Fat;
      Prot 34 g; Carbo 4 g; Fiber <1 g; Chol 95 mg; Sod 205 mg.

Chicken with Cashews
Yield: 4 servings

1 pound chicken breast filets
2 tablespoons light soy sauce
2 teaspoons cornstarch
1 teaspoon sherry
1/2 cup water
3 slices fresh ginger
2 cups coarsely chopped celery
1 cup oil
1 clove of garlic, chopped
1/2 onion, coarsely chopped

1 cup fresh mushrooms
1/2 cup bamboo shoots
1/2 cup water
1 teaspoon sugar
2 teaspoons salt
2 teaspoons cornstarch
2 teaspoons water
1/3 cup cashews
1 teaspoon sesame oil

Rinse chicken and pat dry. Chop into 3/4-inch pieces. Combine with soy sauce, 2 teaspoons cornstarch, wine, water and ginger in bowl. Marinate for 30 minutes. Cook celery in boiling water to cover in saucepan for 5 minutes; drain and rinse in cold water. Stir 1 tablespoon oil into chicken mixture. Heat remaining oil in skillet. Add chicken mixture. Cook until chicken is tender, stirring constantly; remove with slotted spoon. Add garlic and onion to drippings in skillet. Cook for 1 minute, stirring constantly. Add celery, mushrooms and bamboo shoots. Cook for 1 minute, stirring constantly. Stir in 1/2 cup water, sugar and salt. Bring to a boil. Stir in mixture of 2 teaspoons cornstarch and 2 teaspoons water. Cook until thickened, stirring constantly. Add chicken, cashews and sesame oil. Cook just until heated through.

Approx Per Serving: Cal 737; T Fat 64 g; 77% Calories from Fat;
      Prot 30 g; Carbo 12 g; Fiber 3 g; Chol 72 mg; Sod 1381 mg.

Chicken Casserole

Yield: 8 servings

6 ounces thinly sliced dried
   beef or ham
8 chicken breast filets
4 slices bacon, cut into halves

1 cup sour cream
1 10-ounce can cream of
   mushroom soup

Spread dried beef in 8x10-inch baking dish. Rinse chicken and pat dry. Wrap each piece with 1/2 slice of bacon. Arrange over dried beef. Pour mixture of sour cream and soup over chicken. Bake at 275 degrees for 1 1/2 hours.

Approx Per Serving: Cal 290; T Fat 14 g; 46% Calories from Fat;
    Prot 34 g; Carbo 4 g; Fiber <1 g; Chol 100 mg; Sod 698 mg.

Curried Roast Chicken

Yield: 4 servings

1/4 cup chicken stock
3 cloves of garlic, minced
2 teaspoons curry powder
2 teaspoons honey
1 teaspoon marjoram
1 teaspoon fennel
1 teaspoon cumin
1 teaspoon coriander

1/2 teaspoon fenugreek
1/2 teaspoon crushed saffron
   threads
1/2 teaspoon red pepper flakes
1/8 teaspoon black pepper
1/2 cup nonfat yogurt
1 pound chicken breast filets

Combine chicken stock, garlic, curry powder, honey, marjoram, fennel, cumin, coriander, fenugreek, saffron, red pepper and black pepper in large nonstick skillet. Simmer for 1 minute, stirring constantly. Cool for 5 minutes. Stir in yogurt. Rinse chicken and pat dry. Pound 1/3 to 1/2 inch thick between waxed paper. Place in spice mixture, turning to coat well. Marinate in refrigerator for 30 minutes, turning once. Place in lightly oiled baking pan. Place in oven preheated to 500 degrees; reduce oven temperature to 350 degrees. Roast chicken for 45 minutes or until tender.

Approx Per Serving: Cal 173; T Fat 3 g; 17% Calories from Fat;
    Prot 29 g; Carbo 6 g; Fiber <1 g; Chol 73 mg; Sod 134 mg.

Oak leaves do not make the soil too acid for the majority of plants. Most plants like soil on the acid side and grow better in humus made from decomposing oak leaves. Oak leaves are heavy and do not pack and smother like the thinner leaves of maples which may shut out needed air if applied too heavily.

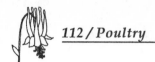

Chicken Dijon

Yield: 4 servings

1 teaspoon olive oil
2 cloves of garlic, minced
2 green onions, thinly sliced
2 tablespoons dry white wine
1 tablespoon fresh lemon juice
¼ cup Dijon mustard

1 teaspoon chopped fresh
   tarragon or ¼ teaspoon dried
   tarragon
Freshly ground pepper to taste
4 4-ounce chicken breast filets

Combine olive oil, garlic and green onions in 10-inch glass dish. Microwave on High for 1 minute. Stir in wine, lemon juice, mustard, tarragon and pepper. Rinse chicken and pat dry. Add to sauce in dish, turning to coat well. Arrange around outer edge of dish. Microwave, covered, for 3 minutes. Turn chicken over; baste with sauce. Microwave, covered, for 3 to 5 minutes longer or until chicken is tender. Serve with sauce.

Approx Per Serving: Cal 172; T Fat 5 g; 27% Calories from Fat;
    Prot 27 g; Carbo 2 g; Fiber <1 g; Chol 72 mg; Sod 260 mg.

Chicken Dinner with Artichokes

Yield: 8 servings

8 chicken breast filets
3 ounces cream cheese, softened
1 10-ounce can cream of
   mushroom soup
1 envelope Italian salad
   dressing mix

½ cup dry white wine
1 8-ounce can mushrooms,
   drained
1 10-ounce package frozen
   artichoke hearts, thawed
12 small red potatoes

Rinse chicken and pat dry. Arrange in baking dish. Combine cream cheese, soup, salad dressing mix and wine in bowl. Add mushrooms and artichoke hearts; mix well. Spoon over chicken. Bake, covered, at 350 degrees for 1 hour. Add potatoes, covering with sauce. Bake until potatoes are tender.

Approx Per Serving: Cal 413; T Fat 10 g; 22% Calories from Fat;
    Prot 33 g; Carbo 46 g; Fiber 7 g; Chol 84 mg; Sod 654 mg.

 Heavy clay soils can be made more workable with the addition of humus such as mushroom compost combined with coarse sand. This combination modifies the soil texture more rapidly than using humus only.

Chicken and Ham Casserole

Yield: 8 servings

1 cup flour
1 teaspoon savory
1 teaspoon each salt and pepper
8 chicken breast filets
1/4 cup butter
4 thin slices cooked ham
1/4 cup butter
8 ounces mushrooms, sliced
2 medium onions, minced
1 clove of garlic, crushed

1 tablespoon chopped parsley
1/4 teaspoon savory
1/8 teaspoon mace
1 teaspoon salt
Pepper to taste
1/2 cup chicken broth
1/2 cup sherry
2 teaspoons light brown sugar
1/2 cup orange juice
1   10-ounce package frozen peas

Mix flour, 1 teaspoon savory, 1 teaspoon salt and 1 teaspoon pepper in paper bag. Rinse chicken well. Add to bag; shake to coat well. Brown in 1/4 cup butter in large skillet; drain on paper towel. Arrange chicken in 9x13-inch baking dish. Trim fat from ham; cut into halves lengthwise. Roll up ham strips; secure with toothpicks. Add ham to drippings in skillet. Cook until brown. Arrange around chicken. Add remaining 1/4 cup butter to skillet. Add mushrooms, onions, garlic, parsley, 1/4 teaspoon savory, mace, 1 teaspoon salt and pepper to taste. Cook until vegetables are tender. Stir in chicken broth, wine, brown sugar and orange juice. Cook for 5 minutes, stirring constantly. Spoon over chicken and ham. Bake, covered with foil, at 325 degrees for 1 hour. Baste chicken with sauce. Add peas; mix gently. Bake for 15 minutes longer or just until peas are tender, basting frequently. Serve with baked rice casserole.

Approx Per Serving: Cal 401; T Fat 16 g; 38% Calories from Fat;
    Prot 35 g; Carbo 24 g; Fiber 3 g; Chol 111 mg; Sod 974 mg.

Curried Chicken Florentine

Yield: 8 servings

2   10-ounce packages frozen
    chopped spinach, thawed
8 chicken breast filets
2   10-ounce cans cream of
    chicken soup

1 cup mayonnaise
1 teaspoon curry powder
1 tablespoon lemon juice
1 cup shredded Cheddar cheese
Paprika to taste

Squeeze spinach to remove excess moisture. Spread in shallow baking dish. Rinse chicken and pat dry. Arrange over spinach. Combine soup, mayonnaise, curry powder and lemon juice in bowl; mix well. Spoon over chicken. Top with cheese; sprinkle with paprika. Bake at 350 degrees for 1 hour.

Approx Per Serving: Cal 481; T Fat 34 g; 63% Calories from Fat;
    Prot 34 g; Carbo 10 g; Fiber 2 g; Chol 109 mg; Sod 925 mg.

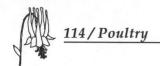
Greek-Style Chicken with Tomatoes   *Yield: 4 servings*

1 pound chicken breast filets
1/4 cup water
2 cups sliced celery
3/4 teaspoon oregano

4 cups chopped tomatoes
3/4 teaspoon salt
1/8 teaspoon pepper
1/4 cup crumbled feta cheese

Rinse chicken and pat dry. Cut into 1/2-inch strips. Bring water to a boil in skillet sprayed with nonstick cooking spray. Add celery; reduce heat. Simmer for 3 to 4 minutes or until celery is tender-crisp. Add chicken, oregano, tomatoes, salt and pepper. Simmer for 5 minutes or until chicken is tender. Sprinkle with cheese. Serve over steamed rice.

Approx Per Serving: Cal 204; T Fat 5 g; 22% Calories from Fat;
    Prot 30 g; Carbo 10 g; Fiber 4 g; Chol 78 mg; Sod 610 mg.

Honey Orange Chicken   *Yield: 4 servings*

2 tablespoons cornstarch
1/2 teaspoon salt
1/8 teaspoon pepper
4 chicken breast filets
2 tablespoons butter

1/2 cup chicken broth
2 tablespoons frozen orange
    juice concentrate
1 teaspoon Dijon mustard
1/2 teaspoon honey

Mix cornstarch, salt and pepper in plastic bag. Rinse chicken and pat dry. Shake in cornstarch mixture in bag. Shake off excess cornstarch, reserving unused mixture in bag. Brown chicken in butter in skillet for 5 minutes on each side. Remove chicken to plate. Stir reserved cornstarch mixture into drippings in skillet. Whisk in chicken broth, orange juice concentrate, mustard and honey. Bring to a boil over medium heat, stirring constantly. Add chicken; reduce heat to medium-low. Simmer, covered, for 5 to 8 minutes or until chicken is tender. Garnish servings with parsley and orange slices.

Approx Per Serving: Cal 228; T Fat 9 g; 37% Calories from Fat;
    Prot 27 g; Carbo 8 g; Fiber <1 g; Chol 88 mg; Sod 492 mg.

Tulips and peonies can be cut in the advanced bud stage, enclosed in plastic bags without water and refrigerated for up to 6 weeks. To arrange, give stems a new cut and place in water. Though they appear wilted when first removed, they soon become turgid and blooms will open.

Festive Chicken

Yield: 6 servings

6 chicken breast filets
1 16-ounce can whole
    cranberry sauce

1 envelope onion soup mix
1 14-ounce bottle of French
    salad dressing

Rinse chicken and pat dry; arrange in 9x13-inch baking dish. Combine cranberry sauce, onion soup mix and salad dressing in bowl; mix well. Spoon over chicken. Marinate in refrigerator for several hours. Bake, covered with foil, at 350 degrees for 30 minutes or until nearly tender. Bake, uncovered, for 15 minutes or until brown.

Approx Per Serving: Cal 608; T Fat 41 g; 60% Calories from Fat;
    Prot 27 g; Carbo 34 g; Fiber 2 g; Chol 72 mg; Sod 967 mg.

Chicken with White Grape Sauce

Yield: 12 servings

12 chicken breast filets
12 slices white bread, cut into
    1/4-inch cubes
1 6-ounce package frozen crab
    meat, thawed, flaked
1/2 cup minced onion
1/2 cup finely chopped celery
1/4 cup melted butter
1/4 teaspoon sage
1/2 teaspoon salt
1/4 teaspoon pepper

1 cup flour
1/2 cup butter
3 tablespoons flour
3 tablespoons butter
1 1/2 cups chicken broth
2 tablespoons sugar
2 teaspoons lemon juice
1/2 teaspoon salt
1 16-ounce can white grapes,
    drained

Rinse chicken and pat dry. Pound 1/4 inch thick between sheets of waxed paper with meat mallet. Combine bread cubes, crab meat, onion, celery, 1/4 cup melted butter, sage, 1/2 teaspoon salt and pepper in bowl; mix well. Spoon stuffing onto filets. Fold over long sides of chicken to cover stuffing. Fold ends over to enclose stuffing completely; secure with toothpicks. Coat chicken with 1 cup flour. Brown on all sides in 1/2 cup butter in skillet. Remove to 10x15-inch baking pan. Bake at 375 degrees for 25 minutes or until tender. Blend 3 tablespoons flour with 3 tablespoons melted butter in heavy saucepan. Cook for 1 minute, stirring constantly. Stir in broth gradually. Cook until thickened, stirring constantly. Stir in sugar, lemon juice and 1/2 teaspoon salt. Fold in grapes. Serve with chicken.

Approx Per Serving: Cal 432; T Fat 19 g; 40% Calories from Fat;
    Prot 33 g; Carbo 31 g; Fiber 1 g; Chol 125 mg; Sod 655 mg.

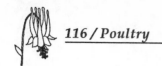

Sweet and Sour Chicken

Yield: 5 servings

1 8-ounce can pineapple
   tidbits
2 pounds chicken breast filets
1/2 teaspoon salt
2 tablespoons cornstarch
2 cloves of garlic
1/3 cup corn oil

1/4 cup pickle juice
2 teaspoons soy sauce
1/2 each red and green bell
   peppers, cut into strips
2 teaspoons cornstarch
2 tablespoons cold water

Drain pineapple, reserving juice. Rinse chicken and pat dry. Freeze chicken partially. Slice into strips. Toss with mixture of salt and cornstarch in bowl, coating well. Stir-fry garlic in oil in wok or skillet; remove garlic. Add chicken to wok gradually, stirring constantly. Stir-fry until opaque. Add reserved pineapple juice, pickle juice and soy sauce. Bring to a boil. Add pineapple and bell peppers. Stir in mixture of cornstarch and water. Cook until thickened, stirring constantly. Serve over brown rice. Garnish with toasted almonds.

Approx Per Serving: Cal 409; T Fat 19 g; 43% Calories from Fat;
   Prot 43 g; Carbo 14 g; Fiber 1 g; Chol 116 mg; Sod 453 mg.
   Nutritional information does not include pickle juice.

Enchiladas Verdes

Yield: 6 servings

12 ounces green tomatoes,
   chopped
2 green chilies
2 cloves of garlic, chopped
1/4 medium onion, chopped
4 tablespoons oil

12 corn tortillas
2 chicken breast filets, cooked,
   chopped
1 cup shredded Monterey Jack
   cheese

Combine green tomatoes and green chilies in saucepan. Cook until heated through. Combine with garlic and onion in blender container. Process until smooth. Fry mixture in 2 tablespoons oil in skillet until thickened to desired consistency. Soften tortillas 1 at a time in remaining 2 tablespoons oil in skillet. Spoon chicken onto tortillas; fold tortillas into halves to enclose filling. Arrange in baking dish. Pour sauce over top; sprinkle with cheese. Bake at 350 degrees just until cheese melts. Serve at once.

Approx Per Serving: Cal 351; T Fat 18 g; 45% Calories from Fat;
   Prot 19 g; Carbo 31 g; Fiber 5 g; Chol 41 mg; Sod 133 mg.

Chicken Gumbo

Yield: 8 servings

Vary the amount of chicken stock in this recipe for a thicker or thinner gumbo. You can substitute gumbo filé for the thyme.

2 cups sliced okra
1 large onion, chopped
2 green bell peppers, chopped
2 stalks celery, chopped
4 cloves of garlic, chopped
1/4 cup olive oil
1/4 cup flour
1/4 cup oil

1   28-ounce can tomatoes
2 quarts chicken stock
2 cups chopped cooked chicken
2 bay leaves
1 teaspoon thyme
1/2 teaspoon Tabasco sauce
Salt and pepper to taste

Sauté okra, onion, green peppers, celery and garlic in olive oil in saucepan for 10 to 15 minutes or until okra is tender; remove from heat. Blend flour and oil in small skillet. Cook until mixture is color of peanut butter, stirring constantly. Add to vegetables; mix well. Add tomatoes and chicken stock. Stir in chicken, bay leaves, thyme, Tabasco sauce, salt and pepper. Simmer, covered, for 1 hour. Remove bay leaves. Serve over rice.

Approx Per Serving: Cal 289; T Fat 18 g; 56% Calories from Fat;
    Prot 18 g; Carbo 15 g; Fiber 3 g; Chol 32 mg; Sod 979 mg.

Chicken in Phyllo

Yield: 16 servings

4 cups chopped cooked chicken
    breasts
1/4 cup chopped parsley
1/2 cup finely chopped scallions
4 eggs, beaten

1/4 teaspoon tarragon
Salt and pepper to taste
8 sheets phyllo pastry
1/2 cup melted butter
1/2 cup fine bread crumbs

Combine chicken, parsley, scallions, eggs, tarragon, salt and pepper in bowl; mix well. Spread 1 sheet phyllo pastry on large damp towel. Brush with melted butter; sprinkle lightly with bread crumbs. Repeat process with 3 additional sheets of pastry. Spread half the chicken mixture down center of dough, leaving 1 inch at either side. Fold in 1-inch edges; roll up pastry to enclose filling using towel to guide. Repeat with remaining ingredients. Place on buttered baking sheet; brush with melted butter. Bake at 375 degrees for 20 minutes or until brown. Slice into 1-inch slices. Serve warm or at room temperature.

Approx Per Serving: Cal 161; T Fat 8 g; 46% Calories from Fat;
    Prot 12 g; Carbo 10 g; Fiber 1 g; Chol 93 mg; Sod 148 mg.

Chicken Potpie

Yield: 12 servings

1   16-ounce package potpie
squares
1 tablespoon oil
Salt to taste
6 cups chicken broth
1/2 cup chopped onion
2 teaspoons Worcestershire
sauce

2 teaspoons salt
3/4 cup flour
3/4 cup water
3/4 teaspoon sage
1/8 teaspoon pepper
4 cups chopped cooked chicken
3 cups chopped potatoes,
cooked

Cook potpie squares with oil and salt to taste in boiling water in saucepan for 10 minutes; drain. Bring chicken broth, onion, Worcestershire sauce and 2 teaspoons salt to a simmer in saucepan. Stir in mixture of flour, 3/4 cup water, sage and pepper. Cook until thickened, stirring constantly. Stir in chicken, potatoes and potpie squares. Spoon into 3-quart baking dish. Bake at 350 degrees for 30 minutes. Garnish with parsley.

Approx Per Serving: Cal 302; T Fat 7 g; 22% Calories from Fat;
Prot 22 g; Carbo 35 g; Fiber 1 g; Chol 42 mg; Sod 799 mg.

Chicken Luau

Yield: 8 servings

*Buy coconut milk in most markets, particularly Asian or Thai markets.
To make coconut milk, chill a mixture of equal amounts of flaked coconut
and cold milk, process in blender for four seconds and strain.*

1   3-pound chicken
2 to 4 cloves of garlic, minced
1 teaspoon grated fresh ginger
Salt and pepper to taste

2   12-ounce packages fresh
spinach
2 cups coconut milk

Rinse chicken well. Combine chicken with garlic, ginger, salt, pepper and water to cover in saucepan. Cook until tender. Drain and chop chicken, discarding skin and bone; keep warm. Spread on serving plate. Cook spinach in a small amount of water in saucepan until tender; drain. Stir in coconut milk. Spoon over chicken.

Approx Per Serving: Cal 321; T Fat 21 g; 57% Calories from Fat;
Prot 29 g; Carbo 7 g; Fiber 3 g; Chol 76 mg; Sod 149 mg.

Wild Rose

Hot Chicken Salad

Yield: 12 servings

4 cups chopped cooked chicken
2 10-ounce cans cream of
    chicken soup
2 cups cooked rice
2 cups chopped celery
1/2 cup chopped onion
1 8-ounce can mushrooms,
    drained

5 hard-boiled eggs, chopped
1 7-ounce can sliced water
    chestnuts, drained
3/4 cup mayonnaise
2 tablespoons lemon juice
1 teaspoon salt
2 cups crushed potato chips

Combine chicken, soup, rice, celery, onion, mushrooms, eggs, water
chestnuts, mayonnaise, lemon juice and salt in bowl; mix well. Spoon
into 9x13-inch baking dish. Top with potato chips. Bake at 350 degrees
for 30 to 40 minutes or until bubbly. May omit mushrooms and/or water
chestnuts if preferred.

Approx Per Serving: Cal 369; T Fat 23 g; 56% Calories from Fat;
    Prot 19 g; Carbo 22 g; Fiber 2 g; Chol 142 mg; Sod 838 mg.

Hot Chicken-Chutney Salad

Yield: 6 servings

2 cups chopped cooked chicken
1 13-ounce can pineapple
    tidbits, drained
1 cup diagonally sliced celery
1/2 cup chopped scallions
1/4 cup salted peanuts
2/3 cup light mayonnaise

2 tablespoons (or more)
    chopped chutney
1/2 teaspoon grated lime rind
2 tablespoons lime juice
1/2 teaspoon curry powder
1/4 teaspoon salt

Combine chicken, pineapple, celery, scallions and peanuts in bowl; mix
gently. Combine mayonnaise, chutney, lime rind, lime juice, curry powder and salt in small bowl. Add to chicken mixture; mix well. Spoon into
1 1/2-quart baking dish. Bake, covered, at 350 degrees for 35 to 45 minutes
or until bubbly. May also serve this dish cold on a bed of lettuce with hot
rolls and a light white wine.

Approx Per Serving: Cal 229; T Fat 12 g; 46% Calories from Fat;
    Prot 16 g; Carbo 16 g; Fiber 2 g; Chol 49 mg; Sod 335 mg.

*Plant bare-root roses only in early spring or late
fall, depending on your climate zone. Immerse
root and stems in water for 24 hours and cut back
broken roots and canes.*

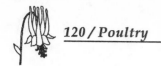

White Chili

Yield: 8 servings

1 16-ounce package dried
    white beans
6 cups chicken broth
2 cloves of garlic, minced
2 medium onions, chopped
1 tablespoon oil
2 4-ounce cans chopped green
    chilies

2 teaspoons cumin
1½ teaspoons oregano
¼ teaspoon cloves
¼ teaspoon cayenne pepper
4 cups chopped cooked chicken
    breasts
3 cups shredded Monterey Jack
    cheese

Soak beans in water to cover in saucepan for several hours; drain. Combine beans with chicken broth, garlic and half the onions in saucepan. Simmer for 3 hours or until beans are tender. Sauté remaining onions in oil in skillet. Stir in green chilies, cumin, oregano, cloves and pepper. Add to beans. Stir in chicken. Simmer, covered, for 1 hour, adding additional broth if needed for desired consistency. Top servings with cheese. Garnish with chopped green onions.

Approx Per Serving: Cal 509; T Fat 18 g; 33% Calories from Fat;
    Prot 44 g; Carbo 41 g; Fiber 2 g; Chol 88 mg; Sod 1061 mg.

Traditional Welsh Duck Dinner

Yield: 4 servings

*This is served at a traditional Christmas dinner in Wales with rutabaga,
peas or Brussels sprouts, applesauce and a trifle.*

1 duck, dressed
3 medium onions, chopped
6 slices stale bread, crumbled
¼ cup melted margarine
2 tablespoons sage

Salt and pepper to taste
2 eggs
6 medium potatoes, peeled,
    chopped, parboiled
1 tablespoon flour

Rinse duck; discard fat and reserve liver and gizzard. Parboil onions; drain, reserving liquid. Mix onions, bread crumbs, margarine, sage, salt and pepper in bowl. Add eggs and enough reserved cooking liquid to make of desired consistency. Stuff duck; truss. Place in roasting pan. Roast at 300 degrees for 1 hour. Arrange potatoes around duck, draining excess drippings. Roast for 1 hour. Cook liver and gizzard in water to cover in saucepan until tender; drain, reserving broth. Chop giblets. Remove duck to serving platter. Blend flour, salt and pepper into pan drippings. Cook for several minutes. Stir in reserved broth and giblets. Cook until thickened, stirring constantly. Serve with duck.

Approx Per Serving: Cal 769; T Fat 26 g; 30% Calories from Fat;
    Prot 26 g; Carbo 108 g; Fiber 10 g; Chol 158 mg; Sod 447 mg.

Pheasant in Cream Sauce
Yield: 8 servings

2 pheasant
1 cup flour
Salt and pepper to taste
3 tablespoons butter
8 ounces fresh mushrooms
1/2 small onion, chopped

3 stalks celery, chopped
1/3 cup sliced almonds
2 cups whipping cream
1 cup dry sherry
1 tablespoon salt
1 teaspoon pepper

Rinse pheasant and pat dry. Cut into quarters. Shake in mixture of flour, salt and pepper to coat well. Brown in butter in skillet; remove to heavy roaster, reserving pan drippings. Sauté mushrooms, onion, celery and almonds in reserved drippings in skillet. Spoon over pheasant. Roast, covered, at 350 degrees for 1 1/2 hours. Add cream, sherry, salt and pepper. Roast, covered, for 30 minutes longer or until pheasant are tender.

Approx Per Serving: Cal 563; T Fat 38 g; 61% Calories from Fat;
    Prot 23 g; Carbo 17 g; Fiber 2 g; Chol 173 mg; Sod 918 mg.

Turkey Crêpes à la King
Yield: 12 servings

1/2 cup sliced mushrooms
1/2 cup chopped green bell pepper
1/2 cup butter
1 1/2 cups flour
1 1/2 teaspoons salt
1/4 teaspoon pepper
2 cups half and half
2 cups chicken or turkey broth
2 cups chopped cooked turkey
1 4-ounce jar chopped pimento

4 eggs
1/2 cup milk
1/2 cup chicken or turkey broth
2 tablespoons melted margarine
1/3 cup mayonnaise
1 egg white, stiffly beaten
2 tablespoons grated Parmesan
  cheese
1/2 cup sliced almonds

Sauté mushrooms and green pepper in butter in skillet for 5 minutes. Stir in 1/2 cup flour, 1 teaspoon salt and pepper. Cook over low heat until bubbly, stirring constantly. Remove from heat. Stir in half and half and 2 cups broth. Bring to a boil, stirring constantly. Cook for 1 minute. Stir in turkey and pimento. Set aside. Combine eggs, milk, 1/2 cup broth, margarine and 1/2 teaspoon salt in mixer bowl; beat at medium speed. Add 1 cup flour gradually, beating constantly until smooth. Bake a small amount at a time in crêpe pan until light brown. Fill crêpes with chicken mixture, rolling to enclose filling. Arrange in baking dish. Fold mayonnaise into egg white. Spread evenly over crêpes. Sprinkle with cheese and almonds. Bake at 375 degrees for 10 minutes or until heated through.

Approx Per Serving: Cal 350; T Fat 25 g; 64% Calories from Fat;
    Prot 15 g; Carbo 16 g; Fiber 1 g; Chol 130 mg; Sod 630 mg.

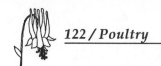

Gardener's Chili

Yield: 12 servings

1 cup chopped onion
1 cup chopped celery
1 cup chopped green bell
  pepper
1/4 cup chopped jalapeño
  peppers
2 large cloves of garlic, minced
2 tablespoons canola oil
3 pounds ground turkey
3 cups puréed plum tomatoes
1 6-ounce can tomato paste

1 4-ounce can mushrooms
1 16-ounce can red kidney
  beans, drained, rinsed
3/4 cup thinly sliced carrot
1 cup thinly sliced zucchini
1 cup beer
2 tablespoons chili powder
1 tablespoon cumin
2 bay leaves
Several drops of Tabasco sauce
Salt and pepper to taste

Sauté onion, celery, green pepper, jalapeño peppers and garlic in canola oil in heavy saucepan. Remove with slotted spoon. Add ground turkey. Cook until light brown and crumbly, stirring constantly. Return sautéed vegetables to saucepan. Add puréed tomatoes, tomato paste, undrained mushrooms, beans, carrot, zucchini, beer, chili powder, cumin, bay leaves, Tabasco sauce, salt and pepper; mix well. Simmer, covered, for 2 to 3 hours or until of desired consistency. Remove bay leaves.

Approx Per Serving: Cal 308; T Fat 14 g; 41% Calories from Fat;
    Prot 27 g; Carbo 20 g; Fiber 6 g; Chol 71 mg; Sod 316 mg.

Grilled Turkey Steak

Yield: 4 servings

Buy turkey steaks or cut turkey breast cross grain into steaks or cutlets. Cut into cubes for shish kabobs.

1/2 cup dry white wine
1/4 cup soy sauce
1 tablespoon oil

1 clove of garlic, crushed
1 pound turkey steaks, 3/4 to 1
  inch thick

Combine wine, soy sauce, oil and garlic in shallow dish. Rinse turkey and pat dry. Add to marinade, turning to coat well. Marinate in refrigerator for 2 to 24 hours, turning steaks several times. Remove steaks from marinade, reserving marinade. Grill steaks over medium coals for 8 to 10 minutes on each side or until cooked through, basting with reserved marinade. May substitute white grape juice for wine.

Approx Per Serving: Cal 164; T Fat 6 g; 35% Calories from Fat;
    Prot 19 g; Carbo 2 g; Fiber <1 g; Chol 47 mg; Sod 1074 mg.

Crowd-Pleasing Turkey Joes

Yield: 25 servings

5 pounds ground turkey
4 medium onions, chopped
1 small bunch celery, chopped
1/2 cup margarine
1 6-ounce can tomato paste
1 18-ounce bottle of barbecue
   sauce

1/3 cup catsup
4 teaspoons dry mustard
4 teaspoons Worcestershire
   sauce
1/3 cup vinegar
1/3 cup brown sugar

Brown ground turkey in saucepan, stirring until crumbly. Sauté onions and celery in margarine in skillet. Add to turkey. Stir in tomato paste, barbecue sauce, catsup, dry mustard, Worcestershire sauce, vinegar and brown sugar. Simmer for 1 1/2 hours. Serve on sandwich buns.

Approx Per Serving: Cal 233; T Fat 13 g; 50% Calories from Fat; Prot 19 g; Carbo 10 g; Fiber 1 g; Chol 57 mg; Sod 365 mg.

Modern Meat Loaf

Yield: 8 servings

1 pound ground turkey
1 pound ground veal
1 envelope onion soup mix
2/3 cup milk
2 eggs

3 cups fresh bread crumbs
Parsley flakes, rosemary, dill,
   basil, cumin and pepper to
   taste

Combine ground turkey, ground veal, soup mix, milk, eggs, bread crumbs and seasonings in bowl; mix well. Pack into large loaf pan. Bake at 375 degrees for 45 to 60 minutes or until done to taste. May add Madeira to taste if desired.

Approx Per Serving: Cal 252; T Fat 10 g; 37% Calories from Fat; Prot 29 g; Carbo 10 g; Fiber <1 g; Chol 150 mg; Sod 276 mg.

Basil

Spinach Swirl Turkey Loaf

Yield: 6 servings

1¼ pounds ground turkey
¾ cup fine bread crumbs
¾ cup finely chopped onion
2 eggs, slightly beaten
1 8-ounce can reduced-sodium
   tomato sauce
1 teaspoon Worcestershire sauce
1 teaspoon prepared mustard

¾ teaspoon oregano
Salt and pepper to taste
1 10-ounce package frozen
   chopped spinach, thawed,
   drained
¾ teaspoon garlic powder
1½ cups shredded low-fat
   Cheddar cheese

Combine ground turkey, bread crumbs, onion, eggs, half the tomato sauce, Worcestershire sauce, mustard, oregano, salt and pepper in bowl; mix well. Press into 8x10-inch rectangle on foil. Spread spinach to within ½ inch of edges. Sprinkle with garlic powder and cheese. Roll from narrow side to enclose filling, lifting foil as guide. Press edges to seal. Place seam side down in greased baking pan. Bake at 350 degrees for 1 hour and 10 minutes. Spread with remaining tomato sauce. Bake for 15 minutes longer. Slice to serve.

Approx Per Serving: Cal 353; T Fat 17 g; 43% Calories from Fat;
    Prot 33 g; Carbo 18 g; Fiber 2 g; Chol 146 mg; Sod 419 mg.

Turkey Tetrazzini

Yield: 6 servings

⅔ cup sliced onion
¼ cup butter
¼ cup flour
¼ teaspoon dry mustard
1 teaspoon salt
¼ teaspoon white pepper
2 cups milk
⅔ cup shredded sharp Cheddar
   cheese
2 tablespoons chopped pimento

2 tablespoons sherry
1 4-ounce can chopped
   mushrooms
1 7-ounce package spaghetti,
   cooked, drained
1 pound cooked turkey, thinly
   sliced
⅓ cup shredded sharp Cheddar
   cheese

Sauté onion in butter in saucepan until tender. Stir in flour, dry mustard, salt and white pepper. Stir in milk gradually. Cook until thickened, stirring constantly. Add ⅔ cup cheese and pimento; stir until cheese melts. Add sherry and undrained mushrooms. Layer spaghetti, turkey and sauce ½ at a time in shallow 2-quart baking dish. Top with ⅓ cup cheese. Bake at 400 degrees for 25 minutes. May freeze casserole and bake at 350 degrees for 1½ hours.

Approx Per Serving: Cal 478; T Fat 25 g; 47% Calories from Fat;
    Prot 27 g; Carbo 35 g; Fiber 2 g; Chol 99 mg; Sod 717 mg.

Seafood

Baked Bluefish Cutlets

Yield: 8 servings

½ cup grated Parmesan cheese
1 cup fine dry bread crumbs
¼ cup chopped parsley
1½ teaspoons salt

1 egg
2 tablespoons milk
3 pounds bluefish filets
2 tablespoons margarine

Mix cheese, bread crumbs, parsley and salt in shallow dish. Beat egg with milk in bowl. Dip fish filets into egg mixture; coat well with crumbs. Brown on both sides in margarine in skillet. Arrange in shallow baking dish. Bake at 350 degrees for 20 minutes. Serve with vinegar.

Approx Per Serving: Cal 326; T Fat 13 g; 36% Calories from Fat;
Prot 40 g; Carbo 10 g; Fiber 1 g; Chol 117 mg; Sod 735 mg.

Ceviche

Yield: 8 servings

2 pounds mackerel
1 cup (or more) lemon juice
½ cup olive oil
1 large onion, chopped
2 tomatoes, peeled, chopped
1 4-ounce jar stuffed green olives

1 4-ounce jar capers
1 manzano or green serrano chili
   pepper, seeded, finely chopped
¼ cup coriander
Salt to taste
2 avocados, chopped

Cut fish into ½-inch cubes. Combine with lemon juice to cover in bowl. Let stand for 20 minutes or until fish is opaque, turning occasionally. Drain off most of the lemon juice. Add next 8 ingredients; mix well. Fold in avocados at serving time. Serve with crackers.

Approx Per Serving: Cal 477; T Fat 40 g; 73% Calories from Fat;
Prot 24 g; Carbo 10 g; Fiber 6 g; Chol 68 mg; Sod 424 mg.
Nutritional information does not include capers.

Flounder and Crab Casserole

Yield: 4 servings

This is a specialty of the North Carolina Outer Banks.

1 pound flounder filets
2/3 cup melted butter
1 cup crushed seasoned
   stuffing mix
6 ounces crab meat
1/2 cup chopped mushrooms
1 egg

2 tablespoons chopped parsley
2 tablespoons lemon juice
1/4 teaspoon hot pepper sauce
1/4 teaspoon salt
1/2 cup crushed seasoned
   stuffing mix
2 tablespoons melted butter

Arrange fish filets in single layer in 9x9-inch baking dish. Combine 2/3 cup melted butter, 1 cup stuffing mix, crab meat, mushrooms, egg, parsley, lemon juice, pepper sauce and salt in bowl; mix well. Spread over fish. Mix 1/2 cup stuffing mix with 2 tablespoons butter in bowl. Sprinkle over top. Bake at 350 degrees for 30 minutes or until fish flakes easily.

Approx Per Serving: Cal 587; T Fat 43 g; 66% Calories from Fat;
   Prot 32 g; Carbo 20 g; Fiber <1 g; Chol 246 mg; Sod 1077 mg.

Orange-Glazed Halibut

Yield: 6 servings

2 pounds halibut steaks
1/4 cup white wine
1 tablespoon cornstarch
1 cup orange juice
1 teaspoon salt

1 chicken bouillon cube or 1
   teaspoon chicken stock base
1 tablespoon chopped chives
Sections of 2 oranges

Arrange steaks in shallow baking dish. Blend wine and cornstarch in small bowl. Combine with orange juice in saucepan. Add salt and bouillon. Cook over medium heat until thickened, stirring constantly. Pour over fish; sprinkle with chives. Arrange orange sections around and over fish. Bake at 350 degrees for 20 minutes, basting once or twice with sauce. Garnish with parsley.

Approx Per Serving: Cal 210; T Fat 4 g; 16% Calories from Fat;
   Prot 28 g; Carbo 11 g; Fiber 1 g; Chol 50 mg; Sod 632 mg.

 Geraniums can be saved if they are removed from soil before frost. The soil around the roots should be shaken off, leaving the foliage and blossoms intact. Store, uncovered, in bushel baskets in complete darkness at cool, but not freezing, temperature. In early March, pot each root in good soil and water as needed. Place in a sunny window when green shoots appear.

Halibut au Gratin

Yield: 1 serving

1 halibut steak or filet
2 tablespoons mayonnaise

1½ tablespoons shredded
   Cheddar cheese

Place fish steak on large piece of foil. Spread with mixture of mayonnaise and cheese. Fold foil to enclose fish; place in baking pan. Bake at 325 degrees for 1 hour.

Approx Per Serving: Cal 388; T Fat 29 g; 69% Calories from Fat;
    Prot 28 g; Carbo 1 g; Fiber 0 g; Chol 74 mg; Sod 300 mg.

Baked Stuffed Rockfish

Yield: 8 servings

1 6 to 8-pound rockfish,
   cleaned
½ lemon
Salt and pepper to taste
1 slice bread
1 pound crab meat

1 egg
1 teaspoon Worcestershire sauce
1 tablespoon mayonnaise
1 teaspoon prepared mustard
1 cup crushed cornflakes
2 tablespoons butter

Rub fish with lemon inside and out; sprinkle with salt and pepper. Dip bread in water and squeeze dry. Combine bread with crab meat, egg, Worcestershire sauce, mayonnaise and mustard in bowl; mix well. Spoon into cavity of fish. Place in greased baking dish. Sprinkle with cornflakes; dot with butter. Bake, loosely covered with foil, at 350 degrees for 1 hour. Bake, uncovered, just until brown.

Approx Per Serving: Cal 727; T Fat 24 g; 32% Calories from Fat;
    Prot 108 g; Carbo 10 g; Fiber <1 g; Chol 321 mg; Sod 618 mg.

Lomi Salmon

Yield: 4 servings

Lomi means "to massage" in Hawaii. This is served as a side dish there.

8 ounces smoked salmon
1 large white onion or 6 green
   onions, chopped

6 large tomatoes, peeled,
   seeded, chopped
8 ice cubes

Shred salmon with fingers, discarding skin and bones. Combine with onion and tomatoes in bowl; mix well with fingers. Add ice cubes. Let stand until chilled. Garnish with lemon slices.

Approx Per Serving: Cal 116; T Fat 3 g; 22% Calories from Fat;
    Prot 12 g; Carbo 11 g; Fiber 3 g; Chol 13 mg; Sod 460 mg.

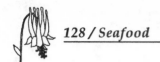

Sole with Leeks and Shrimp
Yield: 4 servings

2 cups thinly sliced leek bulbs
1/4 cup butter
8 ounces shrimp, cooked,
   peeled, chopped
2 tablespoons chopped dill
1 cup whipping cream

2/3 cup dry white wine
Lemon juice to taste
Salt and white pepper to taste
4 4-ounce sole filets
1/2 cup flour
1/4 cup butter

Sauté leeks in 1/4 cup butter in stainless steel or enamel skillet over medium heat for 5 minutes or until tender. Stir in shrimp and dill. Cook for 1 minute. Add whipping cream, wine, lemon juice, salt and white pepper. Simmer for 20 minutes or until thickened to desired consistency. Keep warm, covered, in double boiler over simmering water. Coat fish with flour. Sauté in 1/4 cup butter in skillet over medium-high heat for 2 minutes on each side or until golden brown and flaky. Arrange fish on serving platter. Spoon sauce over top.

Approx Per Serving: Cal 656; T Fat 47 g; 66% Calories from Fat;
    Prot 32 g; Carbo 22 g; Fiber 2 g; Chol 279 mg; Sod 414 mg.

Pecan Trout with Raspberry Sauce
Yield: 8 servings

1/2 cup sugar
1/4 cup red wine vinegar
1/4 cup red wine
1 cup fresh raspberries
1 tablespoon butter
Salt and pepper to taste

1 cup dry white bread crumbs
1 cup chopped roasted pecans
8 8-ounce rainbow trout filets
2 eggs, beaten
3 tablespoons oil

Caramelize sugar in heavy skillet over high heat. Stir in vinegar and wine. Cook until blended. Stir in 3/4 cup raspberries. Simmer for 10 minutes. Purée in blender or food processor. Strain into bowl. Stir in remaining 1/4 cup raspberries, butter, salt and pepper; keep warm. Mix bread crumbs, pecans, salt and pepper in bowl. Dip fish into eggs; coat meaty side with crumb mixture. Place meaty side down in oil in heated skillet. Cook until brown. Turn fish. Cook for 5 minutes longer. Arrange crust side up on serving plates. Spoon sauce over servings.

Approx Per Serving: Cal 563; T Fat 27 g; 43% Calories from Fat;
    Prot 52 g; Carbo 27 g; Fiber 2 g; Chol 190 mg; Sod 184 mg.

*The dainty star-shaped blue flowers of borage add
a cool cucumber-like flavor to any
salad or fruit cup.*

Tuna and Vegetables in Foil

Yield: 4 servings

2 lemons, thinly sliced
1 carrot, juilenned
1 small leek, julienned
1 small turnip, julienned
1 teaspoon butter

2 tablespoons water
4 8-ounce tuna filets
1 tablespoon chopped dill
Salt and freshly ground pepper
   to taste

Arrange 3 lemon slices on each of 4 pieces of foil. Sauté vegetables in butter in skillet. Stir in water. Layer half the vegetables, fish filets and remaining vegetables on prepared foil. Sprinkle with seasonings. Seal tightly. Place in baking pan. Bake at 450 degrees for 12 minutes or until fish flakes easily.

Approx Per Serving: Cal 230; T Fat 3 g; 11% Calories from Fat;
   Prot 43 g; Carbo 7 g; Fiber 2 g; Chol 84 mg; Sod 95 mg.

Marinade for Fish

Yield: enough marinade for 4 servings

1 cup dry white wine
1 tablespoon olive oil
1 tablespoon vinegar
1 small lemon, finely sliced
1 small carrot, finely sliced
1 sprig of thyme

2 small bay leaves
3 cloves, crushed
1 sprig of parsley
Salt to taste
12 peppercorns, slightly
   crushed

Combine all ingredients in glass dish. Use to marinate fish.

Approx Per Serving: Cal 81; T Fat 3 g; 38% Calories from Fat;
   Prot <1 g; Carbo 4 g; Fiber 1 g; Chol 0 mg; Sod 9 mg.

Clam Diggers

Yield: 8 servings

1/2 cup chopped green bell pepper
1/2 cup melted butter
1 teaspoon chopped parsley
1 tablespoon Worcestershire sauce
1/2 teaspoon dry mustard

1 teaspoon oregano
Onion salt to taste
2 7-ounce cans minced clams
12 slices bread, crumbled
Paprika to taste

Sauté green pepper in butter in saucepan until tender. Add next 6 ingredients; mix well. Simmer over medium heat for 5 to 8 minutes. Stir in bread crumbs. Spoon into clam shells. Sprinkle with paprika. Arrange in baking pan. Bake at 350 degrees for 15 minutes.

Approx Per Serving: Cal 244; T Fat 17 g; 55% Calories from Fat;
   Prot 8 g; Carbo 23 g; Fiber 1 g; Chol 62 mg; Sod 352 mg.

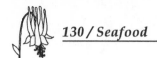

Crab Cakes

Yield: 4 servings

1 pound crab meat
12 crackers, crushed
1/2 green bell pepper, chopped
1 small onion, chopped

1 stalk celery, chopped
1/4 cup mayonnaise
1 teaspoon prepared mustard
2 tablespoons shortening

Combine first 7 ingredients in bowl; mix well. Shape into cakes. Brown on both sides in shortening in skillet; drain.

Approx Per Serving: Cal 324; T Fat 20 g; 57% Calories from Fat; Prot 24 g; Carbo 10 g; Fiber 1 g; Chol 125 mg; Sod 536 mg.

Crab Cioppino

Yield: 12 servings

1 cup chopped onion
1 cup chopped parsley
1 cup chopped green bell pepper
2 cloves of garlic, chopped
1/2 cup olive oil
1   29-ounce can tomatoes
6   15-ounce cans tomato sauce

1 teaspoon Italian seasoning
1 teaspoon oregano
Salt and pepper to taste
4 Dungeness crabs, chopped
1 pound shrimp
1 pound fish filets
2 cups red wine

Sauté onion, parsley, green pepper and garlic in olive oil in saucepan. Add tomatoes, tomato sauce and seasonings; mix well. Simmer, covered, for 30 minutes. Stir in seafood and wine. Simmer, covered, for 30 minutes.

Approx Per Serving: Cal 298; T Fat 12 g; 38% Calories from Fat; Prot 23 g; Carbo 21 g; Fiber 4 g; Chol 97 mg; Sod 1582 mg.

Hot Crab Salad

Yield: 6 servings

1 pound crab meat
1 cup chopped celery
1/2 cup chopped onion
1/4 cup chopped green bell
   pepper

1 slice pimento, chopped
Juice of 1 lemon
2 3/4 cups crumbled stale Cuban
   bread
3/4 cup (about) mayonnaise

Combine crab meat, celery, onion, green pepper, pimento, lemon juice and 2 cups of the bread crumbs in bowl; mix well. Add enough mayonnaise to moisten. Spoon into 2-quart baking dish. Top with remaining 3/4 cup crumbs. Bake at 350 degrees for 40 minutes.

Approx Per Serving: Cal 336; T Fat 24 g; 63% Calories from Fat; Prot 18 g; Carbo 13 g; Fiber 1 g; Chol 92 mg; Sod 568 mg.

Crab Meat Maryland

Yield: 8 servings

3 tablespoons flour
1/4 cup melted butter
2 cups milk
2 tablespoons minced onion
1 tablespoon minced parsley
1 tablespoon minced green bell
  pepper
1 pimento, minced
1/8 teaspoon grated orange rind
Tabasco sauce to taste

1/2 teaspoon celery salt
2 tablespoons sherry
1 egg, beaten
3 cups crab meat
1 teaspoon salt
Pepper to taste
1/2 cup soft bread crumbs
1 tablespoon melted butter
Paprika to taste

Blend flour into 1/4 cup melted butter in double boiler. Stir in milk. Cook over boiling water until thickened, stirring constantly. Add onion, parsley, green pepper, pimento, orange rind, Tabasco sauce and celery salt; mix well. Remove from heat. Add sherry. Stir a small amount of the hot sauce into egg; stir egg into hot sauce. Add crab meat, salt and pepper; mix well. Spoon into greased 1 1/2-quart baking dish. Sprinkle with mixture of bread crumbs and 1 tablespoon butter. Top with paprika. Bake at 350 degrees for 15 to 20 minutes or until brown.

Approx Per Serving: Cal 179; T Fat 11 g; 56% Calories from Fat;
    Prot 12 g; Carbo 7 g; Fiber <1 g; Chol 97 mg; Sod 623 mg.

Mexican Deviled Crab

Yield: 8 servings

2 cups finely chopped green
  onions
6 cloves of garlic, crushed
2 serrano peppers, seeded,
  chopped
8 ounces pimentos, chopped
2 cups olive oil
2 1/4 pounds tomatoes, puréed,
  sieved

1 teaspoon oregano
Bay leaves, salt and pepper to
  taste
2 1/4 pounds crab meat, shredded
1/2 cup chopped fresh parsley
1 cup white wine
1/2 cup chopped fresh coriander

Sauté green onions, garlic, peppers and pimentos in olive oil in skillet. Add tomatoes, oregano, bay leaves, salt and pepper; mix well. Simmer over medium heat for 10 minutes. Stir in crab meat and parsley. Cook for 5 minutes longer. Add wine and coriander just before serving; discard bay leaves. Serve with rice.

Approx Per Serving: Cal 673; T Fat 57 g; 77% Calories from Fat;
    Prot 28 g; Carbo 10 g; Fiber 4 g; Chol 128 mg; Sod 370 mg.

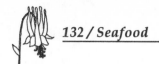

Crawfish Fettucini

Yield: 10 servings

3 onions, chopped
1/2 cup chopped celery
1/2 cup chopped green bell pepper
4 cloves of garlic, minced
1 cup butter
3 pounds crawfish tails
1/4 cup flour
1 tablespoon chopped parsley

2 cups half and half
1 pound jalapeño Velveeta
   cheese, chopped
1   16-ounce package fettucini,
   cooked
1/2 cup grated Parmesan cheese
1/2 cup bread crumbs

Sauté onions, celery, green pepper and garlic in butter in saucepan. Add crawfish. Cook for 15 minutes, stirring frequently. Stir in flour and parsley. Add half and half gradually. Cook until thickened, stirring constantly. Stir in process cheese until melted. Add pasta; mix lightly. Spoon into 9x13-inch baking dish. Sprinkle with Parmesan cheese and bread crumbs. Bake at 350 degrees for 30 minutes.

Approx Per Serving: Cal 733; T Fat 43 g; 53% Calories from Fat;
   Prot 41 g; Carbo 48 g; Fiber 3 g; Chol 240 mg; Sod 1021 mg.

Oyster and Corn Bake

Yield: 12 servings

4 1/2 cups fine cracker crumbs
2   16-ounce cans cream-style corn
4 cups fresh oysters

Salt and pepper to taste
1 cup melted butter
1 cup milk

Layer 1/3 of the cracker crumbs, corn and undrained oysters in greased baking dish, sprinkling with salt and pepper. Top with remaining crumbs. Drizzle with butter and milk. Bake at 350 degrees for 45 minutes; do not overbake.

Approx Per Serving: Cal 391; T Fat 21 g; 49% Calories from Fat;
   Prot 9 g; Carbo 41 g; Fiber 3 g; Chol 100 mg; Sod 852 mg.

Scalloped Oysters

Yield: 4 servings

1/2 cup bread crumbs
2 cups oysters
Salt and pepper to taste

1 cup milk
2 tablespoons butter
1/4 cup shredded Cheddar cheese

Alternate layers of bread crumbs, oysters and seasonings in 1 1/2-quart baking dish until all ingredients are used. Pour milk over layers. Dot with butter; sprinkle with cheese. Bake at 350 degrees for 25 minutes.

Approx Per Serving: Cal 250; T Fat 14 g; 50% Calories from Fat;
   Prot 14 g; Carbo 17 g; Fiber 1 g; Chol 100 mg; Sod 348 mg.

Brochettes de Coquilles St. Jacques
Yield: 4 servings

2 shallots, finely chopped
1 cup dry white wine
12 sea scallops
12 slices bacon, cut into halves

12 small mushrooms
1 yellow or red bell pepper, cut
   into 12 pieces
2 tablespoons oil

Bring shallots to a boil in wine in skillet. Add scallops. Poach for 8 minutes or until opaque; drain and pat dry. Slice into halves; wrap each half with bacon. Thread onto skewers with mushrooms and pepper. Brush with oil; arrange in broiler pan or on grill. Broil or grill until golden brown, turning after 4 minutes. Garnish with chopped parsley.

Approx Per Serving: Cal 270; T Fat 17 g; 56% Calories from Fat;
    Prot 14 g; Carbo 8 g; Fiber 1 g; Chol 29 mg; Sod 366 mg.

Scallop Ceviche
Yield: 4 servings

1 pound scallops
Juice of 8 limes
1 green bell pepper, chopped
1 red bell pepper, chopped
Several hot red pepper seeds
1/2 cup chopped parsley

2 tablespoons minced cilantro
Minced fresh garlic to taste
1/2 red onion, chopped
Freshly ground pepper to taste
1/4 cup olive oil

Marinate scallops in lime juice in bowl for 8 hours to overnight or until opaque. Drain half the lime juice. Stir in remaining ingredients.

Approx Per Serving: Cal 265; T Fat 15 g; 47% Calories from Fat;
    Prot 22 g; Carbo 15 g; Fiber 2 g; Chol 40 mg; Sod 185 mg.

Scallops Florentine
Yield: 6 servings

1 pound scallops
1/4 cup melted butter
1/4 cup flour
1/2 teaspoon salt
1/4 teaspoon white pepper
2 cups half and half

1 10-ounce package frozen
   chopped spinach, thawed,
   drained
1/2 cup sliced mushrooms
1 tablespoon Dijon mustard
6 frozen pastry shells, baked

Steam scallops for 4 minutes; drain. Blend butter, flour, salt and pepper in skillet. Add half and half. Cook until thickened, stirring constantly. Stir in scallops, vegetables and mustard. Cook for 5 minutes. Serve in pastry shells.

Approx Per Serving: Cal 476; T Fat 35 g; 65% Calories from Fat;
    Prot 10 g; Carbo 33 g; Fiber 2 g; Chol 52 mg; Sod 649 mg.

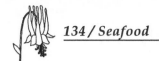

Barbecued Shrimp

Yield: 4 servings

6 ounces olive oil
1/4 cup margarine
1 tablespoon soy sauce
3 tablespoons Worcestershire
  sauce

1 tablespoon oregano
1/4 small can pepper
1 pound large shrimp in shells,
  heads removed

Heat first 6 ingredients in baking pan at 450 degrees until margarine melts. Stir in shrimp. Bake for 20 minutes, stirring several times.

Approx Per Serving: Cal 579; T Fat 55 g; 85% Calories from Fat;
    Prot 20 g; Carbo 3 g; Fiber 0 g; Chol 177 mg; Sod 704 mg.

Oriental Shrimp

Yield: 4 servings

1 pound shrimp, peeled, deveined
1/2 cup orange juice
1/4 cup chicken broth
1/4 cup dry white wine

2 teaspoons minced garlic
2 teaspoons soy sauce
2 teaspoons minced fresh ginger
1/8 teaspoon pepper

Combine all ingredients in large skillet. Let stand for 15 minutes. Bring to a boil, stirring constantly. Cook for 30 seconds or until shrimp are pink. Remove shrimp to warm bowl. Cook sauce for 7 to 8 minutes or until reduced to desired consistency. Serve shrimp and sauce over rice.

Approx Per Serving: Cal 121; T Fat 1 g; 9% Calories from Fat;
    Prot 20 g; Carbo 4 g; Fiber <1 g; Chol 177 mg; Sod 408 mg.

Rockport Shrimp

Yield: 6 servings

1 carrot, chopped
1 onion, chopped
1 green bell pepper, chopped
4 stalks celery, chopped
1/2 cup butter
30 shrimp, peeled
1/3 cup white wine

3 tomatoes, chopped
Salt and pepper to taste
1 teaspoon oregano
6 ounces feta cheese, crumbled
4 ounces grated Parmesan
  cheese

Sauté first 4 ingredients in butter in saucepan. Remove with slotted spoon. Add shrimp. Cook for 2 minutes or until opaque. Stir in wine. Cook for 1 minute. Add cooked vegetables, tomatoes and seasonings. Simmer until liquid has nearly evaporated. Spoon into baking dish. Sprinkle with cheeses. Bake at 450 degrees for 5 minutes. Serve over rice or pasta.

Approx Per Serving: Cal 445; T Fat 29 g; 59% Calories from Fat;
    Prot 37 g; Carbo 9 g; Fiber 2 g; Chol 298 mg; Sod 1078 mg.

Shrimp in Riesling-Dijon Sauce   *Yield: 4 servings*

3 tablespoons olive oil
3 tablespoons butter
4 large cloves of garlic, cut into
   halves lengthwise

1 cup medium dry Riesling
2 tablespoons Dijon mustard
2 pounds shrimp, peeled,
   deveined

Heat olive oil and butter in large heavy skillet. Add garlic. Cook until brown. Remove and discard garlic. Stir in wine. Bring to a boil; reduce heat. Whisk in mustard. Add shrimp. Cook for 3 to 4 minutes or until shrimp are pink. Serve with sourdough bread for dipping in sauce.

Approx Per Serving: Cal 395; T Fat 21 g; 48% Calories from Fat;
   Prot 39 g; Carbo 2 g; Fiber <1 g; Chol 377 mg; Sod 580 mg.

Thai Coconut Shrimp   *Yield: 4 servings*

*The coconut milk sauce for this recipe can also be used with scallops,
firm fish or even poultry. Use purple basil when it is available.*

1 pound medium shrimp
1 tablespoon dry sherry
1 cup unsweetened coconut
   milk
1/2 teaspoon Chinese chili sauce
1/4 teaspoon salt
1 tablespoon peanut oil
1 tablespoon unsalted butter
4 cloves of garlic, finely minced

4 ounces small mushrooms
1/4 cup chopped green onions
1/4 cup chopped fresh mint
   leaves
1/4 cup chopped fresh basil
1 tablespoon cornstarch
1 tablespoon water
1 tablespoon lime juice

Peel, devein and butterfly shrimp; pat dry. Chill in refrigerator. Combine sherry, coconut milk, chili sauce and salt in bowl; mix well. Set aside. Heat peanut oil and butter in wok or sauté pan over high heat until bubbly. Add garlic. Stir-fry for several seconds. Add shrimp. Stir-fry for 2 minutes or until opaque. Add mushrooms, green onions, mint and basil. Stir-fry for 15 seconds. Stir in coconut milk mixture. Bring to a boil. Stir in mixture of cornstarch and water. Cook until thickened, stirring constantly. Stir in lime juice. Spoon onto heated platter. Garnish with basil leaves and/or mint leaves. Serve with steamed white or brown rice.

Approx Per Serving: Cal 312; T Fat 22 g; 62% Calories from Fat;
   Prot 21 g; Carbo 9 g; Fiber 1 g; Chol 185 mg; Sod 358 mg.

*The leaves of anise hyssop make a naturally sweet
tea. The flowers are used in Chinese dishes and
sweet and sour marinades.*

Seafood Strudel

Yield: 6 servings

8 ounces shrimp, peeled,
    deveined
8 ounces scallops
8 ounces fish
1 10-ounce package frozen
    chopped spinach, thawed
2 carrots, thinly sliced

1 medium onion, chopped
1/2 teaspoon sage
1/4 teaspoon salt
1 cup dry bread crumbs
6 sheets frozen phyllo dough,
    thawed

Cut shrimp, scallops and fish into 1-inch pieces. Squeeze spinach to remove excess moisture. Sauté carrots and onion in skillet sprayed with butter-flavored nonstick cooking spray. Add spinach, seafood, sage and salt. Cook until seafood is opaque. Stir in 1/4 cup bread crumbs; remove from heat. Place 1 sheet of phyllo dough on waxed paper. Spray with nonstick cooking spray. Sprinkle with about 2 tablespoons bread crumbs. Repeat process with remaining sheets of dough and bread crumbs. Spread seafood mixture lengthwise down 1 side of dough, covering 1/4 of dough. Roll dough from seafood side to enclose filling. Tuck ends under; place on baking sheet sprayed with nonstick cooking spray. Bake at 400 degrees for 20 minutes. Let stand for 5 minutes. Slice to serve.

Approx Per Serving: Cal 258; T Fat 2 g; 7% Calories from Fat;
    Prot 27 g; Carbo 34 g; Fiber 4 g; Chol 94 mg; Sod 496 mg.

Seafood Tetrazzini

Yield: 8 servings

12 ounces uncooked macaroni
12 ounces shrimp
1 10-ounce can cream of celery
    soup
1 10-ounce can cream of
    Cheddar soup
2 soup cans milk
1 tablespoon chopped onion
1 cup shredded Cheddar cheese

1 teaspoon Worcestershire sauce
1/4 cup chopped parsley
1/2 teaspoon salt
1/4 teaspoon pepper
8 ounces crab meat
8 ounces lobster
8 ounces scallops, cut into
    quarters

Cook macaroni using package directions; drain. Cook shrimp in boiling water in saucepan for 3 to 4 minutes; drain. Peel, devein and cut shrimp into halves. Combine soups and milk in bowl; mix well. Add onion, cheese, Worcestershire sauce, parsley, salt and pepper. Stir in shrimp, crab meat, lobster and scallops. Fold in macaroni. Spoon into 4-quart baking dish. Bake at 375 degrees for 40 minutes.

Approx Per Serving: Cal 438; T Fat 13 g; 28% Calories from Fat;
    Prot 36 g; Carbo 42 g; Fiber 2 g; Chol 157 mg; Sod 1077 mg.

Vegetables & Side Dishes

Midwest Harvest

Central Region

*E*mbracing the Mississippi from its source in Lake Itasca downstream beyond our National Headquarters in St. Louis and reaching eastward to the Great Lakes, this is the Heartland. Orchards, corn and wheat fields and dairy farms combine with ore and coal mines to provide many of the nation's needs, barged on our great waterways. Members make a commitment to guard and protect our resources.

Wisconsin German-Style Dinner

Sauerbraten*
Potato Pancakes* or German Potato Salad*
Applesauce
Sweet and Sour Red Cabbage*
Cheese Tarts

Special Pork Steak Dinner

Herbed Walnuts
Pork Steaks with Apple*
Green Beans with Cherry Tomatoes*
Healthy Spinach Salad
Tarragon Rolls*
Paradise Pumpkin Pie*

*See index for recipes.

Vegetables

Sicilian-Style Stuffed Artichokes

Yield: 4 servings

4 cups bread crumbs
2 cups grated Parmesan cheese
4 cloves of garlic, slivered
1/4 cup chopped fresh parsley
4 teaspoons basil

Salt and pepper to taste
4 artichokes, trimmed
1 tablespoon lemon juice
1/4 cup olive oil

Combine first 7 ingredients in bowl; mix well. Rap top to spread artichoke leaves. Sprinkle with crumb mixture; tap lightly. Arrange upright in deep saucepan. Add 2 inches water, salt and lemon juice. Drizzle with olive oil. Cook, covered, for 15 minutes. Cook, uncovered, for 15 minutes or until top leaf pulls out easily.

Approx Per Serving: Cal 753; T Fat 31 g; 36% Calories from Fat;
Prot 33 g; Carbo 89 g; Fiber 14 g; Chol 36 mg; Sod 1571 mg.

Company Artichoke Casserole

Yield: 10 servings

2 16-ounce cans artichoke
   hearts, drained, cut into
   halves
2 10-ounce packages frozen
   chopped spinach, thawed,
   squeezed dry

1 7-ounce can sliced water
   chestnuts, drained
16 ounces cream cheese
1/4 cup mayonnaise
3/4 cup milk
1/2 cup Parmesan cheese

Layer vegetables in 2-quart baking dish. Blend softened cream cheese, mayonnaise and milk in bowl. Spread over layers. Sprinkle with cheese. Bake at 375 degrees for 30 minutes.

Approx Per Serving: Cal 290; T Fat 23 g; 71% Calories from Fat;
Prot 9 g; Carbo 13 g; Fiber 2 g; Chol 61 mg; Sod 485 mg.

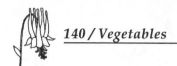

Barbecued Pinto Beans

Yield: 12 servings

1½ pounds dried pinto beans
1 2x2-inch piece pork fatback
1½ cloves of garlic, minced
1 medium onion, chopped

2 tablespoons chili powder
2 teaspoons salt
⅛ teaspoon pepper

Combine beans with pork and water to cover in saucepan for 1½ hours or until beans are nearly tender and liquid is slightly thickened. Add garlic, onion, chili powder, salt and pepper. Simmer for 30 minutes or until done to taste, adding water as needed.

Approx Per Serving: Cal 205; T Fat 1 g; 5% Calories from Fat;
    Prot 14 g; Carbo 36 g; Fiber 13 g; Chol 2 mg; Sod 416 mg.

Ranch-Style Beans

Yield: 75 servings

15 pounds dried pinto beans
3 pounds salt pork, chopped
½ cup salt
2 tablespoons cumin seed

1 16-ounce bottle of catsup
Chopped garlic to taste
3 tablespoons sugar
½ cup chili powder

Soak beans in water to cover in large heavy iron pot overnight. Add salt pork and salt. Simmer for 6 hours, adding hot water as needed. Add cumin seed, catsup, garlic and sugar. Stir in chili powder blended with enough water to make a paste. Simmer for 2 hours longer.

Approx Per Serving: Cal 338; T Fat 3 g; 8% Calories from Fat;
    Prot 23 g; Carbo 57 g; Fiber 20 g; Chol 6 mg; Sod 889 mg.

Green Beans with Cherry Tomatoes

Yield: 4 servings

Salt to taste
1 pound green beans, trimmed
1 pint cherry tomatoes
2 teaspoons olive oil

2 tablespoons chopped fresh
   basil or 1 teaspoon dried
   basil
1 tablespoon red wine vinegar

Bring 1 inch salted water to a boil in large saucepan. Add green beans. Cook for 6 to 7 minutes or just until tender. Drain, reserving 2 tablespoons cooking liquid. Cook cherry tomatoes in olive oil in heavy skillet just until skins begin to burst. Add basil, beans and reserved cooking liquid. Stir in vinegar and ¼ teaspoon salt. Cook for 2 minutes or until heated through.

Approx Per Serving: Cal 80; T Fat 3 g; 26% Calories from Fat;
    Prot 3 g; Carbo 14 g; Fiber 4 g; Chol 0 mg; Sod 16 mg.

Green Beans Supreme

Yield: 6 servings

2 10-ounce packages frozen
   French-style green beans
2 tablespoons minced onion
2 tablespoons butter
1 tablespoon flour
1/4 teaspoon dry mustard
1/2 teaspoon paprika
1/4 teaspoon MSG

1/2 teaspoon Worcestershire
   sauce
1/2 teaspoon salt
1 cup whipping cream
1 cup shredded Cheddar cheese
2 tablespoons fine dry bread
   crumbs

Cook green beans using package directions; drain. Sauté onion in butter in saucepan until transparent; remove from heat. Stir in flour, dry mustard, paprika, MSG, Worcestershire sauce and salt. Heat until bubbly; remove from heat. Stir in cream gradually. Cook for 1 to 2 minutes longer or until heated through. Add beans; toss to mix well. Spoon into baking dish. Sprinkle with cheese and bread crumbs. Broil 2 to 3 inches from heat source for 5 minutes or until golden brown.

Approx Per Serving: Cal 286; T Fat 25 g; 77% Calories from Fat;
   Prot 7 g; Carbo 10 g; Fiber 3 g; Chol 85 mg; Sod 552 mg.

New England Baked Beans

Yield: 8 servings

1 pound dried navy beans or
   pea beans
3/4 cup (about) maple syrup
1 tablespoon catsup
1 teaspoon dry mustard

1 teaspoon salt
1/2 teaspoon pepper
1 medium onion
8 ounces salt pork

Soak beans in water to cover in saucepan overnight. Drain and cover with fresh water. Simmer until bean skins burst when blown upon. Drain, reserving cooking liquid. Combine beans with syrup in bowl. Mix catsup, dry mustard, salt, pepper and a small amount of reserved cooking liquid in small bowl. Add to beans; mix well. Spoon into bean pot. Push whole onion into beans. Add reserved cooking liquid to 3/4 depth of beans. Top with salt pork. Bake at 350 degrees for 6 hours or until done to taste, adding water as needed.

Approx Per Serving: Cal 314; T Fat 4 g; 11% Calories from Fat;
   Prot 16 g; Carbo 55 g; Fiber 13 g; Chol 9 mg; Sod 486 mg.

Broccoli Casserole

Yield: 6 servings

2 10-ounce packages frozen
   broccoli
1/2 cup mayonnaise
1 egg
1 cup shredded Cheddar cheese

1 10-ounce can cream of
   mushroom soup
1 cup bread crumbs
2 tablespoons melted butter

Cook broccoli using package directions; drain. Place in large greased baking dish. Combine mayonnaise, egg, cheese and soup in saucepan. Cook until cheese melts, stirring to mix well. Spoon over broccoli. Top with bread crumbs. Drizzle with butter. Bake at 325 degrees until bubbly and light brown.

Approx Per Serving: Cal 394; T Fat 30 g; 67% Calories from Fat;
    Prot 12 g; Carbo 22 g; Fiber 4 g; Chol 78 mg; Sod 793 mg.

Stuffed Cabbage

Yield: 12 servings

1 medium to large head cabbage
Salt to taste
1/2 cup margarine
4 1/2 to 5 cups cracker crumbs

6 eggs
Pepper to taste
1/2 cup margarine

Line large bowl with cheesecloth. Remove outer leaves of cabbage. Line prepared bowl with leaves; set aside. Chop remaining cabbage. Combine with salt and water to cover in saucepan. Cook until tender; drain. Stir in 1/2 cup margarine. Cool slightly. Add cracker crumbs, eggs, salt and pepper; mix well. Spoon into cabbage leaf-lined bowl. Tie cheesecloth to enclose filling. Place in boiling water to cover in saucepan. Cook for 20 to 30 minutes; drain. Place upside down in serving bowl; remove cheesecloth. Heat 1/2 cup margarine in skillet until brown. Drizzle over cabbage. Slice to serve.

Approx Per Serving: Cal 326; T Fat 21 g; 60% Calories from Fat;
    Prot 5 g; Carbo 27 g; Fiber 1 g; Chol 118 mg; Sod 669 mg.

Blooms of spring flowering woody plants can be easily forced into early bloom indoors. Bathtub soaking of branches, often recommended, is unnecessary. They will open flowers when the ends of cut branches are split upward with pruners and stood in tall containers of water or attractive vases. Mist with water to prevent drying and to coax bloom more easily.

Sweet and Sour Red Cabbage

Yield: 6 servings

1 medium head cabbage,
   shredded
3 tablespoons canola oil
¼ cup cider vinegar

1 medium onion, thinly sliced
1 large red apple, cored, sliced
1 tablespoon sugar
Salt and pepper to taste

Rinse cabbage in water. Add undrained cabbage to oil in skillet. Bring to a boil; reduce heat. Stir in vinegar. Top with onion and apple; do not stir. Simmer, covered, until tender. Season with sugar, salt and pepper; mix gently.

Approx Per Serving: Cal 110; T Fat 7 g; 54% Calories from Fat;
   Prot 1 g; Carbo 13 g; Fiber 2 g; Chol 0 mg; Sod 9 mg.

Carrot Casserole

Yield: 8 servings

12 carrots
2 cups shredded Cheddar
   cheese
2 tablespoons chopped onion
½ cup butter
¼ cup flour

½ teaspoon dry mustard
¼ teaspoon celery salt
1 teaspoon salt
⅛ teaspoon pepper
1 cup bread crumbs

Cook carrots in water in saucepan until tender; drain. Alternate layers of carrots and cheese in 1-quart baking dish until all ingredients are used, ending with carrots. Sauté onion in butter in saucepan. Stir in flour, dry mustard, celery salt, salt and pepper. Stir in milk gradually. Cook until thickened, stirring constantly. Pour over layers. Sprinkle with bread crumbs. Bake at 350 degrees for 25 minutes.

Approx Per Serving: Cal 326; T Fat 22 g; 59% Calories from Fat;
   Prot 10 g; Carbo 24 g; Fiber 4 g; Chol 61 mg; Sod 732 mg.

Carrots à l'Orange

Yield: 8 servings

2 pounds carrots, sliced
1 cup orange juice
2 tablespoons sugar

½ teaspoon lemon juice
1 tablespoon cornstarch
Sections of 2 oranges

Cook carrots in water in saucepan until tender; drain. Blend orange juice, sugar, lemon juice and cornstarch in saucepan. Cook until thickened, stirring constantly. Fold in carrots and orange sections.

Approx Per Serving: Cal 100; T Fat <1 g; 3% Calories from Fat;
   Prot 2 g; Carbo 24 g; Fiber 5 g; Chol 0 mg; Sod 40 mg.

Carrot Pudding

Yield: 10 servings

4 cups mashed cooked carrots
1/4 cup butter
2/3 cup sugar
1 teaspoon salt
1 cup milk

3 eggs, beaten
2 tablespoons (heaping) flour
1 teaspoon baking powder
Cinnamon to taste
1/2 cup broken pecans

Combine hot carrots with butter, sugar and salt; beat until smooth. Stir in milk and eggs. Add mixture of flour, baking powder and cinnamon. Fold in pecans. Spoon into greased 1 1/2-quart baking dish. Bake at 350 degrees for 1 hour.

Approx Per Serving: Cal 232; T Fat 11 g; 42% Calories from Fat;
    Prot 5 g; Carbo 30 g; Fiber 5 g; Chol 80 mg; Sod 399 mg.

Southwestern Cauliflower

Yield: 6 servings

3 cups cauliflowerets and
    chopped stems
1 tablespoon flour
3/4 cup skim milk
1/4 teaspoon salt
1/8 teaspoon (or more) cayenne
    pepper
1/8 teaspoon pepper

1/2 teaspoon melted low-fat
    margarine
1/2 cup shredded low-fat
    Cheddar cheese
2 tablespoons chopped green
    chilies
1/3 cup bread crumbs

Steam cauliflower in saucepan over low heat just until tender; drain. Place in 2-quart baking dish. Shake flour, skim milk, salt, cayenne pepper and pepper in covered jar until smooth. Stir gradually into melted margarine in saucepan. Cook until thickened, stirring constantly. Stir in cheese until melted. Add green chilies. Pour over cauliflower. Top with bread crumbs. Bake at 350 degrees for 10 to 15 minutes or until bubbly.

Approx Per Serving: Cal 79; T Fat 2 g; 25% Calories from Fat;
    Prot 6 g; Carbo 10 g; Fiber 2 g; Chol 6 mg; Sod 207 mg.

Lavender is a member of the mint family. Its purple blossoms, used sparingly, are good in marinades and jellies.

Corn Pudding

Yield: 8 servings

2 cups drained whole kernel
  corn
3 eggs
2 tablespoons sugar
1 tablespoon flour

1¹/₃ cups milk
1 teaspoon salt
¹/₈ teaspoon pepper
1¹/₂ tablespoons butter
Paprika to taste

Combine corn, eggs, sugar, flour, milk, salt and pepper in bowl; mix well. Spoon into greased 1¹/₂-quart baking dish. Dot with butter; sprinkle with paprika. Place dish in larger pan of hot water. Bake at 350 degrees for 45 minutes or until set.

Approx Per Serving: Cal 122; T Fat 6 g; 42% Calories from Fat;
  Prot 5 g; Carbo 14 g; Fiber 1 g; Chol 91 mg; Sod 423 mg.

Broiled Basil Eggplant

Yield: 8 servings

¹/₄ cup olive oil
2 tablespoons lemon juice
2 tablespoons chopped parsley
2 tablespoons chopped basil
Salt and pepper to taste

8 large ¹/₃-inch thick eggplant
  slices
3 tablespoons olive oil
3 ounces mozzarella cheese,
  sliced ¹/₈ inch thick

Whisk ¹/₄ cup olive oil, lemon juice, parsley, basil, salt and pepper in bowl until smooth. Brush both sides of eggplant slices with 3 tablespoons olive oil. Arrange in single layer on baking sheet; season with salt and pepper. Broil until tender and light brown, turning once. Arrange on ovenproof platter, overlapping slices slightly. Top with cheese. Broil just until cheese melts. Whisk basil sauce to mix again. Spoon over eggplant. Garnish with sprigs of fresh basil. Serve immediately.

Approx Per Serving: Cal 147; T Fat 14 g; 84% Calories from Fat;
  Prot 3 g; Carbo 3 g; Fiber 1 g; Chol 8 mg; Sod 42 mg.

Chive

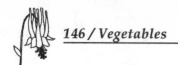

Fiddlehead Fern Stir-Fry

Yield: 4 servings

1 tablespoon oil
1 pound tightly curled
  fiddlehead ferns

⅛ teaspoon garlic powder
2 to 3 tablespoons water

Heat oil in wok. Add ferns and garlic powder. Stir-fry for several minutes, coating well with oil. Add 2 tablespoons water. Stir-fry for 2 to 3 minutes, adding remaining 1 tablespoon water if necessary to prevent sticking.

Approx Per Serving: Cal 82; T Fat 4 g; 41% Calories from Fat;
   Prot 3 g; Carbo 10 g; Fiber 2 g; Chol 0 mg; Sod 87 mg.

Mustard Greens with Ham Hock

Yield: 4 servings

1 pound mustard greens
1 meaty ham hock

Salt and pepper to taste

Add mustard greens to a small amount of water in saucepan. Add ham hock. Simmer, covered, until tender. Drain, removing ham hock. Chop ham and return to saucepan. Season to taste.

Approx Per Serving: Cal 72; T Fat 3 g; 36% Calories from Fat;
   Prot 7 g; Carbo 6 g; Fiber 3 g; Chol 11 mg; Sod 236 mg.

Out-of-this-World Mushrooms

Yield: 6 servings

1 pound fresh mushrooms
1 teaspoon chervil
1 teaspoon Bovril
1 teaspoon tarragon
2 teaspoons lemon juice

¼ teaspoon salt
¼ cup melted butter
1 cup whipping cream
1 tablespoon cornstarch

Remove stems of mushrooms. Slice stems and caps. Stir chervil, Bovril, tarragon, lemon juice and salt into butter in skillet over medium heat. Add mushrooms. Cook for 5 minutes. Reduce heat. Stir in mixture of cream and cornstarch. Cook for 7 minutes or until thickened, stirring constantly. Serve with steaks, roasts or on toast points.

Approx Per Serving: Cal 229; T Fat 23 g; 86% Calories from Fat;
   Prot 2 g; Carbo 6 g; Fiber 1 g; Chol 75 mg; Sod 171 mg.
   Nutritional information does not include Bovril.

Southern Okra

Yield: 6 servings

1 tablespoon sugar
1 teaspoon flour
1/2 teaspoon salt
1/2 teaspoon pepper
2 cups sliced okra

1 medium onion, chopped
1 green bell pepper, chopped
2 tablespoons oil
3 tomatoes, peeled, chopped

Mix sugar, flour, salt and pepper in small bowl; set aside. Cook okra in boiling water to cover in saucepan for 10 minutes or until tender; drain. Sauté onion and green pepper in oil in skillet over medium heat. Stir in sugar mixture and tomatoes. Cook for 5 minutes. Add okra. Simmer until heated through; stir as little as possible. Serve with rice.

Approx Per Serving: Cal 96; T Fat 5 g; 43% Calories from Fat;
    Prot 2 g; Carbo 13 g; Fiber 3 g; Chol 0 mg; Sod 186 mg.

Onions in Wine Sauce

Yield: 8 servings

2 pounds tiny boiling onions,
    peeled
2 cups water
1 cup white wine
1/2 teaspoon salt
1/4 cup flour

1/4 cup melted butter
1 cup half and half
2 tablespoons chopped parsley
White pepper to taste
3 tablespoons grated Parmesan
    cheese

Combine onions with water, wine and salt in saucepan. Simmer for 20 minutes or until onions are tender. Drain, reserving liquid. Blend flour into butter in saucepan. Stir in half and half and 1 cup reserved cooking liquid. Cook until thickened, stirring constantly. Stir in parsley, onions and white pepper. Spoon into 1 1/2-quart baking dish. Sprinkle with cheese. Bake at 375 degrees for 15 minutes.

Approx Per Serving: Cal 171; T Fat 10 g; 53% Calories from Fat;
    Prot 4 g; Carbo 13 g; Fiber 2 g; Chol 28 mg; Sod 233 mg.

*In areas where temperatures may dip to 15 below
zero or colder, cut branches of forsythia early
in the winter to force and enjoy before the flower
buds are killed by deep frost.*

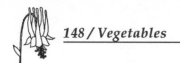

Garlic and Rosemary Peas

Yield: 4 servings

1 large clove of garlic, minced
1 small onion, chopped
4 slices bacon, chopped
1 tablespoon oil

1   10-ounce package frozen peas
1   16-ounce can tomatoes,
      chopped
Rosemary, salt and pepper to taste

Sauté garlic, onion and bacon in oil in saucepan until bacon is crisp. Add remaining ingredients. Cook until peas are thawed. Add water if necessary to cover peas. Simmer, covered, for 1 hour.

Approx Per Serving: Cal 154; T Fat 7 g; 40% Calories from Fat;
    Prot 7 g; Carbo 17 g; Fiber 5 g; Chol 5 mg; Sod 366 mg.

German Hot Potato Salad

Yield: 8 servings

3 pounds new potatoes
6 slices bacon, chopped
2 tablespoons flour
1 small onion, minced
1 cup sugar
1 cup water

1/2 cup vinegar
1 cup chopped celery
2 hard-boiled eggs, sliced
Salt, pepper and celery salt to
    taste

Cook potatoes in water to cover in saucepan until tender. Peel and slice potatoes. Fry bacon in skillet; remove bacon with slotted spoon, reserving drippings. Stir in flour and onion. Cook for 1 minute, stirring constantly. Add sugar, water and vinegar. Cook until thickened and smooth. Layer potatoes, celery, eggs, seasonings and vinegar sauce 1/2 at a time in serving bowl. Toss lightly to mix. Sprinkle with bacon. Garnish with additional sliced egg and paprika.

Approx Per Serving: Cal 320; T Fat 6 g; 16% Calories from Fat;
    Prot 6 g; Carbo 63 g; Fiber 3 g; Chol 68 mg; Sod 133 mg.

Potato Pancakes

Yield: 12 servings

2 eggs
1/2 small onion
2 tablespoons flour

1/4 teaspoon baking powder
1 teaspoon salt
3 cups cubed potatoes

Combine eggs, onion, flour, baking powder, salt and 1/2 cup potatoes in food processor fitted with grater blade. Process just until potatoes are grated. Add remaining potatoes. Process just until grated. Spoon onto hot greased griddle. Bake until golden brown on both sides; drain.

Approx Per Serving: Cal 75; T Fat 1 g; 12% Calories from Fat;
    Prot 2 g; Carbo 14 g; Fiber 1 g; Chol 36 mg; Sod 200 mg.

Golden Potato Surprise

Yield: 4 servings

4 white potatoes, peeled,
   chopped
Salt to taste
2 medium red onions, chopped
2 tablespoons butter
2 tablespoons flour
1/2 teaspoon thyme

1/2 teaspoons salt
1/2 teaspoon pepper
1 cup half and half
1 teaspoon Dijon mustard
1/2 cup mayonnaise
4 slices crisp-fried bacon,
   crumbled

Cook potatoes in salted water to cover in saucepan until tender; drain. Place in 2-quart baking dish. Sauté onions in butter in saucepan. Stir in flour, thyme, salt and pepper. Add half and half gradually. Cook until thickened, stirring constantly. Cool slightly. Stir in mustard and mayonnaise. Spoon over potatoes. Bake at 350 degrees for 30 minutes. Top with bacon.

Approx Per Serving: Cal 432; T Fat 38 g; 78% Calories from Fat;
   Prot 6 g; Carbo 18 g; Fiber 3 g; Chol 59 mg; Sod 620 mg.

Potatoes Extraordinaire

Yield: 10 servings

8 or 9 medium-large potatoes
1/4 cup margarine
1 1/2 cups shredded Cheddar
   cheese
1/2 cup grated Parmesan cheese

1/2 teaspoon paprika
1 1/2 teaspoons salt
1/2 teaspoon pepper
2 cups whipping cream

Bring unpeeled potatoes and water to cover to a boil in saucepan. Cook for just 10 minutes; drain. Peel and grate potatoes. Layer half the potatoes in large baking dish. Dot with margarine. Layer half the cheeses and seasonings over potatoes. Top with remaining potatoes, cheeses and seasonings. Pour cream over layers. Bake at 350 degrees for 45 minutes. Serve immediately. May prepare casserole and chill for 1 hour prior to baking if desired.

Approx Per Serving: Cal 316; T Fat 29 g; 82% Calories from Fat;
   Prot 8 g; Carbo 7 g; Fiber 1 g; Chol 86 mg; Sod 576 mg.

The mild and sweet white flowers of chamomile can be used for tea, salads or as a garnish.

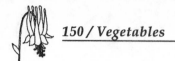

Mashed Potato Casserole

Yield: 8 servings

6 medium potatoes, peeled,
   chopped
1/2 cup warm milk
1 large onion, finely chopped
4 stalks celery with leaves,
   finely chopped

6 tablespoons butter
1 cup bread cubes
1 egg, beaten
1 teaspoon chopped parsley
Salt and pepper to taste

Cook potatoes in water to cover in saucepan until tender; drain. Mash potatoes with warm milk until light and fluffy. Sauté onion and celery in butter in skillet just until tender. Add bread, egg, parsley, salt and pepper; mix well. Add to potatoes; mix well. Spoon into greased baking dish; do not smooth top. Bake at 350 degrees for 15 minutes.

Approx Per Serving: Cal 136; T Fat 10 g; 65% Calories from Fat;
   Prot 3 g; Carbo 9 g; Fiber 2 g; Chol 52 mg; Sod 129 mg.

Peruvian-Style Stuffed Potatoes

Yield: 6 servings

8 ounces ground beef
1 small onion, chopped
1 clove of garlic, shopped
1 teaspoon oil
2 tablespoons tomato paste
1 teaspoon chopped parsley
1/4 cup seedless raisins
4 black olives, chopped

1 hard-boiled egg, chopped
1/4 cup white wine
Salt and pepper to taste
4 potatoes, peeled, chopped
1 egg, beaten
1/2 cup flour
Oil for browning

Brown ground beef with onion and garlic in oil in skillet, stirring frequently; drain. Stir in tomato paste, parsley, raisins, olives, hard-boiled egg, wine, salt and pepper. Cook potatoes in water to cover in saucepan until tender; drain. Mash until smooth. Add beaten egg, salt and pepper; mix well. Shape into balls. Fill balls with ground beef mixture, shaping potato to enclose filling. Coat balls with flour. Brown in hot oil in skillet.

Approx Per Serving: Cal 210; T Fat 9 g; 39% Calories from Fat;
   Prot 12 g; Carbo 20 g; Fiber 2 g; Chol 96 mg; Sod 77 mg.
   Nutritional information does not include oil for browning.

Plant marigolds among your tomatoes and other vegetables. The roots produce a chemical in the soil that kill nematodes.

Pumpkin Puff

Yield: 6 servings

This is a favorite dish for Thanksgiving.

1 29-ounce can pumpkin
1/2 cup packed brown sugar
5 tablespoons melted butter
1/2 teaspoon nutmeg
1/2 teaspoon cinnamon
1/2 teaspoon ginger

1 teaspoon salt
3 eggs, beaten
1/2 cup whipping cream
2 tablespoons honey
1/2 cup chopped walnuts

Combine pumpkin, brown sugar, butter, nutmeg, cinnamon, ginger and salt in bowl; mix well. Mix in eggs and cream. Spoon into greased baking dish. Top with mixture of honey and walnuts. Bake at 375 degrees for 50 minutes or until puffed. Serve at once.

Approx Per Serving: Cal 410; T Fat 26 g; 55% Calories from Fat;
   Prot 7 g; Carbo 42 g; Fiber 3 g; Chol 160 mg; Sod 496 mg.

Stuffed Pumpkin

Yield: 20 servings

1 3 to 5-pound pumpkin
8 slices bread, lightly toasted,
   cubed
1 cup raisins
1 cup packed brown sugar
1 cup melted margarine
1 cup evaporated milk

1 8-ounce can crushed
   pineapple
1 cup chopped apple
1 cup chopped walnuts
1 teaspoon cinnamon
1 teaspoon cloves

Cut top from pumpkin and discard seed. Combine bread cubes, raisins, brown sugar, margarine, evaporated milk, undrained pineapple, apple, walnuts, cinnamon and cloves in bowl; mix well. Spoon into pumpkin; replace top. Place on baking sheet. Bake at 350 degrees for 2 1/2 hours. Serve whole pumpkin on serving platter. Allow guests to scoop out servings of stuffing and pumpkin.

Approx Per Serving: Cal 279; T Fat 14 g; 44% Calories from Fat;
   Prot 4 g; Carbo 36 g; Fiber 3 g; Chol 3 mg; Sod 187 mg.

Tomato

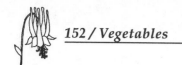

Tomatoes Supreme

Yield: 4 servings

4 medium tomatoes
¼ cup sherry
Basil, salt and pepper to taste

¼ cup mayonnaise
¼ cup shredded Cheddar cheese

Slice off tops of tomatoes; pierce several times. Place in baking dish. Pour sherry over tomatoes; sprinkle with basil, salt and pepper. Let stand for 15 minutes. Bake at 325 degrees for 15 minutes. Spread with mixture of mayonnaise and cheese. Broil just until cheese melts.

Approx Per Serving: Cal 169; T Fat 14 g; 77% Calories from Fat; Prot 3 g; Carbo 6 g; Fiber 2 g; Chol 16 mg; Sod 133 mg.

Spinach Soufflé

Yield: 12 servings

2 10-ounce packages frozen chopped spinach
2 pounds large curd cottage cheese
8 ounces brick cheese, shredded

8 ounces American cheese, shredded
6 tablespoons flour
½ cup butter
6 eggs, beaten

Cook spinach using package directions; drain. Combine with cottage cheese and shredded cheeses in bowl; mix well. Spoon into 9x13-inch baking dish. Sprinkle with flour; dot with butter. Pour eggs over top. Bake at 350 degrees for 1 hour.

Approx Per Serving: Cal 354; T Fat 25 g; 64% Calories from Fat; Prot 23 g; Carbo 9 g; Fiber 1 g; Chol 175 mg; Sod 822 mg.

Apple and Pecan Squash

Yield: 4 servings

2 medium acorn squash
½ cup butter
2 cups finely chopped apples
2 teaspoons lemon juice

1 teaspoon cinnamon
½ teaspoon salt
1 cup chopped pecans
Nutmeg to taste

Cut squash into halves crosswise, discarding seed. Place cut side down in shallow baking dish. Bake at 350 degrees for 45 minutes. Scoop out pulp, reserving shells. Combine pulp with butter, apples, lemon juice, cinnamon, salt and ¾ cup pecans in bowl; mix well. Spoon into reserved shells. Top with remaining ¼ cup pecans and nutmeg. Bake at 350 degrees for 10 minutes.

Approx Per Serving: Cal 557; T Fat 44 g; 66% Calories from Fat; Prot 5 g; Carbo 46 g; Fiber 9 g; Chol 62 mg; Sod 470 mg.

Summer Squash Casserole

Yield: 6 servings

6 cups sliced summer squash
1 large onion, sliced
1 cup shredded carrot
1 cup sour cream

1 10-ounce can cream of
  chicken soup
1 cup stuffing mix
½ cup melted butter

Steam squash and onion in saucepan for 5 minutes; drain. Add carrot, sour cream and soup; mix well. Add mixture of stuffing mix and butter. Spoon into 9x9-inch baking dish. Bake at 350 degrees for 30 minutes.

Approx Per Serving: Cal 348; T Fat 27 g; 67% Calories from Fat;
    Prot 6 g; Carbo 23 g; Fiber 3 g; Chol 62 mg; Sod 686 mg.

Texas Squash

Yield: 8 servings

1 medium spaghetti squash
6 medium tomatoes, chopped
¾ cup coarsely chopped onion
½ cup oat bran
1 tablespoon Italian seasoning

2 teaspoons sugar
¼ teaspoon salt
1 cup sliced fresh mushrooms
2 cups cooked mixed vegetables

Cut squash into halves, discarding seed. Place cut side down on lightly oiled baking sheet. Bake at 350 degrees for 35 to 45 minutes or until tender. Scoop out strands of squash with fork; drain and keep warm. Combine tomatoes, onion, oat bran, Italian seasoning, sugar and salt in saucepan. Bring to a boil; reduce heat. Simmer for 15 minutes. Add mushrooms and mixed vegetables. Cook until heated through. Spoon squash onto platter. Spoon sauce over top.

Approx Per Serving: Cal 92; T Fat 1 g; 6% Calories from Fat;
    Prot 4 g; Carbo 22 g; Fiber 7 g; Chol 0 mg; Sod 106 mg.
    Nutritional information does not include Italian seasoning.

Tropical flowers that grow from bulbs provide out-standing material for flower arrangers—eucomis, acidanthera, crocosmia, gladiolus, dahlia, sprekelia and canna. Many gardeners pass them by because they must be planted in spring, dug in fall and stored through the winter. Gardening has always been work, and planting summer bulbs is well worth the effort.

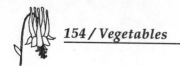

Old-Fashioned Sweet Potatoes

Yield: 4 servings

4 medium sweet potatoes,
    peeled
1½ cups sugar
½ teaspoon cinnamon

¼ teaspoon nutmeg
¼ cup butter
1 cup (about) orange juice

Grate sweet potatoes into baking dish. Sprinkle with mixture of sugar, cinnamon and nutmeg; dot with butter. Add enough orange juice to be visible; do not cover with orange juice. Bake at 350 degrees for 1½ hours.

Approx Per Serving: Cal 578; T Fat 12 g; 18% Calories from Fat;
    Prot 3 g; Carbo 118 g; Fiber 5 g; Chol 31 mg; Sod 119 mg.

Sweet Potato Casserole

Yield: 8 servings

4 cups mashed cooked sweet
    potatoes
¾ cup sugar
2 eggs
6 tablespoons melted margarine
1 teaspoon lemon juice
1 teaspoon vanilla extract

¼ teaspoon cinnamon
¼ teaspoon nutmeg
¼ teaspoon salt
1 cup packed brown sugar
⅓ cup flour
¼ cup margarine, softened
⅔ cup chopped pecans

Combine first 9 ingredients in bowl; mix well. Spoon into lightly greased 8x8-inch baking dish. Mix brown sugar, flour, ¼ cup margarine and pecans in bowl. Sprinkle over casserole. Bake at 350 degrees for 30 minutes or until golden brown.

Approx Per Serving: Cal 604; T Fat 23 g; 33% Calories from Fat;
    Prot 6 g; Carbo 98 g; Fiber 2 g; Chol 53 mg; Sod 288 mg.

Whipped Turnips

Yield: 8 servings

4 cups mashed cooked turnips
2 cups soft bread crumbs
½ cup melted butter
2 tablespoons sugar

4 eggs, slightly beaten
2 teaspoons salt
¼ teaspoon pepper

Combine turnips with bread crumbs in bowl; mix well. Add butter, sugar, eggs, salt and pepper; mix well. Spoon into 2-quart baking dish sprayed with butter-flavored nonstick cooking spray. Bake at 350 degrees for 1 hour or until set.

Approx Per Serving: Cal 211; T Fat 15 g; 61% Calories from Fat;
    Prot 5 g; Carbo 17 g; Fiber 3 g; Chol 138 mg; Sod 800 mg.

Italian Zucchini Pie

Yield: 6 servings

4 cups thinly sliced zucchini
1 cup coarsely chopped onion
¼ cup margarine
½ cup chopped fresh parsley
¼ teaspoon garlic powder
¼ teaspoon sweet basil
¼ teaspoon oregano

½ teaspoon salt
½ teaspoon pepper
2 eggs, beaten
2 cups shredded mozzarella
 cheese
1 8-count can crescent rolls
2 teaspoons Dijon mustard

Sauté zucchini and onion in margarine in skillet for 10 minutes or until tender. Stir in parsley, garlic powder, basil, oregano, salt and pepper. Beat eggs and cheese in large bowl. Add zucchini mixture; mix well. Separate roll dough into wedges. Arrange in ungreased 10 or 11-inch pie plate, pressing edges to seal. Spread with mustard. Spoon zucchini mixture into crust. Bake at 375 degrees for 18 to 20 minutes or until knife inserted into center comes out clean and top is light brown. Let stand for 10 minutes.

Approx Per Serving: Cal 359; T Fat 25 g; 62% Calories from Fat;
    Prot 13 g; Carbo 21 g; Fiber 2 g; Chol 100 mg; Sod 764 mg.

Zucchini Casserole

Yield: 12 servings

1 large zucchini, sliced
1 10-ounce can cream of
   mushroom soup
2 cups grated carrots

½ cup chopped onion
2 cups sour cream
4½ cups Stove-Top stuffing mix
¼ cup melted margarine

Cook zucchini in water in saucepan until tender; drain. Add soup, carrots, onion and sour cream; mix well. Stir in 2½ cups stuffing mix. Spoon into 9x13-inch baking dish. Brown remaining 2 cups stuffing mix in margarine in skillet. Sprinkle on casserole. Bake at 350 degrees for 35 minutes.

Approx Per Serving: Cal 251; T Fat 14 g; 52% Calories from Fat;
    Prot 5 g; Carbo 25 g; Fiber 1 g; Chol 17 mg; Sod 613 mg.

Sage

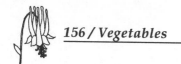

Fall Garden Casserole

Yield: 6 servings

1 cup shredded carrots
½ cup shredded rutabaga
¼ cup shredded sweet potato
2 tablespoons chopped onion
½ cup water
1½ cups cooked rice
¼ cup milk

¾ cup shredded Monterey Jack
  cheese
½ teaspoon basil
Salt and pepper to taste
¼ cup shredded Monterey Jack
  cheese

Cook carrots, rutabaga, sweet potato and onion in water in saucepan for 5 minutes or until tender. Drain, reserving cooking liquid. Add enough additional water to reserved liquid to measure ¼ cup liquid. Combine vegetables with rice, milk and ¾ cup cheese; mix well. Add reserved liquid, basil, salt and pepper; mix well. Spoon into lightly greased 1-quart baking dish. Bake, covered, at 350 degrees for 20 minutes. Sprinkle with remaining ¼ cup cheese. Bake, uncovered, for 5 minutes.

Approx Per Serving: Cal 164; T Fat 6 g; 34% Calories from Fat;
  Prot 7 g; Carbo 20 g; Fiber 2 g; Chol 19 mg; Sod 118 mg.

Ratatouille

Yield: 8 servings

1 medium onion, chopped
2 cloves of garlic, chopped
1 bay leaf
¼ cup oil
1 eggplant, peeled, chopped
¾ cup tomato juice
3 tablespoons sherry
2 tablespoons tomato paste
½ teaspoon basil

½ teaspoon marjoram
½ teaspoon oregano
½ teaspoon salt
⅛ teaspoon pepper
2 medium green bell peppers,
  cut into strips
1 medium zucchini, chopped
2 tomatoes, chopped
2 tablespoons chopped parsley

Sauté onion, garlic and bay leaf in oil in small skillet for 3 to 5 minutes or until onion is tender. Add eggplant, tomato juice, sherry, tomato paste, basil, marjoram, oregano, salt and pepper. Simmer, covered, for 10 minutes. Stir in green peppers and zucchini. Simmer, covered, for 10 minutes. Add tomatoes. Cook just until heated through. Stir in parsley; discard bay leaf. Serve over brown rice. Garnish with mozzarella cheese and black olives.

Approx Per Serving: Cal 108; T Fat 7 g; 59% Calories from Fat;
  Prot 2 g; Carbo 9 g; Fiber 3 g; Chol 0 mg; Sod 225 mg.

Vegetable Medley

Yield: 8 servings

This Hungarian recipe, called Tzitayough Sempoog, utilizes end-of-the-season vegetables. The combination is delicious but can be varied to suit individual tastes and availability of vegetables. Serve it hot as a vegetable or cold as a salad or relish with sandwiches. It is especially good with brisket dinner or baked dinner.

1   8-ounce can tomato sauce
²/₃ cup olive oil
¹/₄ cup chopped fresh parsley
¹/₂ cup thinly sliced celery
¹/₂ teaspoon whole allspice
1 teaspoon salt
¹/₂ teaspoon coarsely ground
   red pepper

¹/₂ teaspoon pepper
1   1 to 1¹/₂-pound eggplant
3 medium tomatoes, cut into
   ³/₄-inch cubes
2 medium onions, thinly sliced
1 large green bell pepper, cut
   into ³/₄-inch squares

Combine tomato sauce, olive oil, parsley, celery, allspice, salt, red pepper and pepper in small bowl; mix well. Let stand for several minutes. Cut eggplant into 1-inch pieces. Layer eggplant, tomatoes, onions, green pepper and tomato sauce mixture ¹/₂ at a time in 9x13-inch baking dish. Bake, covered, at 400 degrees for 30 minutes. Bake, uncovered, for 30 minutes longer.

Approx Per Serving: Cal 215; T Fat 18 g; 73% Calories from Fat;
   Prot 2 g; Carbo 13 g; Fiber 5 g; Chol 0 mg; Sod 453 mg.

Batter that Matters

Yield: enough batter for 4 servings

Make an herb-flavored batter by the addition of 1 minced clove of garlic and 1 teaspoon basil. Substitute water for beer if you prefer.

¹/₂ cup cornstarch
¹/₂ cup flour
1 teaspoon baking powder
¹/₂ teaspoon salt

¹/₂ teaspoon pepper
¹/₂ cup beer
1 egg, slightly beaten

Mix cornstarch, flour, baking powder, salt and pepper in bowl. Add beer and egg; mix until smooth. Use as batter for deep frying bite-sized vegetables such as carrots, zucchini, onions, tomatoes, broccoli or cauliflower.

Approx Per Serving: Cal 148; T Fat 2 g; 10% Calories from Fat;
   Prot 3 g; Carbo 27 g; Fiber 1 g; Chol 53 mg; Sod 368 mg.

Side Dishes

Manicotti in Béchamel Sauce
Yield: 12 servings

1/2 cup grated fresh pecorino or Romano cheese
1/2 cup grated Parmesan cheese
1 cup cubed mozzarella cheese
16 ounces ricotta cheese
3 eggs, beaten
2 tablespoons chopped parsley
12 pecan halves, chopped
Nutmeg and pepper to taste
3 1/2 cups flour
Salt to taste

2 tablespoons olive oil
1 tablespoon water
4 eggs, at room temperature
6 quarts water
1 tablespoon olive oil
1 cup shredded Monterey Jack cheese
1/4 cup butter
1/4 cup flour
1   14-ounce can chicken broth
1   5-ounce can evaporated milk

Combine pecorino cheese, Parmesan cheese, cubed mozzarella cheese, ricotta cheese, 3 eggs, parsley, pecans, nutmeg and pepper in bowl; mix well. Set aside. Combine 3 1/2 cups flour and salt to taste in bowl. Add 2 tablespoons olive oil, 1 tablespoon water and 4 eggs; mix well to form dough. Knead until smooth. Roll on floured surface or in pasta machine. Cut into twelve 4x4-inch squares. Combine with 6 quarts salted boiling water and 1 tablespoon olive oil in saucepan. Cook for 4 to 5 minutes or until tender. Remove to damp towel with slotted spoon. Place spoonful of cheese filling on each square. Roll gently to enclose filling; arrange in buttered 9x13-inch baking dish. Sprinkle with shredded Monterey Jack cheese. Melt butter in saucepan. Blend in 1/4 cup flour. Cook for 1 minute; remove from heat. Stir in chicken broth. Cook for 1 minute or until thickened, stirring constantly. Stir in evaporated milk. Spoon over manicotti. Bake at 375 degrees for 35 minutes.

Approx Per Serving: Cal 440; T Fat 25 g; 51% Calories from Fat; Prot 20 g; Carbo 33 g; Fiber 1 g; Chol 180 mg; Sod 418 mg.

Fettucini with Tomato-Basil Sauce   Yield: 6 servings

4 large tomatoes, peeled,
   seeded, coarsely chopped
1 clove of garlic, crushed
1 bunch fresh basil, chopped

2 tablespoons olive oil
Salt and pepper to taste
1   16-ounce package fettucini,
   cooked, drained

Drain tomatoes partially. Combine with garlic, basil, olive oil, salt and pepper in large bowl; mix well. Serve over hot fettucini. Garnish with grated Parmesan cheese and pepper.

Approx Per Serving: Cal 343; T Fat 6 g; 15% Calories from Fat;
    Prot 10 g; Carbo 61 g; Fiber 4 g; Chol 0 mg; Sod 8 mg.

Pesto alla Genovese   Yield: 32 one-tablespoon servings

4 cups chopped fresh basil
1/2 cup chopped parsley
4 large cloves of garlic
1/2 cup pine nuts

1 cup olive oil
1 1/2 teaspoons salt
1 teaspoon pepper
2/3 cup grated Parmesan cheese

Process first 7 ingredients in blender at high speed until smooth. Stir in cheese. Freeze until ready to use over pasta, in soups and stews or over sliced tomatoes.

Approx Per Serving: Cal 83; T Fat 8 g; 92% Calories from Fat;
    Prot 1 g; Carbo 1 g; Fiber <1 g; Chol 1 mg; Sod 132 mg.

Holiday Spinach Noodles   Yield: 8 servings

16 ounces spinach noodles
6 tablespoons flour
1/4 teaspoon nutmeg
1 teaspoon salt
1/4 teaspoon pepper
1/2 cup melted unsalted butter
4 cups milk

3 chicken bouillon cubes
1/4 cup finely chopped onion
1/4 cup finely chopped red bell
   pepper
1 pound muenster cheese, sliced
1 pound fresh mushrooms,
   sliced

Cook noodles using package directions; drain. Blend flour, nutmeg, salt, and pepper into melted butter in 2-quart saucepan over medium heat. Stir in milk gradually. Add bouillon. Cook until thickened, stirring constantly. Stir in onion and red pepper. Spread 1/4 of the sauce in 9x13-inch baking dish. Layer noodles, cheese, mushrooms and remaining sauce 1/3 at a time in prepared dish. Bake at 350 degrees for 35 minutes.

Approx Per Serving: Cal 641; T Fat 35 g; 49% Calories from Fat;
    Prot 27 g; Carbo 55 g; Fiber 5 g; Chol 102 mg; Sod 1129 mg.

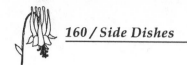

Pasta Fagioli

Yield: 6 servings

1 medium onion, chopped
1 clove of garlic, minced
1 small green bell pepper,
   chopped
1/4 cup olive oil
4 medium tomatoes, chopped
4 fresh basil leaves

12 Swiss chard leaves
2 cups beef broth
3 cups cooked white beans
Salt and pepper to taste
6 ounces uncooked spaghetti,
   cooked

Sauté onion, garlic and green pepper in olive oil in 5-quart saucepan for 5 minutes. Add tomatoes and basil. Sauté for 5 minutes. Add chard. Simmer for 5 minutes. Stir in beef broth. Simmer for 5 minutes. Add beans, salt and pepper. Heat to serving temperature. Stir in spaghetti at serving time. Garnish servings with Parmesan cheese. Serve with toasted garlic bread and tossed green salad.

Approx Per Serving: Cal 345; T Fat 10 g; 27% Calories from Fat;
   Prot 14 g; Carbo 51 g; Fiber 10 g; Chol <1 mg; Sod 281 mg.

Macaroni and Cheese

Yield: 8 servings

1 cup uncooked elbow macaroni
2 tablespoons flour
2 tablespoons melted butter
1/2 cup half and half
1 cup milk

2 cups shredded sharp Cheddar
   cheese
1/2 teaspoon dry mustard
1/4 teaspoon paprika
1 cup crushed Triscuits

Cook macaroni using package directions; drain. Blend flour into melted butter in saucepan. Stir in half and half and milk. Cook until thickened, stirring constantly. Add cheese, dry mustard and paprika; stir until cheese melts. Stir in macaroni. Spoon into greased shallow baking dish. Sprinkle with cracker crumbs. Bake at 350 degrees for 30 minutes or until casserole is bubbly.

Approx Per Serving: Cal 284; T Fat 18 g; 56% Calories from Fat;
   Prot 11 g; Carbo 20 g; Fiber 1 g; Chol 47 mg; Sod 218 mg.

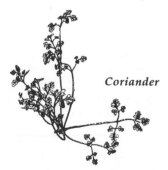

Coriander

Chilies Rellenos

Yield: 6 servings

4 egg yolks
4 egg whites
¼ cup flour
¾ teaspoon baking powder
¼ teaspoon salt

1 small onion, chopped
2 cups shredded sharp Cheddar
  cheese
6 canned green chilies
3 tablespoons oil

Beat egg yolks in mixer bowl until thick and lemon-colored. Beat egg whites in mixer bowl until stiff peaks form. Fold into egg yolks. Sift in flour, baking powder and salt; mix well. Combine onion and cheese in bowl; mix well. Stuff carefully into chilies. Dip chilies into batter, coating well. Fry in oil in skillet until brown on both sides, turning once. May substitute seeded fresh chilies or frozen chilies for canned chilies.

Approx Per Serving: Cal 298; T Fat 23 g; 70% Calories from Fat;
    Prot 15 g; Carbo 8 g; Fiber <1 g; Chol 182 mg; Sod 604 mg.

Enchiladas

Yield: 6 servings

You can top with lightly fried eggs for New Mexico-style enchiladas.

1 medium onion, chopped
1 tablespoon shortening
1 cup drained canned tomatoes
1 cup chopped green chilies

½ cup whipping cream
6 corn tortillas
Shortening for frying tortillas
1 cup shredded Cheddar cheese

Sauté onion in 1 tablespoon shortening in skillet. Add tomatoes and green chilies; mix well. Stir in cream gradually. Simmer for 5 minutes. Fry tortillas in hot shortening in heavy skillet for 5 minutes on each side. Layer tortillas, sauce and cheese on serving plates. Garnish with shredded lettuce.

Approx Per Serving: Cal 255; T Fat 17 g; 58% Calories from Fat;
    Prot 8 g; Carbo 20 g; Fiber 4 g; Chol 47 mg; Sod 192 mg.
    Nutritional information does not include shortening for
    frying tortillas.

*The earlier a woody plant flowers in spring, the
more easily it will force. Good candidates are
forsythia, cornelian cherry, pussy willow and fruits
like cherry or apricot. Later flowering plants
like lilac, crabapple and mock orange are
not as easy to force.*

Frittata with Spinach and Tarragon
Yield: 2 servings

4 egg whites
1 egg
1 teaspoon water
½ cup chopped spinach
¼ cup chopped scallions

¼ cup whole kernel corn
2 tablespoons shredded part-
 skim mozzarella cheese
½ teaspoon tarragon

Whisk egg whites with whole egg and water in medium bowl until smooth. Stir in spinach, scallions, corn, cheese and tarragon. Spoon into 6-inch baking dish sprayed with nonstick cooking spray. Bake at 400 degrees for 10 to 12 minutes or until puffed and golden brown. May broil for several seconds if browner top is desired.

Approx Per Serving: Cal 118; T Fat 4 g; 32% Calories from Fat;
    Prot 13 g; Carbo 8 g; Fiber 2 g; Chol 110 mg; Sod 182 mg.

Panhellenic Casserole
Yield: 8 servings

4 slices firm white bread, crusts
 trimmed
2 tablespoons butter, softened
2 cups shredded sharp Cheddar
 cheese
2 cups shredded Monterey Jack
 cheese
1 7-ounce can chopped green
 chilies

6 eggs
2 cups milk
¼ teaspoon garlic powder
1 teaspoon oregano
1 teaspoon paprika
¼ teaspoon dry mustard
1 teaspoon salt
½ teaspoon red pepper

Spread bread with butter. Arrange bread buttered side down in 9x13-inch baking dish. Sprinkle with cheeses and green chilies. Beat eggs with milk, garlic powder, oregano, paprika, dry mustard, salt and red pepper in bowl. Pour over bread. Chill for 4 hours to overnight. Bake at 325 degrees for 50 minutes.

Approx Per Serving: Cal 385; T Fat 28 g; 65% Calories from Fat;
    Prot 22 g; Carbo 12 g; Fiber <1 g; Chol 231 mg; Sod 943 mg.

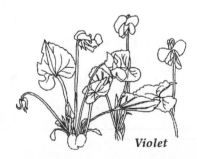

Violet

Hominy Casserole

Yield: 12 servings

1 16-ounce cans white or
   yellow hominy
2 cups shredded Monterey Jack
   cheese

16 ounces sour cream
2 4-ounce cans chopped green
   chilies
1 cup shredded Cheddar cheese

Layer hominy and Monterey Jack cheese in large greased baking dish. Mix sour cream and green chilies in bowl. Spoon over layers. Top with Cheddar cheese. Bake at 300 degrees for 45 minutes to 1 hour or until brown and bubbly.

Approx Per Serving: Cal 214; T Fat 17 g; 70% Calories from Fat;
    Prot 9 g; Carbo 7 g; Fiber 0 g; Chol 44 mg; Sod 424 mg.

Festive Rice Casserole

Yield: 8 servings

6 slices bacon
1 15-ounce can black-eyed peas
   with jalapeño peppers

1 16-ounce can stewed tomatoes
2 cups uncooked instant rice
1 medium onion, thinly sliced

Fry bacon in skillet until crisp. Remove bacon; drain all but 2 table-spoons of drippings. Add peas, tomatoes, rice and onion to drippings in skillet; mix well. Spoon into 9x13-inch baking dish. Crumble bacon over top. Bake at 350 degrees for 30 minutes or until bubbly. Serve with beef or chicken.

Approx Per Serving: Cal 213; T Fat 6 g; 26% Calories from Fat;
    Prot 7 g; Carbo 33 g; Fiber 5 g; Chol 25 mg; Sod 453 mg.

Mexican Rice

Yield: 8 servings

2 cups uncooked rice
2 cloves of garlic, chopped
1/2 onion, chopped
2 tablespoons oil
2 sprigs of parsley

3 tomatoes, peeled, puréed
1 cup fresh peas
2 carrots, finely chopped
4 cups chicken broth
Salt to taste

Soak rice in lukewarm water in bowl for 15 minutes; rinse in cold water and drain. Sauté rice with garlic and onion in oil in skillet until light brown. Stir in parsley and tomatoes. Add peas, carrots, chicken broth and salt. Simmer, covered, for 30 minutes or until rice is tender and liquid is absorbed. Discard parsley.

Approx Per Serving: Cal 254; T Fat 5 g; 16% Calories from Fat;
    Prot 7 g; Carbo 45 g; Fiber 3 g; Chol 1 mg; Sod 402 mg.

Pilaf

Yield: 8 servings

2 cloves of garlic, minced
1 onion, chopped
1/2 cup margarine
1 4-ounce can chopped
  mushrooms, drained

1 cup uncooked rice
2 10-ounce cans beef
  consommé
1 10-ounce can water
1/2 teaspoon oregano

Sauté garlic and onion in margarine until translucent. Add mushrooms. Sauté for 1 minute. Stir in rice. Spoon into 1 1/2-quart baking dish. Stir in consommé and water. Sprinkle with oregano. Bake at 400 degrees for 1 hour or until liquid is absorbed.

Approx Per Serving: Cal 214; T Fat 12 g; 49% Calories from Fat;
    Prot 5 g; Carbo 22 g; Fiber 1 g; Chol 0 mg; Sod 564 mg.

Rice and Corn Dressing

Yield: 10 servings

1/2 cup chopped celery
1/2 cup chopped green bell pepper
1 cup chopped onion
Salt and red pepper to taste

1/2 cup margarine
2 cups uncooked long grain rice
1 11-ounce can Mexicorn
2 10-ounce cans beef broth

Sauté celery, green pepper and onion with salt and red pepper in margarine in skillet until translucent. Add rice. Cook until rice is light brown. Stir in corn and beef broth. Simmer, covered, for 30 minutes or until rice is tender and liquid is absorbed.

Approx Per Serving: Cal 246; T Fat 10 g; 35% Calories from Fat;
    Prot 4 g; Carbo 36 g; Fiber 1 g; Chol <1 mg; Sod 378 mg.

Wild Rice

Yield: 6 servings

1 cup wild rice
1 small onion, chopped
1 green bell pepper, chopped

4 ounces slivered almonds
2 tablespoons margarine
1 1/2 cups thin white sauce

Rinse rice well. Soak in water to cover in saucepan for 2 hours; drain. Add cold water to cover. Cook for 45 minutes to 1 hour or until rice is tender; drain. Let stand, covered, in warm place for 2 hours. Sauté onion, green pepper and almonds in margarine in skillet. Add to rice; mix well. Spoon into buttered baking dish. Top with white sauce. Bake at 350 degrees for 30 to 40 minutes or until bubbly. Serve with fowl.

Approx Per Serving: Cal 348; T Fat 22 g; 53% Calories from Fat;
    Prot 10 g; Carbo 32 g; Fiber 3 g; Chol 8 mg; Sod 271 mg.

Autumn Apples

Yield: 10 servings

2 cups sugar
2 cups water
Juice of 1½ lemons
Grated rind of 1 lemon
1 cinnamon stick

⅛ teaspoon cardamom
½ teaspoon red food coloring
8 large cooking apples, cut into
   1-inch slices

Combine first 7 ingredients in skillet. Boil for 1 minute. Add apples. Cook for 12 minutes or until tender. Remove to serving bowl with slotted spoon. Cook syrup until thickened to desired consistency. Pour over apples. Chill until serving time. May use 12 small whole cooking apples if desired.

Approx Per Serving: Cal 256; T Fat 1 g; 2% Calories from Fat;
    Prot <1 g; Carbo 66 g; Fiber 4 g; Chol 0 mg; Sod 2 mg.

Apple and Cranberry Casserole

Yield: 8 servings

4 cups chopped unpeeled apples
1 12-ounce package cranberries
½ cup chopped pecans
1¼ cups sugar

½ cup melted margarine
½ cup packed brown sugar
1½ cups quick-cooking oats
¾ teaspoon salt

Combine apples and cranberries in buttered 2-quart baking dish. Sprinkle with pecans and sugar. Mix margarine with brown sugar, oats and salt in bowl. Pat over top. Bake at 350 degrees for 40 to 45 minutes or until brown. May add ¼ cup orange juice.

Approx Per Serving: Cal 455; T Fat 18 g; 34% Calories from Fat;
    Prot 3 g; Carbo 75 g; Fiber 6 g; Chol 0 mg; Sod 343 mg.

Pineapple Casserole

Yield: 6 servings

1 20-ounce can crushed
   pineapple or pineapple
   tidbits
½ cup sugar

3 tablespoons flour
1 cup shredded Cheddar cheese
¼ cup melted butter
½ cup butter cracker crumbs

Drain pineapple, reserving 3 tablespoons juice. Mix sugar and flour in bowl. Stir in reserved pineapple juice. Add cheese and pineapple; mix well. Spoon into greased 1-quart baking dish. Top with mixture of melted butter and cracker crumbs. Bake at 350 degrees for 20 to 30 minutes or until light brown.

Approx Per Serving: Cal 331; T Fat 16 g; 42% Calories from Fat;
    Prot 6 g; Carbo 44 g; Fiber 1 g; Chol 41 mg; Sod 253 mg.

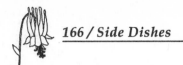

Pineapple Salsa

Yield: 12 servings

Serve this salsa with broiled fish, grilled chicken, pork chops or tortilla chips.

1 large pineapple
1 each red, green and yellow
    bell peppers, chopped
2 hot peppers with seed, chopped
1/4 cup (or more) fresh cilantro

1/4 cup fresh parsley
1 small onion
3 or 4 green onions with tops
1/4 cup safflower oil
2 tablespoons fresh lime juice

Peel pineapple and cut into quarters, discarding core. Place in baking pan. Broil for several minutes until warm but not brown. Drain and chop pineapple. Combine peppers in food processor container; process just until chopped. Combine with pineapple in large bowl. Process cilantro, parsley, onion and green onions until chopped. Add to pineapple with oil and lime juice. Season to taste. Chill, covered, for 2 hours or longer.

Approx Per Serving: Cal 77; T Fat 5 g; 53% Calories from Fat;
    Prot 1 g; Carbo 9 g; Fiber 1 g; Chol 0 mg; Sod 3 mg.

Tomato-Peach Conserve

Yield: 160 servings

9 large peaches
12 large tomatoes

6 cups sugar

Scald peaches and tomatoes in boiling water in saucepan. Remove skins and cut into pieces. Combine with sugar in large heavy saucepan. Cook for 3 hours or to desired consistency, stirring frequently with wooden spoon. Spoon into 10 small jars, leaving 1/4 inch headspace. Seal with 2-piece lids.

Approx Per Serving: Cal 33; T Fat <1 g; 1% Calories from Fat;
    Prot <1 g; Carbo 8 g; Fiber <1 g; Chol 0 mg; Sod 1 mg.

Red Eggs and Pickled Beets

Yield: 6 servings

1   16-ounce can beets
1 cup vinegar

3 tablespoons sugar
6 hard-boiled eggs, peeled

Combine beets, vinegar and sugar in saucepan. Heat just until sugar dissolves, mixing gently. Combine with eggs in bowl. Marinate in refrigerator for 4 hours or until eggs are as red as desired.

Approx Per Serving: Cal 130; T Fat 6 g; 38% Calories from Fat;
    Prot 7 g; Carbo 14 g; Fiber 1 g; Chol 213 mg; Sod 265 mg.

Crisp Onion Rings

Yield: 12 servings

3 sweet Texas onions
Sugar to taste

Dillweed, alum and vinegar to taste

Slice onions into thick slices; separate into rings. Mix ice water, sugar, dillweed, alum and vinegar in bowl. Add onions. Chill, covered, for several hours.

Nutritional information for this recipe is not available.

Grandmother's Pickles

Yield: 36 servings

2 16-ounce jars kosher dill
    pickles
4 cups sugar
1 cup white vinegar
1 cup (scant) water

3 bay leaves
3 cinnamon sticks
1 tablespoon whole cloves
1 clove of garlic

Drain and rinse pickles; cut each pickle into 3 pieces. Return to jars. Combine sugar, vinegar, water, bay leaves, cinnamon, cloves and garlic in saucepan. Boil for 10 minutes. Pour over pickles; seal. Chill in refrigerator for 10 to 14 days before serving.

Approx Per Serving: Cal 88; T Fat <1 g; 0% Calories from Fat;
    Prot <1 g; Carbo 23 g; Fiber <1 g; Chol 0 mg; Sod 288 mg.

Easy Apple Butter

Yield: 80 servings

8 cups applesauce
2 cups sugar
1/2 teaspoon cloves

1/2 teaspoon cinnamon
1/2 teaspoon allspice

Combine applesauce, sugar, cloves, cinnamon and allspice in baking dish; mix well. Cover loosely with baking parchment. Bake at 275 degrees for 6 to 7 hours or until of desired consistency, stirring occasionally. Freeze or can as desired.

Approx Per Serving: Cal 39; T Fat <1 g; 1% Calories from Fat;
    Prot <1 g; Carbo 10 g; Fiber <1 g; Chol 0 mg; Sod 1 mg.

*The petals of daisies have a light mint or clover flavor;
discard the hard centers of the blossoms.*

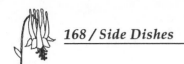

Honey Jelly
Yield: 64 servings

3 cups honey
1 cup water

½ bottle of liquid pectin

Blend honey and water in saucepan. Cook over high heat until bubbly. Stir in pectin. Bring to a full rolling boil, stirring constantly. Pour into 4 hot sterilized ½-pint jars; seal with 2-piece lids.

Approx Per Serving: Cal 49; T Fat 0 g; 0% Calories from Fat;
    Prot <1 g; Carbo 13 g; Fiber 0 g; Chol 0 mg; Sod 1 mg.

Microwave Marmalade
Yield: 24 servings

1 large 8 to 10-ounce orange

1½ cups (about) sugar

Chop orange, discarding seed and thick membrane. Process in food processor until finely chopped. Measure pulp and juice. Combine with equal amount of sugar in 2 or 3-quart glass bowl; mix well. Microwave on High for 6 to 8 minutes or until thick enough to coat metal spoon, stirring every 2 minutes. Cool to room temperature; mixture will thicken as it cools. Store in refrigerator for up to 1 month.

Approx Per Serving: Cal 54; T Fat <1 g; 0% Calories from Fat;
    Prot <1 g; Carbo 14 g; Fiber <1 g; Chol 0 mg; Sod <1 mg.

Pepper Jelly
Yield: 64 servings

This is delicious with any meat. It also makes
a beautiful gift at Christmas.

2 large green peppers, chopped
3 cayenne peppers
1½ cups vinegar
6 cups sugar

¼ teaspoon Tabasco sauce
¼ teaspoon green food coloring
1 package pectin

Process green peppers and cayenne peppers in several batches with vinegar in blender until smooth. Combine with sugar in saucepan; mix well. Let stand for 20 minutes. Cook until sugar dissolves, stirring constantly; remove from heat. Stir in Tabasco sauce, food coloring and pectin. Pour into hot sterilized jars; seal with 2-piece lids. Jelly will thicken as it cools.

Approx Per Serving: Cal 74; T Fat <1 g; 0% Calories from Fat;
    Prot <1 g; Carbo 19 g; Fiber <1 g; Chol 0 mg; Sod 1 mg.

Fruity Persimmon Jam

Yield: 112 servings

2¼ cups persimmon pulp
1   10-ounce package frozen
    sliced strawberries, thawed
1   20-ounce can unsweetened
    crushed pineapple

½ cup lemon juice
1 package pectin
6 cups sugar
¼ teaspoon margarine

Combine persimmon pulp, strawberries, pineapple and lemon juice in 6 to 8-quart saucepan. Add pectin. Stir until pectin dissolves. Bring to a boil over high heat, stirring constantly. Stir in sugar. Bring to a full rolling boil. Stir in margarine to reduce foaming. Boil for 5 minutes, stirring constantly; remove from heat. Skim foam. Spoon into 7 sterilized ½-pint jars. Let stand for 24 hours. Seal with ¼ inch thick paraffin.

Approx Per Serving: Cal 48; T Fat <1 g; 0% Calories from Fat;
    Prot <1 g; Carbo 13 g; Fiber <1 g; Chol 0 mg; Sod 1 mg.

Rhubarb Jam

Yield: 112 servings

8 cups ¾-inch rhubarb pieces
4 cups sugar
1   6-ounce package raspberry
    gelatin

1   21-ounce can blueberry pie
    filling

Cook rhubarb with sugar in saucepan until tender, stirring frequently; remove from heat. Stir in gelatin until dissolved. Stir in pie filling. Spoon into 7 hot sterilized ½-pint jars; seal with 2-piece lids. Store in refrigerator.

Approx Per Serving: Cal 40; T Fat <1 g; 0% Calories from Fat;
    Prot <1 g; Carbo 10 g; Fiber <1 g; Chol 0 mg; Sod 7 mg.

Opal Basil Jelly

Yield: 64 servings

Opal basil is also called purple basil.

1½ cups packed opal basil
    leaves
3 cups water

2 tablespoons lemon juice
4 cups sugar
1 package pectin

Crush basil leaves. Combine with water in saucepan. Bring to a boil over high heat; remove from heat. Steep for 10 minutes; strain. Combine 3 cups infusion and lemon juice in saucepan. Prepare jelly with sugar using pectin package directions. Serve as condiment with meats or on toast.

Approx Per Serving: Cal 49; T Fat <1 g; 0% Calories from Fat;
    Prot <1 g; Carbo 13 g; Fiber <1 g; Chol 0 mg; Sod <1 mg.

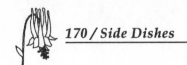

Tomato Marmalade

Yield: 198 servings

8 pounds tomatoes
8 pounds (about) sugar
3 oranges, quartered, seeded

2 lemons, quartered, seeded
1/2 ounce cinnamon sticks
1/2 ounces whole cloves

Slice tomatoes into bowl; drain half the liquid. Weigh tomatoes. Combine with equal amount of sugar in large saucepan; stir to dissolve sugar. Cut fruit into thin slices. Add to tomatoes with cinnamon and cloves. Boil until thickened to desired consistency, stirring frequently. Cool slightly. Pour into 12 hot sterilized 1/2-pint jars; seal with 2-piece lids.

Approx Per Serving: Cal 75; T Fat <1 g; 0% Calories from Fat;
Prot <1 g; Carbo 19 g; Fiber <1 g; Chol 0 mg; Sod 2 mg.

Zesty Mustard

Yield: 16 servings

1/4 cup flour
2 tablespoons sugar
1 tablespoon dry mustard

1 teaspoon sugar
Turmeric to taste

Mix flour, sugar, dry mustard and salt in bowl. Add enough cold water to make a thin paste. Stir in enough boiling water to thicken to desired consistency. Add turmeric to color as desired. May thin with white vinegar or add 1/3 cup salad dressing if desired.

Approx Per Serving: Cal 17; T Fat <1 g; 11% Calories from Fat;
Prot <1 g; Carbo 4 g; Fiber 0 g; Chol 0 mg; Sod <1 mg.

Creole Seasoning

Yield: 36 servings

Use this seasoning on steak or buttered vegetables, or add 3/4 to 1 teaspoon seasoning to 1/4 cup mayonnaise for a zippy salad dressing.

1/4 cup ground red pepper
1 tablespoon chili powder
1 tablespoon coriander
2 teaspoons cloves
1 tablespoon paprika

1 tablespoon freshly ground
   pepper
1 1/2 teaspoons garlic powder
3 tablespoons salt

Mix all ingredients in airtight container. Store in cool place.

Approx Per Serving: Cal 3; T Fat <1 g; 36% Calories from Fat;
Prot <1 g; Carbo <1 g; Fiber <1 g; Chol 0 mg; Sod 536 mg.

Breads

Sunrise in Santa Fe

South Central

Arkansas • New Mexico • Oklahoma • Texas

*G*eographic diversity of the Region includes cactus-spiked deserts, citrus groves, vast dry plains, forested highlands and towering snow-capped mountains. As in other wide-spread jurisdictions, Regional meetings serve as an excellent means of emphasizing goals of the National Council, and expanding interest in horticulture, conservation, highway beautification, junior clubs and flower show schools.

Texas Barbecue for Seventy Five

*Lone Star Brisket**

*Ranch-Style Beans**   *Texas Potato Salad**

Garlic-Butter French Bread

*Crisp Onion Rings**   *Home-Grown Tomatoes*

Pickles and Jalapeño Peppers

Pecan Pralines and/or Homemade Ice Cream*

Coffee, Iced Tea and Beer

New Mexico Feast

New Mexican cooking is as distinctive and colorful as the State of New Mexico. It is a superb blend of the cultures of the indian, Spanish, Mexican and Anglo people. The local people have taken materials from each culture and produced a cuisine that is forever distinctive in taste, aroma and color. The food is unlike any other you will ever taste!

Margaritas, Sangria or Mexican Beer

*Chilies Rellenos**   *Enchiladas**

*Beef Tacos**   *Posole**

Sopaipillas with Honey   Biscochitos**

Coffee

*See index for recipes.

Breads

Angel Biscuits

Yield: 30 servings

1 envelope dry yeast
2 tablespoons lukewarm water
5 to 5½ cups sifted flour
1 tablespoon baking powder
1 teaspoon baking soda
¼ cup sugar
1 teaspoon salt
1 cup shortening
2 cups buttermilk, at room
  temperature

Dissolve yeast in lukewarm water. Sift dry ingredients into large bowl. Cut in shortening until crumbly. Add yeast and buttermilk; mix well. Knead until smooth. Roll ½ to ¾ inch thick on floured surface. Cut with biscuit cutter; fold over. Place on lightly greased baking sheet. Bake at 400 degrees for 15 to 20 minutes or until golden brown.

Approx Per Serving: Cal 151; T Fat 7 g; 43% Calories from Fat;
    Prot 3 g; Carbo 19 g; Fiber 1 g; Chol 1 mg; Sod 127 mg.

Applescotch Biscuits

Yield: 10 servings

2 10-count cans biscuits
¼ cup melted butter
½ cup sugar
1 tablespoon cinnamon
2 apples, peeled, sliced
½ cup chopped pecans
1 4-ounce package butterscotch
   pudding and pie filling mix

Separate biscuits. Dip 1 at a time into melted butter; coat with mixture of sugar and cinnamon. Arrange in 9-inch round baking pan. Place apple slices around and between biscuits. Mix any remaining cinnamon-sugar mixture with pecans and pudding mix. Sprinkle over biscuits. Bake at 400 degrees for 20 to 25 minutes or until golden brown.

Approx Per Serving: Cal 296; T Fat 13 g; 39% Calories from Fat;
    Prot 3 g; Carbo 43 g; Fiber 2 g; Chol 14 mg; Sod 593 mg.

Tiny Hot Cheese Biscuits
Yield: 50 servings

½ cup margarine, softened
1 6-ounce jar Old English
   cheese spread, softened
½ teaspoon salt
½ teaspoon red pepper
1 cup flour

Cream margarine and cheese spread in mixer bowl. Mix in salt and red pepper. Add flour gradually, mixing until smooth. Drop by teaspoonfuls onto greased baking sheet. Chill, lightly covered, for 3 hours to overnight. Bake at 400 degrees for 8 minutes or until lightly browned.

Approx Per Serving: Cal 37; T Fat 3 g; 66% Calories from Fat;
    Prot 1 g; Carbo 2 g; Fiber <1 g; Chol 2 mg; Sod 83 mg.

Sweet Potato Biscuits
Yield: 30 servings

2 cups flour
4 teaspoons baking powder
2 tablespoons sugar
½ teaspoon salt
½ cup shortening
1 cup mashed cooked sweet
   potatoes

Combine flour, baking powder, sugar and salt in bowl. Cut in shortening until crumbly. Add sweet potatoes; mix well. Knead until smooth. Pat or roll on floured surface; cut with small biscuit cutter. Place on baking sheet. Bake at 400 degrees for 15 minutes.

Approx Per Serving: Cal 76; T Fat 4 g; 42% Calories from Fat;
    Prot 1 g; Carbo 10 g; Fiber <1 g; Chol 0 mg; Sod 81 mg.

Sweet Potato Ham Biscuits
Yield: 48 servings

3 cups flour
2 tablespoons sugar
2 teaspoons baking powder
½ teaspoon baking soda
Salt to taste
¼ cup butter-flavored shortening
¾ cup mashed cooked sweet
   potatoes
1 cup buttermilk
8 ounces baked ham, very
   thinly sliced

Combine flour, sugar, baking powder, baking soda and salt in large bowl. Cut in shortening until crumbly. Mix in sweet potatoes. Add buttermilk; stir with fork until moistened. Knead 4 or 5 times on floured surface. Roll ½ inch thick; cut with 2-inch biscuit cutter. Place on lightly greased baking sheet. Bake at 450 degrees for 8 to 10 minutes or until lightly browned. Split biscuits; fill with ham. Serve hot or at room temperature.

Approx Per Serving: Cal 55; T Fat 1 g; 24% Calories from Fat;
    Prot 2 g; Carbo 8 g; Fiber <1 g; Chol 3 mg; Sod 91 mg.

Favorite Drop Doughnuts

Yield: 60 servings

4 eggs, beaten
2 cups sugar
1 tablespoon nutmeg
1 teaspoon vanilla extract
Salt to taste
2 teaspoons baking soda

2 cups buttermilk
2 cups whole wheat flour
3¹/₂ to 4 cups all-purpose flour
¹/₄ cup canola oil
Oil for deep frying

Beat eggs with sugar in large bowl. Add nutmeg, vanilla and salt. Dissolve baking soda in buttermilk. Add to egg mixture alternately with mixture of flours, mixing well after each addition. Add canola oil. Spray doughnut press with nonstick cooking spray; fill with batter. Press doughnut batter into deep 375-degree oil. Deep-fry until golden brown on both sides; drain on paper towels.

Approx Per Serving: Cal 86; T Fat 2 g; 16% Calories from Fat;
Prot 2 g; Carbo 16 g; Fiber 1 g; Chol 15 mg; Sod 41 mg.
Nutritional information does not include oil for deep frying.

Beignets (French Doughnuts)

Yield: 60 servings

Serve these in the New Orleans manner with café au lait.

1 envelope dry yeast
¹/₂ cup lukewarm water
¹/₄ cup shortening
¹/₂ cup sugar
1 teaspoon salt

1 cup boiling water
1 cup evaporated milk
2 eggs, beaten
8 cups sifted flour
Oil for deep frying

Dissolve yeast in lukewarm water. Combine shortening, sugar and salt in large bowl. Add boiling water. Cool to lukewarm. Add yeast, evaporated milk, eggs and enough flour to make soft dough; mix well. Knead on floured surface; shape into ball. Place in greased container; cover with greased tight-fitting lid. Heat 5 inches oil to 350 degrees in large deep pan. Roll portion of dough the size of an orange to ¹/₄-inch thickness on floured surface; cut into 2x3-inch pieces. Deep-fry in hot oil until brown on both sides; drain in paper towels. Dust with confectioners' sugar. Do not allow dough to rise before frying; rising will occur as beignets cook.

Approx Per Serving: Cal 79; T Fat 2 g; 18% Calories from Fat;
Prot 2 g; Carbo 14 g; Fiber <1 g; Chol 8 mg; Sod 43 mg.
Nutritional information does not include oil for deep frying.

German Apple Coffee Cake

Yield: 12 servings

3 eggs	2 teaspoons cinnamon
1 cup vegetable oil	1 teaspoon baking soda
2 cups sugar	1/2 teaspoon salt
1 teaspoon vanilla extract	4 cups sliced peeled tart apples
2 cups sifted flour	1 cup chopped walnuts

Beat eggs in mixer bowl until thick and lemon-colored. Add oil and sugar; beat until creamy. Add vanilla. Sift in flour, cinnamon, baking soda and salt; mix well. Arrange apple slices in 9x13-inch baking dish. Sprinkle with walnuts. Pour batter over top. Bake at 350 degrees for 40 to 50 minutes or until golden brown.

Approx Per Serving: Cal 464; T Fat 26 g; 49% Calories from Fat;
Prot 5 g; Carbo 55 g; Fiber 2 g; Chol 53 mg; Sod 177 mg.

Springtime Coffee Cake

Yield: 12 servings

1 pound fresh rhubarb, chopped	1 teaspoon baking soda
16 ounces fresh or frozen strawberries	1 cup margarine
2 tablespoons lemon juice	2 eggs, slightly beaten
1/3 cup cornstarch	1 cup buttermilk
1 cup sugar	1 teaspoon vanilla extract
3 cups flour	3/4 cup sugar
1 cup sugar	1/2 cup flour
1 teaspoon baking powder	1/4 cup margarine

Combine rhubarb and strawberries in saucepan. Cook, covered, for 5 minutes. Add lemon juice and mixture of cornstarch and 1 cup sugar. Cook until thickened, stirring constantly. Let stand until cool. Combine 3 cups flour, 1 cup sugar, baking powder and baking soda in bowl. Cut in 1 cup margarine until crumbly. Beat eggs with buttermilk and vanilla in bowl. Add to flour mixture; mix until moistened. Spread half the batter in greased 9x13-inch baking pan. Spread strawberry mixture over batter. Spoon remaining batter over top. Mix 3/4 cup sugar, 1/2 cup flour and 1/4 cup margarine in small bowl until crumbly. Sprinkle over coffee cake. Bake at 350 degrees for 45 minutes or until golden brown.

Approx Per Serving: Cal 534; T Fat 21 g; 34% Calories from Fat;
Prot 6 g; Carbo 82 g; Fiber 3 g; Chol 36 mg; Sod 356 mg.

Finnish Coffee Bread

Yield: 30 servings

Add candied fruit for a festive Christmas bread.

2 cups lukewarm milk	1/2 cup shortening
1/2 cup sugar	7 to 71/2 cups flour
2 teaspoons salt	10 cardamom seed, ground
2 cakes compressed yeast	2 to 4 tablespoons coffee
2 eggs	2 to 4 tablespoons sugar

Combine milk, 1/2 cup sugar and salt in large bowl. Crumble yeast into mixture. Add eggs and shortening; mix well. Add enough flour to make stiff batter. Add cardamom. Let rise, covered, in warm place until doubled in bulk. Divide into 2 portions. Shape each into braided loaf; place on greased baking sheet. Let rise until doubled in bulk. Bake at 350 degrees for 20 to 25 minutes or until golden brown. Brush tops with coffee; sprinkle with remaining sugar.

Approx Per Serving: Cal 180; T Fat 5 g; 24% Calories from Fat; Prot 4 g; Carbo 30 g; Fiber 1 g; Chol 16 mg; Sod 155 mg.

Sweet Petals Coffee Cake

Yield: 12 servings

1 envelope dry yeast	1/2 cup melted margarine
1/4 cup warm water	3/4 cup sugar
3/4 cup milk, scalded	1 tablespoon cinnamon
3 tablespoons shortening	3/4 cup chopped pecans
2 tablespoons sugar	1 cup confectioners' sugar
11/2 teaspoons salt	2 to 3 tablespoons milk
21/2 to 3 cups flour	

Dissolve yeast in warm water. Let stand for 5 minutes. Combine hot milk, shortening, 2 tablespoons sugar and salt in large bowl. Let stand until cooled to lukewarm. Stir in yeast. Add enough flour gradually to make stiff dough. Knead on floured surface until smooth and elastic. Place in greased bowl, turning to coat surface. Let rise, covered, for 1 hour or until doubled in bulk. Place 15-inch square foil sheet on baking sheet. Grease foil and turn edges up to form 12-inch circle. Knead dough; shape into log. Slice 1/2 inch thick. Shape each slice into 3 to 4-inch roll. Dip each into margarine; coat with mixture of 3/4 cup sugar, cinnamon and pecans. Coil rolls in large spiral starting in center of foil circle. Sprinkle with any remaining pecan mixture. Let rise, covered, for 1 hour or until doubled in bulk. Bake at 350 degrees for 25 to 30 minutes or until golden brown. Cool slightly. Drizzle mixture of confectioners' sugar and milk over coffee cake.

Approx Per Serving: Cal 368; T Fat 17 g; 40% Calories from Fat; Prot 5 g; Carbo 51 g; Fiber 2 g; Chol 3 mg; Sod 365 mg.

Texas Pecan Coffee Ring

Yield: 20 servings

¹/₂ cup margarine
¹/₄ cup maple syrup
³/₄ cup packed brown sugar

1 cup chopped pecans
2   10-count cans biscuits

Melt margarine in small saucepan. Stir in syrup, brown sugar and pecans. Pour enough into bottom of greased bundt pan to coat bottom. Arrange biscuits on edge around pan. Pour remaining brown sugar mixture over top. Bake at 350 degrees for 25 to 30 minutes or until golden brown. Let stand for 3 minutes. Invert onto serving plate.

Approx Per Serving: Cal 194; T Fat 11 g; 49% Calories from Fat;
        Prot 2 g; Carbo 23 g; Fiber 1 g; Chol 1 mg; Sod 308 mg.

Corn Bread

Yield: 8 servings

1   16-ounce can cream-style
        corn
³/₄ cup milk
¹/₃ cup oil
2 eggs, beaten
1 cup cornmeal

¹/₂ teaspoon baking soda
1 teaspoon salt
¹/₂ cup shredded Cheddar
        cheese
1   4-ounce can chopped green
        chilies, drained

Combine corn, milk, oil and eggs in bowl; mix well. Add mixture of cornmeal, baking soda and salt; mix well. Pour into greased 9-inch square baking pan. Top with cheese and green chilies. Bake at 350 degrees for 45 to 60 minutes or until golden brown.

Approx Per Serving: Cal 249; T Fat 14 g; 49% Calories from Fat;
        Prot 7 g; Carbo 26 g; Fiber 3 g; Chol 64 mg; Sod 651 mg.

Corny Corn Bread

Yield: 8 servings

1¹/₂ cups self-rising cornmeal
1 cup cream-style corn
1 large onion, chopped
¹/₂ cup vegetable oil

1 cup sour cream
2 eggs, slightly beaten
¹/₂ teaspoon salt

Combine all ingredients in bowl; mix just until moistened. Pour into greased and floured 8-inch square baking pan. Bake at 350 degrees for 45 minutes or until brown.

Approx Per Serving: Cal 342; T Fat 22 g; 56% Calories from Fat;
        Prot 6 g; Carbo 32 g; Fiber 1 g; Chol 66 mg; Sod 685 mg.

Old-Fashioned Corn Bread

Yield: 4 servings

This recipe from 1910 is best when made with coarse water-ground meal.

1 cup cornmeal
2 tablespoons flour
1 tablespoon baking powder
1/4 teaspoon baking soda

1 teaspoon salt
1 teaspoon sugar
1 cup buttermilk
1 egg, beaten

Combine cornmeal, flour, baking powder, baking soda, salt and sugar in bowl. Beat buttermilk and egg in small bowl. Preheat oven to 400 degrees. Heat well-greased 8-wedge cast-iron corn bread skillet in oven. Add buttermilk mixture to dry ingredients; mix just until blended. Fill wedges of hot skillet 3/4 full. Bake for 20 minutes or until golden brown. Serve with butter, honey or apple butter.

Approx Per Serving: Cal 192; T Fat 2 g; 11% Calories from Fat;
  Prot 7 g; Carbo 35 g; Fiber 3 g; Chol 56 mg; Sod 913 mg.

Paraguayan Embassy Corn Bread

Yield: 10 servings

3 large onions, sliced
1 cup oil
1/2 cup water
1 cup milk
1 1/2 cups white cornmeal
1 1/2 teaspoons baking powder

8 ounces Muenster cheese,
  shredded
2 teaspoons reduced-sodium
  salt
4 eggs

Sauté onions in oil in skillet until tender but not brown. Add water. Simmer for 20 minutes. Let stand until cool. Mix in milk. Combine cornmeal, baking powder, cheese and salt in bowl; mix well. Beat eggs until fluffy. Add onion mixture to cornmeal mixture; mix well. Add eggs, mix well. Pour into greased 8x11-inch baking pan. Bake at 425 degrees for 25 minutes. Remove from pan. May cut into small portions to serve as appetizer.

Approx Per Serving: Cal 399; T Fat 31 g; 69% Calories from Fat;
  Prot 9 g; Carbo 21 g; Fiber 2 g; Chol 68 mg; Sod 437 mg.

Chicken wire netting supported in a rigidly upright position makes a good light frame for displaying large flowering clematis, which climbs by clinging with tendrils. The vine top should grow in sun; the roots benefit from being shaded.

Fluffy Spoon Bread

Yield: 8 servings

2 eggs, beaten
1/3 cup cornmeal
1/4 teaspoon baking soda
2 teaspoons baking powder

1/2 teaspoon salt
1 cup milk
1 cup buttermilk
1/4 cup melted butter

Combine all ingredients in bowl; mix well. Pour into greased 8-inch square baking dish. Bake at 425 degrees for 30 minutes or until brown.

Approx Per Serving: Cal 124; T Fat 9 g; 62% Calories from Fat; Prot 4 g; Carbo 8 g; Fiber <1 g; Chol 74 mg; Sod 352 mg.

Grits Spoon Bread

Yield: 6 servings

1/2 cup margarine
1 cup quick-cooking grits
3 cups boiling water
2/3 cup nonfat dry milk powder

2 eggs, beaten
2 tablespoons sugar
1 teaspoon salt

Melt margarine in 1-quart casserole. Add grits to boiling water in saucepan. Cook over low heat for 5 minutes, stirring occasionally; remove from heat. Add melted margarine, dry milk powder, eggs, sugar and salt. Beat for 1 minute. Pour into casserole. Bake at 350 degrees for 50 to 60 minutes or until golden brown.

Approx Per Serving: Cal 302; T Fat 17 g; 52% Calories from Fat; Prot 7 g; Carbo 29 g; Fiber 3 g; Chol 72 mg; Sod 598 mg.

Sweet Milk Spoon Bread

Yield: 6 servings

1 cup cornmeal
1 teaspoon salt
1 tablespoon sugar
2 cups boiling water

1/4 cup butter
1 cup cold milk
1 tablespoon baking powder
3 eggs, slightly beaten

Mix cornmeal with salt and sugar in saucepan. Moisten with a small amount of cold water; stir to remove lumps. Stir boiling water into cornmeal mixture gradually. Cook until thickened into mush, stirring frequently; remove from heat. Stir in butter, milk and baking powder. Add eggs; mix well. Pour into hot buttered casserole. Bake at 375 degrees for 30 to 40 minutes or until brown. Serve immediately.

Approx Per Serving: Cal 226; T Fat 12 g; 48% Calories from Fat; Prot 6 g; Carbo 23 g; Fiber 2 g; Chol 133 mg; Sod 636 mg.

West Virginia Corn Pone

Yield: 12 servings

A variation of this recipe is 150 years old.

4 cups cornmeal	1 teaspoon baking powder
1 tablespoon salt	1 cup flour
1 cup boiling water	1/4 teaspoon baking soda
2 cups warm water	1 cup buttermilk
2 eggs	1/4 cup boiling water
3/4 cup sugar	

Combine cornmeal and salt in large bowl. Stir in 1 cup boiling water gradually. Add warm water; mix well. Let stand, covered, overnight. Add eggs, sugar, baking powder, flour and baking soda dissolved in buttermilk; mix well. Pour into greased 12-inch cast-iron skillet. Bake at 400 degrees for 45 minutes. Remove from oven. Pour 1/4 cup boiling water over top. Let stand, covered, until serving time.

Approx Per Serving: Cal 275; T Fat 2 g; 6% Calories from Fat;
     Prot 7 g; Carbo 57 g; Fiber 4 g; Chol 36 mg; Sod 611 mg.

Hush Puppies

Yield: 36 servings

1 cup cornmeal	1/2 teaspoon salt
1/2 cup flour	1 cup milk
2 teaspoons baking powder	Oil for deep frying
1 tablespoon sugar	

Combine cornmeal, flour, baking powder, sugar and salt in bowl. Add milk; mix well. Drop by teaspoons into 375-degree oil. Deep-fry for 3 to 5 minutes or until golden brown; drain on paper towels.

Approx Per Serving: Cal 26; T Fat <1 g; 10% Calories from Fat;
     Prot 1 g; Carbo 5 g; Fiber <1 g; Chol 1 mg; Sod 51 mg.
     Nutritional information does not include oil for deep frying.

*Winter mulch of any suitable material keeps the soil
frozen to prevent alternate freezing and thawing.
It can be applied before the ground is frozen
just as the leaves in the forest cover the plants
below the trees as the leaves fall and before
the earth has frozen.*

Lefse

Yield: 12 servings

*Five pounds of potatoes will make three recipes of lefse;
mix 1 recipe at a time with flour to roll.*

4 cups mashed potatoes	**1 tablespoon sugar**
1/2 teaspoon salt	**1/4 cup butter**
1/4 to 1/2 cup half and half	**2 cups flour**

Peel and cook potatoes. Put potatoes through ricer or mash well with potato masher. Add salt, half and half, sugar and butter; mix well. Chill in refrigerator until ready to use. Add flour; mix well. Shape 1/3 cup at a time into balls; roll out very thin. Bake on lefse grill or electric skillet at highest temperature setting until golden brown, turning once. Cover with moistened dish towel to prevent drying. Spread with butter; sprinkle with sugar when ready to eat.

Approx Per Serving: Cal 181; T Fat 6 g; 27% Calories from Fat;
    Prot 4 g; Carbo 30 g; Fiber 2 g; Chol 15 mg; Sod 338 mg.

Skyline Apple Muffins

Yield: 25 servings

1 1/2 cups packed brown sugar	**1 teaspoon vanilla extract**
2/3 cup vegetable oil	**2 1/2 cups flour**
1 egg	**1 1/2 cups chopped peeled apples**
1 cup buttermilk	**1/2 cup chopped pecans**
1 teaspoon baking soda	**1/3 cup sugar**
1 teaspoon salt	**1 teaspoon melted butter**

Combine brown sugar, oil and egg in large bowl. Mix buttermilk with baking soda, salt and vanilla. Add to brown sugar mixture alternately with flour, mixing well after each addition. Fold in apples and pecans. Spoon into paper-lined muffin cups. Sprinkle with mixture of sugar and melted butter. Bake at 325 degrees for 30 minutes or until golden brown.

Approx Per Serving: Cal 197; T Fat 8 g; 36% Calories from Fat;
    Prot 2 g; Carbo 30 g; Fiber 1 g; Chol 9 mg; Sod 140 mg.

*The petals of scented geraniums range in taste from
lemon to rose to mint. Use the leaves sparingly;
they have a stronger flavor than the petals.*

Banana Muffins

Yield: 12 servings

1 cup all-purpose flour
1/2 cup whole wheat flour
1 cup wheat germ
1/3 cup packed brown sugar
1 tablespoon baking powder

1/4 teaspoon salt
1 cup mashed bananas
1/2 cup low-fat milk
1/4 cup canola oil
2 eggs

Combine flours, wheat germ, brown sugar, baking powder and salt in bowl; mix well. Mix bananas with milk, oil and eggs in bowl. Add to dry ingredients; mix just until moistened. Fill greased muffin cups 2/3 full. Bake at 400 degrees for 22 to 25 minutes or until brown.

Approx Per Serving: Cal 182; T Fat 7 g; 32% Calories from Fat;
     Prot 5 g; Carbo 27 g; Fiber 2 g; Chol 36 mg; Sod 147 mg.

Low-Cholesterol Berry Muffins

Yield: 18 servings

2 cups flour
1 cup oats
1 cup sugar
4 teaspoons baking powder
1 teaspoon salt

1/2 teaspoon cinnamon
2 egg whites
1/2 cup canola oil
1 cup skim milk
11/2 cup fresh blueberries

Combine flour, oats, sugar, baking powder, salt and cinnamon in blender. Add mixture of egg whites, oil and milk. Process until well mixed. Fold in blueberries. Fill paper-lined muffin cups 3/4 full. Bake at 400 degrees for 20 minutes or until golden brown. May substitute raspberries or blackberries for blueberries. Frozen berries may be substituted for fresh if thawed and well drained. May omit berries and add 1 cup apples and 1/2 cup raisins or substitute ginger for cinnamon and peaches for berries.

Approx Per Serving: Cal 179; T Fat 7 g; 33% Calories from Fat;
     Prot 3 g; Carbo 27 g; Fiber 1 g; Chol <1 mg; Sod 206 mg.

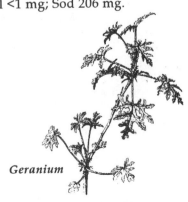

Geranium

Refrigerator Bran Muffins

Yield: 60 servings

1 15-ounce package raisins
4 shredded wheat biscuits,
  crumbled
4 cups All-Bran
2 cups boiling water
3 cups flour
1 cup bran flakes
1/2 cup wheat germ

1/2 cup soy flour
1 teaspoon baking powder
1 teaspoon salt
4 eggs
3/4 cup vegetable oil
4 cups buttermilk
1/4 cup Sweet-10
1 teaspoon vanilla extract

Layer raisins, shredded wheat and cereal in bowl. Pour boiling water over layers. Let stand until cool. Combine flour, bran flakes, wheat germ, soy flour, baking powder and salt in bowl; mix well. Beat eggs with oil, buttermilk, Sweet-10 and vanilla in very large bowl. Add flour mixture; mix well. Add raisin mixture; mix well. Spoon desired amount of batter into muffin cups sprayed with nonstick cooking spray. Bake at 400 degrees for 15 to 18 minutes or until brown. Store remaining batter in tightly covered jars in refrigerator for up to 1 month. Do not stir batter before spooning into muffin cups. May bake batter as soft cookies if desired.

Approx Per Serving: Cal 105; T Fat 4 g; 29% Calories from Fat;
Prot 3 g; Carbo 17 g; Fiber 3 g; Chol 15 mg; Sod 135 mg.

Two-Bran Muffins

Yield: 12 servings

The fruit makes the muffins moist, thus requiring less oil.

1 cup whole wheat flour
3/4 cup wheat bran
1/4 cup oat bran
3/4 teaspoon baking soda
1/4 teaspoon salt

1 cup skim milk
2 egg whites
1/4 cup honey
1 tablespoon vegetable oil
1 small banana

Combine flour, wheat bran, oat bran, baking soda and salt in bowl. Combine skim milk, egg whites, honey, oil and banana in blender container. Process until smooth. Add to dry ingredients; mix well with spoon. Spoon into greased muffin cups. Bake at 375 degrees for 20 minutes or until toothpick inserted in center comes out clean. May substitute apple for banana.

Approx Per Serving: Cal 90; T Fat 2 g; 14% Calories from Fat;
Prot 3 g; Carbo 18 g; Fiber 3 g; Chol <1 mg; Sod 116 mg.

Currant Oat Muffins

Yield: 12 servings

1 cup oat bran
2/3 cup oats
1/3 cup whole wheat pastry flour
1/3 cup unbleached flour
1/4 cup chopped walnuts
3 tablespoons currants

1 tablespoon baking powder
1 egg, slightly beaten
1 1/4 cups buttermilk
1/4 cup maple syrup
1 tablespoon vegetable oil
1 1/2 teaspoons vanilla extract

Combine oat bran, oats, flours, walnuts, currants and baking powder in bowl. Beat egg with buttermilk, maple syrup, oil and vanilla in medium bowl. Add to dry mixture. Mix 10 to 15 strokes with rubber spatula; do not overmix. Spoon into muffin cups sprayed with nonstick cooking spray. Bake at 400 degrees for 20 minutes or until light brown.

Approx Per Serving: Cal 124; T Fat 4 g; 27% Calories from Fat;
  Prot 5 g; Carbo 21 g; Fiber 2 g; Chol 19 mg; Sod 118 mg.

South Dakota Fiber Muffins

Yield: 12 servings

2 eggs, beaten
1 1/3 cups milk
1/4 cup honey
1/4 cup oil
1/4 cup finely chopped onion

1 cup whole wheat flour
1 cup cornmeal
4 teaspoons baking powder
1/2 teaspoon salt
1/4 cup sunflower seed

Combine eggs, milk, honey, oil and onion in bowl. Add flour, cornmeal, baking powder and salt; mix just until moistened. Batter will be thin. Spoon into greased or paper-lined muffin cups. Sprinkle with sunflower seed. Bake at 400 degrees for 18 to 20 minutes or until brown.

Approx Per Serving: Cal 186; T Fat 8 g; 39% Calories from Fat;
  Prot 5 g; Carbo 24 g; Fiber 2 g; Chol 39 mg; Sod 222 mg.

When winter leaves are raked from the woodland garden in the spring, you may find large numbers of beneficial lady bugs, which feed on other insect pests, particularly aphids. When you find lady bugs, let the leaves stay in place a while longer.

Peachy Muffins

Yield: 40 servings

1 cup finely chopped peeled
   peaches
1 tablespoon sugar
1 teaspoon lemon juice
1½ cups flour
½ cup packed brown sugar
1 teaspoon baking soda

¼ teaspoon salt
1½ teaspoons ginger
½ teaspoon cinnamon
½ cup sour cream
2 eggs, slightly beaten
2 tablespoons molasses
½ cup melted unsalted butter

Toss peaches with sugar and lemon juice in bowl. Let stand for several minutes. Mix flour, brown sugar, baking soda, salt, ginger and cinnamon together. Add sour cream, eggs, molasses and butter to peach mixture; mix well. Add ½ cup flour mixture; beat until well blended. Add remaining flour mixture; beat until smooth. Fill greased miniature muffin cups ⅔ full. Bake at 350 degrees for 12 to 15 minutes or until top is dry and springy. Serve warm.

Approx Per Serving: Cal 67; T Fat 3 g; 43% Calories from Fat;
   Prot 1 g; Carbo 9 g; Fiber <1 g; Chol 18 mg; Sod 41 mg.

Sour Cream Muffins

Yield: 12 servings

1 cup sour cream
1 egg
½ cup sugar
¼ teaspoon salt

½ teaspoon baking soda
1 cup flour
¼ cup cinnamon-sugar

Blend sour cream and egg in bowl. Add sugar, salt, baking soda and flour; mix well. Spoon into greased muffin cups. Sprinkle cinnamon-sugar on top. Bake at 350 degrees for 20 minutes or until golden brown.

Approx Per Serving: Cal 134; T Fat 5 g; 31% Calories from Fat;
   Prot 2 g; Carbo 21 g; Fiber <1 g; Chol 26 mg; Sod 95 mg.

Zucchini

Zucchini Muffins

Yield: 12 servings

1¹/2 cups whole wheat flour
1 cup bran cereal
1 tablespoon baking powder
1 teaspoon baking soda
¹/4 teaspoon salt
1 teaspoon cinnamon
2 eggs, beaten

¹/3 cup canola oil
¹/2 cup honey
¹/2 cup milk
1 cup packed shredded zucchini
1 tablespoon lemon juice
¹/2 cup raisins
¹/2 cup chopped pecans

Mix flour, cereal, baking powder, baking soda, salt and cinnamon together. Beat eggs with oil, honey and milk in bowl. Add zucchini, lemon juice and flour mixture; mix just until moistened. Fold in raisins and pecans. Fill paper-lined muffin cups almost full. Bake at 400 degrees for 20 minutes.

Approx Per Serving: Cal 239; T Fat 11 g; 39% Calories from Fat;
    Prot 5 g; Carbo 34 g; Fiber 5 g; Chol 37 mg; Sod 252 mg.

Apricot Tea Bread

Yield: 12 servings

1 cup dried apricots
2 cups sifted flour
4 teaspoons baking powder
¹/2 teaspoon baking soda
¹/3 cup sugar
¹/2 teaspoon salt
¹/2 teaspoon nutmeg
1 cup All-Bran

¹/2 cup coarsely chopped
    walnuts
Grated rind of 1 lemon
1 egg, beaten
1¹/4 cups buttermilk
¹/4 cup melted butter
Juice of 1 lemon

Cut apricots into fourths; place in sieve or steamer over boiling water in saucepan. Steam for 10 minutes or until slightly tender. Sift flour, baking powder, baking soda, sugar, salt and nutmeg into bowl. Add apricots, cereal, walnuts and lemon rind. Beat egg in bowl until frothy. Beat in buttermilk, melted butter and lemon juice. Add to dry mixture; mix well but do not beat. Pour into greased loaf pan. Bake at 350 degrees for 1 hour. Cool on wire rack. Cut into thin slices.

Approx Per Serving: Cal 220; T Fat 8 g; 31% Calories from Fat;
    Prot 6 g; Carbo 35 g; Fiber 4 g; Chol 29 mg; Sod 380 mg.

Cholesterol-Free Banana Bread

Yield: 12 servings

2¼ cups flour
1 cup oats
¼ cup packed brown sugar
1 tablespoon baking powder
½ teaspoon salt
¼ teaspoon baking soda
10 tablespoons light corn oil
  margarine

1½ cups mashed bananas
1 6-ounce can frozen apple
  juice concentrate, thawed
½ cup egg substitute
1 teaspoon vanilla extract
½ cup chopped pecans

Combine flour, oats, brown sugar, baking powder, salt and baking soda in bowl. Cut in margarine until crumbly. Add bananas, apple juice concentrate, egg substitute and vanilla; mix just until moistened. Stir in pecans. Spoon into greased 5x9-inch loaf pan. Bake at 350 degrees for 1 hour or until loaf tests done. Cool in pan on wire rack for 10 minutes. Remove to wire rack. Serve warm or cool completely.

Approx Per Serving: Cal 266; T Fat 9 g; 30% Calories from Fat;
  Prot 6 g; Carbo 42 g; Fiber 2 g; Chol <1 mg; Sod 327 mg.

Baked Brown Bread

Yield: 48 servings

1 cup (or more) golden raisins
3 cups All-Bran
1 pound brown sugar
3 cups flour

1 teaspoon salt
1 tablespoon baking soda
3 cups buttermilk, at room
  temperature

Plump raisins in hot water to cover for several minutes; drain. Mix cereal and brown sugar in bowl. Sift in flour, salt and baking soda. Add raisins and buttermilk; mix well. Pour into 6 buttered 16-ounce cans. Bake at 350 degrees for 1 hour. Let stand until cool enough to handle. Remove from cans. Cool on wire rack. Store in refrigerator or freezer.

Approx Per Serving: Cal 93; T Fat <1 g; 3% Calories from Fat;
  Prot 2 g; Carbo 23 g; Fiber 2 g; Chol 1 mg; Sod 177 mg.

 The deep violet, mauve, yellow and white petals of pansies have a mild grape or clover taste.

Boston Brown Bread

Yield: 24 servings

3 cups flour
3 cups All-Bran
2 cups packed brown sugar

1 tablespoon baking soda
3 cups milk
1¹/2 cup raisins

Combine flour, cereal, brown sugar, baking soda and milk in bowl; mix well. Stir in raisins. Pour into 2 greased loaf pans. Bake at 375 degrees for 1 hour or until loaves test done.

Approx Per Serving: Cal 216; T Fat 1 g; 5% Calories from Fat;
Prot 4 g; Carbo 51 g; Fiber 4 g; Chol 4 mg; Sod 248 mg.

Wonderful Coconut Bread

Yield: 12 servings

³/4 cup butter, softened
1¹/4 cups sugar
³/4 cup milk
3 eggs
1 teaspoon vanilla extract
2 teaspoons coconut extract

2¹/2 cups flour
1 teaspoon baking powder
¹/2 teaspoon salt
³/4 cup milk
1 cup shredded coconut

Cream butter and sugar in mixer bowl until light. Beat in eggs, vanilla and coconut extracts. Add mixture of dry ingredients alternately with milk, mixing well after each addition. Fold in coconut. Pour into greased and floured loaf pan. Bake at 350 degrees for 1 hour and 20 minutes, covering with foil if loaf browns too quickly.

Approx Per Serving: Cal 354; T Fat 17 g; 43% Calories from Fat;
Prot 6 g; Carbo 46 g; Fiber 1 g; Chol 88 mg; Sod 264 mg.

Grape Nuts Bread

Yield: 12 servings

2 cups buttermilk
1 cup Grape Nuts
1 egg, beaten
³/4 cup sugar
4 cups flour

1 teaspoon baking soda
2 teaspoons baking powder
¹/2 teaspoon salt
1 cup chopped pecans

Pour buttermilk over cereal in bowl. Let stand for several minutes. Mix in egg and sugar. Sift in dry ingredients; mix well. Stir in pecans; batter will be thick. Spread in greased 5x9-inch loaf pan. Bake at 350 degrees for 50 to 60 minutes or until loaf tests done.

Approx Per Serving: Cal 324; T Fat 8 g; 22% Calories from Fat;
Prot 8 g; Carbo 56 g; Fiber 2 g; Chol 19 mg; Sod 328 mg.

Irish Tea Loaf

Yield: 20 servings

4 cups flour
³/₄ cup sugar
1 tablespoon baking powder
1 teaspoon baking soda
1 teaspoon salt
¹/₂ cup butter

¹/₂ cup raisins
2 tablespoons caraway seed
3 extra-large eggs, beaten
2 cups sour cream
1 teaspoon vanilla extract

Combine flour, sugar, baking powder, baking soda and salt in bowl; mix well. Cut in butter until crumbly. Stir in raisins and caraway seed. Reserve 1 tablespoon beaten eggs. Blend remaining eggs with sour cream and vanilla in bowl. Add to flour mixture; mix well but do not overmix. Dough will be sticky. Spoon into greased 3³/₄x11¹/₂-inch loaf pan; smooth top. Brush with reserved eggs. Bake at 350 degrees for 1 hour or until toothpick inserted in center comes out clean, covering loosely with foil if loaf browns too quickly.

Approx Per Serving: Cal 238; T Fat 11 g; 40% Calories from Fat;
   Prot 5 g; Carbo 31 g; Fiber 1 g; Chol 63 mg; Sod 262 mg.

Lemon Bread

Yield: 24 servings

1 cup margarine, softened
2 cups sugar
4 eggs
3 cups flour
¹/₂ teaspoon salt
1 teaspoon baking soda

1 cup buttermilk
1 cup chopped pecans
1 cup sugar
10 tablespoons lemon juice
Grated rind of 1 lemon

Cream margarine and 2 cups sugar in mixer bowl until light and fluffy. Beat in eggs 1 at a time. Sift in flour, salt and baking soda alternately with buttermilk, mixing well after each addition. Pour into 2 greased 5x9-inch loaf pans. Sprinkle with pecans. Bake at 350 degrees for 1 hour or until bread tests done. Combine 1 cup sugar, lemon juice and lemon rind in small saucepan. Warm for 2 minutes over low heat; do not melt sugar. Brush over warm loaves until all sugar mixture is used. Let stand in pans until cool.

Approx Per Serving: Cal 272; T Fat 12 g; 40% Calories from Fat;
   Prot 3 g; Carbo 39 g; Fiber 1 g; Chol 36 mg; Sod 173 mg.

 *Try coralbells, meadow rue, goatsbeard, lady's
mantle or Solomon's seal in the shady
spots in your garden.*

Nectarine-Blueberry Bread

Yield: 12 servings

²/₃ cup chopped almonds
1 tablespoon sugar
1 cup flour
³/₄ cup sugar
2 teaspoons baking powder
¹/₂ teaspoon allspice
¹/₄ teaspoon baking soda
¹/₄ teaspoon salt

¹/₃ cup margarine, softened
1 teaspoon grated orange rind
¹/₄ cup orange juice
2 eggs
¹/₂ cup flour
²/₃ cup coarsely chopped
   nectarine
¹/₂ cup fresh blueberries

Mix ¹/₄ cup of the almonds with 1 tablespoon sugar in bowl. Set aside. Combine flour, ³/₄ cup sugar, baking powder, allspice, baking soda and salt in mixer bowl. Add margarine, orange rind and orange juice; beat at low speed until blended. Beat at high speed for 2 minutes. Add eggs and ¹/₂ cup flour. Beat at low speed just until mixed. Fold in nectarine, blueberries and remaining almonds. Pour into greased 4x8-inch loaf pan. Sprinkle with mixture of almonds and sugar. Bake at 350 degrees for 55 to 60 minutes or until bread tests done.

Approx Per Serving: Cal 228; T Fat 10 g; 40% Calories from Fat;
    Prot 5 g; Carbo 30 g; Fiber 2 g; Chol 36 mg; Sod 189 mg.

Orange Marmalade Bread

Yield: 12 servings

2¹/₂ cups flour
1 teaspoon baking soda
1 teaspoon salt
³/₄ cup sugar
1 egg, beaten

¹/₂ cup orange marmalade
¹/₄ cup white vinegar
1 cup milk
2 tablespoons oil

Combine flour, baking soda, salt and sugar in bowl. Beat egg with marmalade, vinegar, milk and oil in bowl. Add to dry ingredients all at once; stir just until mixed. Pour into greased 5x9-inch loaf pan. Bake at 350 degrees for 1 hour.

Approx Per Serving: Cal 217; T Fat 4 g; 15% Calories from Fat;
    Prot 4 g; Carbo 43 g; Fiber 1 g; Chol 21 mg; Sod 264 mg.

Mint

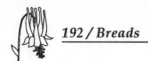

Raisin Bread

Yield: 30 servings

2¹/₂ cups water
¹/₄ cup sugar
1   15-ounce package golden
     raisins
1 cup sugar
¹/₂ cup margarine, softened

¹/₂ teaspoon salt
2 eggs
¹/₂ teaspoon vanilla extract
1 cup chopped pecans
2¹/₄ cups flour
2 teaspoons baking soda

Combine water, ¹/₄ cup sugar and raisins in saucepan. Boil for 10 minutes. Cool. Drain, reserving juice. Cream 1 cup sugar, margarine, salt, eggs and vanilla in mixer bowl until light. Add pecans and 1 cup reserved raisin juice; mix well. Add flour and baking soda; mix well. Stir in raisins. Pour into 3 greased 4x8-inch loaf pans. Bake at 375 degrees for 1 hour.

Approx Per Serving: Cal 168; T Fat 6 g; 32% Calories from Fat;
     Prot 2 g; Carbo 28 g; Fiber 1 g; Chol 14 mg; Sod 133 mg.

Strawberry Bread

Yield: 24 servings

3 cups flour
1 teaspoon baking soda
1 teaspoon salt
2 teaspoons cinnamon
2 cups sugar

2   10-ounce packages frozen
     strawberries, thawed
4 eggs, beaten
1¹/₄ cups vegetable oil
1¹/₄ cups chopped pecans

Mix flour, baking soda, salt, cinnamon and sugar in bowl. Combine undrained strawberries, eggs, oil and pecans in bowl; mix well. Add to dry ingredients; mix well. Pour into 2 greased 5x9-inch loaf pans. Bake at 350 degrees for 1¹/₄ hours or until loaves test done. Cool in pans for 10 minutes. Remove to wire rack to cool completely. For high altitudes, use 1³/₄ cups sugar and 3¹/₂ cups flour; bake at 375 degrees for 55 minutes.

Approx Per Serving: Cal 284; T Fat 17 g; 52% Calories from Fat;
     Prot 3 g; Carbo 32 g; Fiber 1 g; Chol 36 mg; Sod 136 mg.

*Broccoli is probably the favorite edible flower of
most Americans. The part we eat is
actually the blossom.*

Broccoli Bread

Yield: 12 servings

1 16-ounce loaf frozen bread dough, thawed	1/2 10-ounce package frozen chopped broccoli, thawed
3 1-ounce slices provolone cheese	1 cup shredded American cheese
1/2 package pepperoni (about 15 slices)	1 cup shredded mozzarella cheese

Roll bread dough into 11x12-inch rectangle on floured surface. Arrange provolone cheese slices down center of rectangle. Add layers of pepperoni, broccoli, American and mozzarella cheeses. Fold ends over filling; fold sides over. Prick with fork. Place on baking sheet. Let stand for 10 minutes. Bake at 325 degrees for 20 to 25 minutes or until brown.

Approx Per Serving: Cal 224; T Fat 11 g; 46% Calories from Fat;
    Prot 11 g; Carbo 20 g; Fiber 1 g; Chol 24 mg; Sod 567 mg.

Chive Bread

Yield: 12 servings

1 envelope dry yeast	1 teaspoon salt
1/4 cup warm water	1/4 teaspoon baking soda
2 tablespoons sugar	1 egg
2 cups (or more) flour	1 cup sour cream
1/4 cup chopped chives	1 tablespoon melted shortening

Dissolve yeast in warm water. Add pinch of sugar. Combine remaining sugar, 1 cup flour, chives, salt, baking soda, egg and sour cream in food processor container. Process for 30 seconds. Add enough remaining flour gradually to make soft dough, processing after each addition. Pour into greased 9-inch round cake pan. Brush with melted shortening. Let rise until doubled in bulk. Bake at 350 degrees for 40 to 45 minutes or until golden brown.

Approx Per Serving: Cal 143; T Fat 6 g; 37% Calories from Fat;
    Prot 4 g; Carbo 19 g; Fiber 1 g; Chol 26 mg; Sod 212 mg.

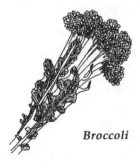

Broccoli

Dilly Casserole Bread

Yield: 12 servings

1 envelope dry yeast
1/4 cup warm water
1 cup lukewarm cottage cheese
2 tablespoons sugar
1 tablespoon minced onion
1 tablespoon butter

2 tablespoons dillseed
1 teaspoon salt
1/2 teaspoon baking soda
1 egg, beaten
21/4 to 21/2 cups flour

Dissolve yeast in warm water in large bowl. Add cottage cheese, sugar, onion, butter, dillseed, salt, baking soda and egg; mix well. Add enough flour to make stiff dough. Let rise, covered, for 50 to 60 minutes until doubled in bulk. Stir dough down. Place in greased 8-inch casserole. Let rise for 30 to 40 minutes or until almost doubled in bulk. Bake at 350 degrees for 40 to 50 minutes or until golden brown. May bake in loaf pan for 50 minutes. May brush with melted butter if desired.

Approx Per Serving: Cal 138; T Fat 2 g; 16% Calories from Fat;
    Prot 6 g; Carbo 23 g; Fiber 1 g; Chol 23 mg; Sod 297 mg.

Whole Wheat Dill Bread

Yield: 12 servings

1 envelope dry yeast
1/4 cup warm water
1 teaspoon sugar
1 cup cream-style low-fat
    cottage cheese
2 tablespoons minced onion

2 tablespoons margarine
1 tablespoon dillseed
1 teaspoon salt
1/4 teaspoon baking soda
1 egg
21/2 cups whole wheat flour

Dissolve yeast in warm water. Add sugar. Heat cottage cheese, onion, margarine, dillseed, salt and baking soda in saucepan or microwave until heated to lukewarm. Add yeast mixture and egg; mix well. Add flour. Knead on lightly floured surface until smooth and elastic. Place in greased bowl, turning to coat surface. Let rise, covered, in warm place until doubled in bulk. Knead several times on lightly floured surface. Place in greased 5x9-inch loaf pan. Bake at 350 degrees for 35 minutes or until loaf tests done.

Approx Per Serving: Cal 128; T Fat 3 g; 22% Calories from Fat;
    Prot 7 g; Carbo 19 g; Fiber 3 g; Chol 19 mg; Sod 300 mg.

Dill

Shepherd's Bread
Yield: 36 servings

3 cups very hot water
1/2 cup butter
1/2 cup sugar

2 1/2 teaspoons salt
2 envelopes dry yeast
9 1/2 cups (about) flour

Combine hot water, butter, sugar and salt in large bowl; stir until butter melts. Let stand until cooled to lukewarm. Stir in yeast. Let stand, covered, for 15 minutes or until bubbly. Add 5 cups flour; beat to make thick batter. Stir in about 3 1/2 cups flour or enough to make stiff dough. Knead on floured surface for 10 minutes or until smooth and elastic, adding flour as necessary. Place in greased bowl, turning to coat surface. Let rise, covered, in warm place for 1 1/2 hours or until doubled in bulk. Knead on floured surface; shape into ball. Cut circle of foil to fit bottom of Dutch oven. Grease foil, side and lid of oven with oil. Place dough in oven. Let rise, covered with lid, in warm place for 1 hour or until dough pushes lid up about 1/2 inch. Bake, covered with lid, at 375 degrees for 12 minutes. Bake, uncovered, for 30 to 35 minutes or until loaf is golden brown and sounds hollow when tapped. Invert onto wire rack to cool.

Approx Per Serving: Cal 154; T Fat 3 g; 17% Calories from Fat;
    Prot 4 g; Carbo 28 g; Fiber 1 g; Chol 7 mg; Sod 171 mg.

Sweet Yellow Greek Bread
Yield: 36 servings

4 eggs
1 cup sugar
1 cup melted butter
1 teaspoon salt

2 envelopes dry yeast
1 1/2 cups very warm milk
8 cups flour

Beat eggs with sugar in large bowl. Mix in butter and salt. Dissolve yeast in warm milk. Stir into egg mixture. Mix in flour gradually. Knead on floured surface for 5 minutes. Place in greased bowl, turning to coat surface. Let rise, covered, for 2 hours or until doubled in bulk. Shape into 3 loaves; place in greased 5x9-inch loaf pans. Let rise for 1 hour or until doubled in bulk. Bake at 450 degrees for 10 minutes. Reduce temperature to 350 degrees. Bake for 30 minutes longer.

Approx Per Serving: Cal 203; T Fat 7 g; 31% Calories from Fat;
    Prot 4 g; Carbo 29 g; Fiber 1 g; Chol 43 mg; Sod 170 mg.

Store bulbs through the winter in old nylon stockings. They will be well aired and easy to hang out of the way. Knot the stockings to separate kinds and colors of bulbs.

Tomato Bread

Yield: 24 servings

This unusual bread is wonderful for grilled cheese sandwiches.

2 cups tomato juice
2 tablespoons butter
3 tablespoons sugar
1 teaspoon salt
1/2 teaspoon basil
1/2 teaspoon oregano

1/4 cup catsup
1/4 cup shredded Cheddar
   cheese
1 envelope dry yeast
1/4 cup warm water
7 cups sifted flour

Heat tomato juice and butter in saucepan until butter melts. Stir in sugar, salt, basil, oregano, catsup and cheese. Let stand until cooled to lukewarm. Dissolve yeast in warm water in large mixer bowl. Add tomato mixture and 3 cups flour. Beat at medium speed for 2 minutes. Add enough remaining flour to make soft dough. Knead on floured surface for 8 to 10 minutes or until smooth and elastic. Place in greased bowl, turning to coat surface. Let rise, covered, for 1 to 1 1/2 hours or until doubled in bulk. Punch dough down; divide into 2 portions. Let rest, covered, for 10 minutes. Shape into loaves; place in 2 greased 5x9-inch loaf pans. Let rise, covered, for 1 hour or until almost doubled in bulk. Bake at 375 degrees for 25 minutes or until loaves test done.

Approx Per Serving: Cal 149; T Fat 2 g; 10% Calories from Fat;
   Prot 4 g; Carbo 29 g; Fiber 1 g; Chol 4 mg; Sod 208 mg.

Shredded Wheat Bread

Yield: 60 servings

This bread is especially good toasted for breakfast or with soup.

6 shredded wheat biscuits,
   crumbled
1/2 cup margarine
1 tablespoon salt

1 1/3 cups packed brown sugar
4 cups boiling water
10 cups flour
3 envelopes quick-rising yeast

Combine shredded wheat, margarine, salt, brown sugar and boiling water in large bowl. Let stand for 30 minutes or until cooled to lukewarm. Stir in 3 cups flour and yeast. Add remaining 7 cups flour; mix well. Knead on floured surface until smooth and elastic. Place in greased bowl, turning to coat surface. Let rise, covered, until doubled in bulk. Knead several times. Shape into 5 loaves; place in greased loaf pans. Let rise until doubled in bulk. Bake at 350 degrees for 30 minutes.

Approx Per Serving: Cal 120; T Fat 2 g; 13% Calories from Fat;
   Prot 3 g; Carbo 23 g; Fiber 1 g; Chol 0 mg; Sod 128 mg.

Whole Wheat Bread

Yield: 24 servings

2 envelopes dry yeast	1 tablespoon salt
1 teaspoon sugar	1/4 cup shortening
1/4 cup warm water	3/4 cup cool water
1 cup milk, scalded	1 cup all-purpose flour
1/4 cup packed brown sugar	3 1/2 cups whole wheat flour
2 tablespoons molasses	1/2 cup all-purpose flour

Dissolve yeast and sugar in warm water. Let stand for 5 minutes. Combine hot milk, brown sugar, molasses, salt and shortening in large bowl; stir until blended. Add cool water. Stir in yeast, 1 cup all-purpose flour and 1 1/2 cups whole wheat flour; mix until smooth. Add 2 cups whole wheat flour or enough to make soft dough. Place on surface sprinkled with 1/2 cup all-purpose flour. Knead 100 strokes. Place in greased bowl, turning to coat surface. Let rise, covered, until doubled in bulk. Divide into 2 portions. Let rest for 5 minutes. Shape into loaves; place in 2 greased 5x9-inch loaf pans. Let rise until doubled in bulk. Bake at 400 degrees for 40 minutes.

Approx Per Serving: Cal 129; T Fat 3 g; 20% Calories from Fat;
Prot 4 g; Carbo 23 g; Fiber 3 g; Chol 1 mg; Sod 273 mg.

Best-Ever Rolls

Yield: 48 servings

1 cup milk	1 1/2 cups cold water
3/4 cup instant potato flakes	3 eggs, beaten
3/4 cup sugar	8 cups flour
1 tablespoon salt	2 envelopes quick-rising yeast
1 cup butter-flavored shortening	1/2 cup warm water

Combine milk, potato flakes, sugar, salt and shortening in saucepan. Heat to the boiling point; remove from heat. Add cold water. Let stand until cooled to lukewarm. Combine with eggs in large bowl; beat until smooth. Beat in 4 cups flour. Dissolve yeast in warm water. Stir into batter. Mix in remaining 4 cups flour. Knead on floured surface until smooth and elastic. Place in greased bowl, turning to coat surface. Let rise, covered, until doubled in bulk. Shape into balls; place on greased baking sheet. Let rise until doubled in bulk. Bake at 350 degrees for 25 to 30 minutes or until golden brown.

Approx Per Serving: Cal 146; T Fat 5 g; 31% Calories from Fat;
Prot 3 g; Carbo 22 g; Fiber 1 g; Chol 14 mg; Sod 145 mg.

Caramel Rolls

Yield: 12 servings

1½ cups pecans
12 frozen dinner rolls, thawed
1   4-ounce package butterscotch
    instant pudding mix

½ cup packed brown sugar
1 stick butter, sliced

Sprinkle half the pecans in buttered bundt pan. Arrange rolls in pan. Sprinkle with pudding mix. Top with remaining pecans, brown sugar and butter. Let rise, covered with plastic wrap, for 8 hours. Bake at 350 degrees for 20 minutes. Invert onto serving plate. Let stand for 3 to 4 minutes before removing pan.

Approx Per Serving: Cal 321; T Fat 20 g; 54% Calories from Fat;
    Prot 3 g; Carbo 34 g; Fiber 2 g; Chol 21 mg; Sod 272 mg.

Cornmeal Yeast Rolls

Yield: 40 servings

2 cups milk
⅓ cup cornmeal
½ cup margarine
½ cup sugar
1 teaspoon salt

2 eggs, beaten
1 envelope dry yeast
¼ cup warm water
4½ to 5 cups flour

Pour milk into saucepan. Sprinkle with cornmeal; mix well. Bring to a boil, stirring constantly. Cook for 3 minutes, stirring constantly; remove from heat. Stir in margarine, sugar and salt. Let stand until cooled to lukewarm. Dissolve yeast in warm water. Combine cornmeal mixture, yeast and eggs in large bowl. Mix in flour; dough will be soft. Knead on floured surface until smooth and elastic. Place in greased bowl, turning to coat surface. Let rise, covered, until doubled in bulk. Stir dough down. Let rise until doubled in bulk. Roll on floured surface; cut with biscuit cutter. Arrange in greased baking pan. Let rise until doubled in bulk. Bake at 350 degrees for 20 to 25 minutes or until golden brown.

Approx Per Serving: Cal 103; T Fat 3 g; 28% Calories from Fat;
    Prot 3 g; Carbo 16 g; Fiber 1 g; Chol 12 mg; Sod 89 mg.

Marigold

Kolaches

Yield: 40 servings

2 envelopes dry yeast
1/4 cup lukewarm water
1 cup butter, softened
1/4 cup sugar
2 teaspoons salt
6 egg yolks
2 cups milk, scalded
6 cups flour

1/4 cup melted butter
2   16-ounce sour cherries
1 cup sugar
6 tablespoons cornstarch
1/4 teaspoon salt
1 teaspoon red food coloring
1 teaspoon vanilla extract
1/2 teaspoon almond extract

Dissolve yeast in lukewarm water. Cream butter with 1/4 cup sugar and 2 teaspoons salt in large bowl. Beat in egg yolks 1 at a time. Stir in milk. Cool to lukewarm. Add yeast. Beat in flour. Let rise, covered, in warm place until doubled in bulk. Roll to 3/4-inch thickness on floured surface. Cut with small biscuit cutter or juice glass. Arrange 1 inch apart on greased baking sheet. Brush with melted butter. Let rise until light. Drain cherries, reserving juice. Blend a small amount of reserved juice with 1 cup sugar, cornstarch and 1/4 teaspoon salt in small bowl. Bring remaining juice to a boil in saucepan. Stir in cornstarch mixture. Cook until thickened, stirring constantly. Add food coloring, flavorings and cherries. Cool. Press centers of kolaches to make indentations. Fill with cherry mixture. Let rise until light. Bake at 450 degrees for 8 to 10 minutes or until golden brown.

Approx Per Serving: Cal 174; T Fat 7 g; 37% Calories from Fat;
    Prot 3 g; Carbo 24 g; Fiber 1 g; Chol 49 mg; Sod 177 mg.

Hot Oatmeal Rolls

Yield: 48 servings

2 cakes compressed yeast
1 cup warm water
1 cup oats
1/3 cup oil
1/2 cup molasses

1 tablespoon salt
2 cups boiling water
2 eggs, beaten
8 to 9 cups flour

Soften yeast in warm water. Combine oats, oil, molasses, salt and boiling water in large bowl; mix well. Let stand until cooled to lukewarm. Beat in yeast, eggs and enough flour to make medium dough. Knead on floured surface until smooth and elastic. Place in greased bowl, turning to coat surface. Let rise, covered, in warm place for 1 hour or until doubled in bulk. Shape into rolls; place on greased baking sheet. Let rise, covered, until doubled in bulk. Bake at 375 degrees for 15 minutes.

Approx Per Serving: Cal 116; T Fat 2 g; 16% Calories from Fat;
    Prot 3 g; Carbo 21 g; Fiber 1 g; Chol 9 mg; Sod 137 mg.

Raised Cinnamon Rolls

Yield: 24 servings

2 envelopes dry yeast
1¼ cups warm water
¼ cup melted butter
2 4-ounce packages golden
    egg custard mix
1 teaspoon salt

3 to 3½ cups flour
2 cups packed brown sugar
1 teaspoon cinnamon
2 tablespoons light corn syrup
½ cup melted margarine

Dissolve yeast in warm water in large bowl. Add butter, custard mix, salt and enough flour to make medium dough. Knead until smooth and elastic. Place in greased bowl, turning to coat surface. Roll to ¼-inch thickness on floured surface. Sprinkle with half the brown sugar. Roll as for jelly roll. Cut into 1½-inch slices. Mix remaining brown sugar with cinnamon, corn syrup and ½ cup margarine in 9x13-inch baking pan. Arrange rolls in prepared baking pan. Let rise until doubled in bulk. Bake at 350 degrees for 20 minutes or until golden brown. Invert onto serving tray.

Approx Per Serving: Cal 243; T Fat 6 g; 22% Calories from Fat;
    Prot 3 g; Carbo 45 g; Fiber 1 g; Chol 5 mg; Sod 221 mg.

Refrigerator Rolls

Yield: 54 servings

2 envelopes dry yeast
½ cup lukewarm water
1 cup milk, scalded
¾ cup shortening
¾ cup sugar

2 eggs, beaten
2 teaspoons salt
1 cup cold water
6¼ cups sifted flour

Dissolve yeast in lukewarm water. Combine milk, shortening and sugar in saucepan. Heat until shortening melts. Beat eggs with salt and cold water in large bowl. Add milk mixture and yeast; mix well. Stir in flour. Place in greased 6-quart bowl. Chill, tightly covered, overnight. Shape as desired; place in greased baking pan. Let rise until doubled in bulk. Bake at 350 degrees for 20 to 25 minutes or until golden brown. May use dough for dinner rolls, crescent rolls, cinnamon rolls, etc.

Approx Per Serving: Cal 91; T Fat 3 g; 33% Calories from Fat;
    Prot 2 g; Carbo 13 g; Fiber <1 g; Chol 9 mg; Sod 84 mg.

Tarragon Rolls

Yield: 12 servings

1 envelope dry yeast
¼ cup warm water
⅓ cup shortening
½ cup boiling water
1 egg
¼ cup sugar

½ teaspoon salt
½ cup cold water
3⅔ cups unbleached flour
3 tablespoons crushed dried
    tarragon leaves

Dissolve yeast in warm water. Let stand until bubbly. Combine shortening and boiling water in large bowl. Beat in egg, sugar, salt and cold water. Add yeast, flour and tarragon; mix well. Chill, covered, overnight. Shape into rolls; place in greased baking pan. Let rise for 2 to 3 hours or until doubled in bulk. Bake at 350 degrees for 20 minutes.

Approx Per Serving: Cal 196; T Fat 7 g; 31% Calories from Fat;
    Prot 4 g; Carbo 30 g; Fiber <1 g; Chol 18 mg; Sod 96 mg.

Whole Wheat Cottage Cheese Rolls

Yield: 24 servings

2 cups all-purpose flour
1¾ cups whole wheat flour
2 envelopes dry yeast
½ teaspoon baking soda
1½ cups cream-style low-fat
    cottage cheese

½ cup water
¼ cup packed brown sugar
2 tablespoons margarine
2 teaspoons salt
2 tablespoons dark molasses
2 eggs

Mix all-purpose and whole wheat flours. Combine 1½ cups mixture with dry yeast and baking soda in large mixer bowl. Combine cottage cheese, water, brown sugar, margarine, salt and molasses in saucepan. Heat to 115 to 120 degrees, stirring constantly. Add to yeast mixture. Add eggs. Beat at low speed for 30 seconds. Beat at high speed for 3 minutes. Stir in enough remaining flour mixture to make moderately stiff dough. Knead on floured surface for 8 to 10 minutes or until smooth and elastic. Place in greased bowl, turning to coat surface. Let rise, covered, until almost doubled in bulk. Punch dough down. Let rise until almost doubled in bulk. Shape into rolls; place in greased muffin cups. Let rise until almost doubled in bulk. Bake at 375 degrees for 12 to 15 minutes or until rolls test done.

Approx Per Serving: Cal 111; T Fat 2 g; 16% Calories from Fat;
    Prot 5 g; Carbo 19 g; Fiber 2 g; Chol 19 mg; Sod 273 mg.

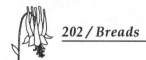

Sopaipillas

Yield: 16 servings

2 cups flour
1½ teaspoons baking powder
1 teaspoon sugar

2 tablespoons lard
¾ cups (or more) water
Oil for deep frying

Sift dry ingredients into bowl. Cut in lard until crumbly. Add water; mix well. Knead 10 to 15 times on floured surface. Roll ⅛ inch thick. Cut into 3-inch squares. Deep-fry in 3 inches hot oil until golden brown, turning once; drain on paper towels. Serve immediately with honey.

Approx Per Serving: Cal 73; T Fat 2 g; 22% Calories from Fat;
Prot 2 g; Carbo 12 g; Fiber <1 g; Chol 2 mg; Sod 31 mg.
Nutritional information does not include oil for deep frying.

Puffy Pancake

Yield: 4 servings

3 eggs
½ cup flour
¼ teaspoon salt

½ cup milk
2 tablespoons melted butter

Beat eggs in bowl. Add flour, salt, milk and butter; beat until smooth. Pour into greased 9-inch pie plate. Bake at 350 degrees for 20 minutes. Serve immediately with syrup.

Approx Per Serving: Cal 186; T Fat 11 g; 54% Calories from Fat;
Prot 7 g; Carbo 14 g; Fiber <1 g; Chol 179 mg; Sod 246 mg.

Irish Scones

Yield: 6 servings

2 cups self-rising flour
3 tablespoons butter

½ cup milk
Salt to taste

Sift flour into bowl. Add butter; mix lightly with fingertips. Add milk and salt; mix lightly. Knead lightly into soft dough, adding a small amount of milk if necessary. Roll about ½ inch thick on floured surface; cut with biscuit cutter. Place on greased baking sheet. Bake on top oven rack at 425 degrees for 12 to 15 minutes. Serve hot with tea. May add 1 tablespoon sugar and 2 tablespoons minced dried fruit before adding milk.

Approx Per Serving: Cal 210; T Fat 7 g; 30% Calories from Fat;
Prot 5 g; Carbo 32 g; Fiber 1 g; Chol 18 mg; Sod 507 mg.

Scotch Tea Scones

Yield: 18 servings

½ cup raisins
2 cups sifted flour
2 teaspoons (rounded) baking
    powder
½ teaspoon salt

½ cup sugar
¾ cup shortening
2 eggs, beaten
⅓ cup evaporated milk

Plump raisins in hot water to cover in bowl for several minutes; drain. Mix flour, baking powder, salt and sugar in bowl. Cut in shortening until crumbly. Stir in raisins. Make well in center. Add eggs and evaporated milk; mix well. Knead several times on floured surface. Pat into ½-inch thick rectangle. Cut into 18 triangles. Place on greased baking sheet; do not allow scones to touch. Brush lightly with additional milk; sprinkle lightly with sugar if desired. Bake on bottom oven rack at 375 degrees for 18 minutes. Bake on top rack for 5 minutes longer or until golden brown. Serve warm. Reheat scones by sprinkling cool scones with several drops of water and warming in toaster oven.

Approx Per Serving: Cal 173; T Fat 10 g; 50% Calories from Fat;
    Prot 2 g; Carbo 20 g; Fiber 1 g; Chol 25 mg; Sod 114 mg.

Breakfast Custard Toast

Yield: 4 servings

2 cups milk
¼ cup sugar
¼ teaspoon salt
3 eggs, beaten
Vanilla extract to taste

4 thick slices bread
2 tablespoons butter
1 tablespoon sugar
Cinnamon to taste

Combine milk, ¼ cup sugar and salt in saucepan over low heat. Bring to a simmer. Stir a small amount of hot mixture into eggs; stir eggs into hot mixture. Cook until thickened, stirring constantly; remove from heat. Stir in vanilla. Spread bread with butter; sprinkle with 1 tablespoon sugar and cinnamon. Toast under broiler until bubbly. Place toast in soup plates. Spoon hot custard mixture over top.

Approx Per Serving: Cal 333; T Fat 15 g; 41% Calories from Fat;
    Prot 16 g; Carbo 38 g; Fiber <1 g; Chol 192 mg; Sod 455 mg.

*The flower bracts of the hibiscus are used for herbal
tea in the Middle East, in Africa and in
the Caribbean.*

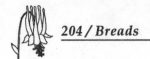

Buttermilk Belgian Waffles

Yield: 8 servings

2 eggs, separated
1½ cups flour
¼ cup cornstarch
2 teaspoons baking powder
1 teaspoon baking soda

½ teaspoon salt
6 tablespoons melted
   shortening
2 cups buttermilk
½ teaspoon vanilla extract

Beat egg whites just until stiff peaks form. Beat egg yolks until light and lemon-colored. Sift flour, cornstarch, baking powder and baking soda together twice. Combine egg yolks, shortening, buttermilk and vanilla in bowl. Add to dry ingredients; mix just until moistened. Fold in stiffly beaten egg whites gently. Bake on lightly greased preheated Belgian waffle iron until light brown and crisp. Serve with heated syrup or sliced fresh fruit.

Approx Per Serving: Cal 230; T Fat 12 g; 46% Calories from Fat;
    Prot 6 g; Carbo 25 g; Fiber 1 g; Chol 56 mg; Sod 400 mg.

Norwegian Lemon Waffles

Yield: 6 servings

5 eggs
⅓ cup sugar
½ teaspoon freshly grated
   lemon rind

1 cup unbleached flour, sifted
1 cup sour cream
¼ cup melted butter
1 teaspoon lemon juice

Combine eggs with sugar in mixer bowl. Beat for 10 minutes or until light and fluffy. Fold in mixture of lemon rind and flour alternately with sour cream. Stir in butter and lemon juice. Let rest for 10 to 15 minutes. Bake in lightly greased hot waffle iron until steaming stops and waffle is golden brown. Serve hot or cold.

Approx Per Serving: Cal 325; T Fat 21 g; 57% Calories from Fat;
    Prot 8 g; Carbo 27 g; Fiber 0 g; Chol 215 mg; Sod 143 mg.

*Pussy willow branches used as cuttings are more
likely to grow if they are stuck into a muddy
spot in the spring garden. The new roots will grow
better than roots developed by standing in jars
of water, which are better adapted to water than soil.*

Desserts

Rocky Mountain High

Rocky Mountain

Colorado • Kansas • Montana • Nebraska
North Dakota • South Dakota • Utah • Wyoming

A vast region with majestic mountains, rolling plains and the "big sky," this diversity poses a wide variety of challenges to its gardeners to meet the National Council goals. Planting living memorials to our American war heros has continued a heartfelt garden club activity. From floral remembrances honoring the fallen soldiers of World War I through the Montana-initiated movement to "Plant a million trees to honor our Vietnam war dead," that remains a priority of the Region.

Rocky Mountain Pheasant Dinner

Pheasant in Cream Sauce*
Wild Rice*
Buttered Broccoli Spears
Hot Buttered Rolls
Amaretto Banana-Coconut Pie*

Colorado Ranch Meal

Rancher's Steak*
Baked Potato with Sour Cream and Chives
Green Beans
Tossed Salad
Strawberry Glaze Pie*

*See index for recipes.

Desserts

Pot O' Dirt

Yield: 16 servings

16 ounces Oreo cookies
1/2 cup melted butter
2 4-ounce packages French
   vanilla instant pudding mix

2 cups milk
2 pints English toffee ice
   cream, softened
12 ounces whipped topping

Crush 2/3 of the cookies in plastic bag. Mix with butter in bowl. Press over bottom and side of new 8-inch clay flowerpot lined with plastic wrap. Combine pudding mix with milk in bowl; mix well. Stir in ice cream. Spoon into flowerpot. Top with whipped topping. Discard icing from remaining cookies; crush cookies. Sprinkle over dessert. Chill for 3 hours or longer. Garnish with fresh flowers and gummy worm.

Approx Per Serving: Cal 395; T Fat 22 g; 48% Calories from Fat;
   Prot 4 g; Carbo 48 g; Fiber <1 g; Chol 34 mg; Sod 324 mg.

Apple and Raspberry Crisp

Yield: 8 servings

6 cups sliced peeled apples
1 1/2 cups raspberries
2 tablespoons flour
1/3 cup sugar

3 teaspoons cinnamon
1 cup quick-cooking oats
1/4 cup packed brown sugar
1/4 cup margarine, softened

Mix apples and raspberries in 2-quart baking dish. Mix flour, sugar and 2 teaspoons cinnamon in bowl. Mix with fruit in baking dish. Combine oats, brown sugar and 1 teaspoon cinnamon in bowl. Cut in margarine until crumbly. Sprinkle over fruit. Bake at 350 degrees for 55 minutes or until fruit is tender. Serve warm or cool.

Approx Per Serving: Cal 214; T Fat 7 g; 27% Calories from Fat;
   Prot 2 g; Carbo 38 g; Fiber 4 g; Chol 0 mg; Sod 71 mg.

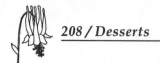

Old-Fashioned Apple Dumplings   *Yield: 6 servings*

2 cups sugar
2 cups water
2 tablespoons butter
1 teaspoon cinnamon
1/4 teaspoon nutmeg
2 1/2 cups flour

4 teaspoons baking powder
3/4 teaspoon salt
1 cup (scant) shortening
3/4 cup milk
6 medium apples

Combine sugar, water, butter, cinnamon and nutmeg in saucepan. Cook for 5 minutes. Combine flour, baking powder and salt in bowl. Cut in shortening until crumbly. Add milk; mix to form dough. Divide into 6 portions. Roll each portion on floured surface. Slice apples into wedges. Place 1 apple in center of each circle of dough. Pull dough up to enclose apple; press edges to seal. Place in 9x13-inch baking pan. Pour hot syrup over top. Bake at 350 degrees for 35 to 40 minutes or until apples are tender and pastry is brown.

Approx Per Serving: Cal 884; T Fat 40 g; 40% Calories from Fat;
     Prot 7 g; Carbo 129 g; Fiber 5 g; Chol 15 mg; Sod 535 mg.

No-Bake Apricot Cheesecake   *Yield: 12 servings*

1/2 cup butter
1/3 cup sugar
1 1/2 cups cornflake crumbs
1 30-ounce can apricot halves
1 envelope unflavored gelatin
16 ounces cream cheese, softened

1 14-ounce can sweetened
   condensed milk
2 tablespoons lemon juice
4 ounces whipped topping
1 teaspoon cornstarch

Bring butter and sugar to a boil in small saucepan; remove from heat. Stir in cornflake crumbs. Reserve 2 tablespoons crumb mixture. Press remaining crumbs over bottom of 9-inch springform pan. Chill in refrigerator. Drain apricots, reserving 1 cup syrup. Soften gelatin in 1/2 cup reserved syrup in saucepan. Heat over low heat until gelatin is dissolved. Reserve 4 apricot halves for top of cheesecake. Purée remaining apricots in blender. Add to gelatin; set aside. Beat cream cheese in mixer bowl until smooth. Beat in condensed milk and lemon juice. Stir in apricot mixture. Fold in whipped topping. Spoon into prepared springform pan. Slice reserved apricot halves. Arrange in 2-slice clusters on top of cheesecake. Sprinkle reserved crumbs around outer edge. Chill for 3 hours. Blend cornstarch with remaining 1/2 cup reserved apricot syrup in saucepan. Cook until thickened, stirring constantly. Cool to room temperature. Spoon over cheesecake.

Approx Per Serving: Cal 452; T Fat 26 g; 51% Calories from Fat;
     Prot 7 g; Carbo 50 g; Fiber 1 g; Chol 73 mg; Sod 329 mg.

Heavenly Low-Fat Cheesecake

Yield: 12 servings

³/₄ cup graham cracker crumbs
2 tablespoons melted reduced-
   calorie margarine
15 ounces part-skim ricotta cheese
1 cup nonfat plain yogurt
1 cup sugar

2 tablespoons flour
2 tablespoons lemon juice
8 ounces Neufchâtel cheese,
   softened
³/₄ cup (6 ounces) egg substitute
2¹/₂ teaspoons vanilla extract

Mix graham cracker crumbs and margarine in bowl. Press over bottom of 9-inch springform pan. Bake at 325 degrees for 5 minutes. Cool to room temperature. Process next 5 ingredients in blender until smooth. Beat Neufchâtel cheese in mixer bowl until light. Beat in egg substitute and vanilla. Add ricotta mixture gradually, mixing well. Spoon into crust. Place on baking sheet. Bake at 325 degrees for 1 hour or until center is nearly set. Cool for 15 minutes. Loosen from side of pan with knife. Cool for 30 minutes longer. Place on serving plate; remove side of pan. Cool completely. Chill for 4 to 6 hours.

Approx Per Serving: Cal 235; T Fat 10 g; 36% Calories from Fat;
   Prot 10 g; Carbo 28 g; Fiber <1 g; Chol 26 mg; Sod 231 mg.

Margarita Cheesecake

Yield: 12 servings

1¹/₄ cups finely crushed pretzels
1 tablespoon sugar
¹/₂ cup melted butter
16 ounces cream cheese, softened
¹/₂ cup sugar
2 envelopes Margarita mix
4 eggs

¹/₃ cup Tequila
1 teaspoon grated lime rind
¹/₂ teaspoon vanilla extract
2 cups sour cream
¹/₄ cup sugar
1 tablespoon lime juice
¹/₂ teaspoon grated lime rind

Mix first 3 ingredients in bowl. Press over bottom and part of the way up the side of 9-inch springform pan. Bake at 375 degrees for 6 minutes or until golden brown. Beat cream cheese in mixer bowl until fluffy. Add ¹/₂ cup sugar and Margarita mix; beat until light. Beat in eggs 1 at a time. Stir in Tequila, 1 teaspoon lime rind and vanilla. Pour into crust. Bake at 375 degrees for 25 to 30 minutes or until center is nearly set. Cool for 30 minutes. Increase temperature to 425 degrees. Combine sour cream and remaining ingredients in bowl; mix well. Spread over cheesecake. Bake at 425 degrees for 10 minutes. Cool on wire rack. Chill overnight. Place on serving plate; remove side of pan. Garnish with lime slices. May omit Tequila and reduce number of eggs to 3.

Approx Per Serving: Cal 411; T Fat 31 g; 70% Calories from Fat;
   Prot 7 g; Carbo 24 g; Fiber <1 g; Chol 150 mg; Sod 363 mg.
   Nutritional information does not include Margarita mix.

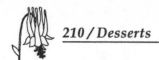

Coffee Delight

Yield: 16 servings

1¹/₂ tablespoons instant coffee
8 ounces miniature
    marshmallows
³/₄ cup boiling water

2 cups whipping cream,
    whipped
1 angel food cake, torn
1 cup chopped pecans

Dissolve coffee and marshmallows in boiling water in bowl. Cool. Fold in whipped cream. Place cake in two 8-inch pans. Sprinkle with pecans. Top with whipped cream mixture. Chill for 24 hours.

Approx Per Serving: Cal 291; T Fat 16 g; 48% Calories from Fat;
    Prot 4 g; Carbo 35 g; Fiber 1 g; Chol 41 mg; Sod 226 mg.

Creamy Coconut Mold

Yield: 12 servings

2 envelopes unflavored gelatin
1¹/₂ cups cold water
1 14-ounce can sweetened
    condensed milk
3 ounces cream cheese,
    softened, chopped

24 ounces cottage cheese
1 cup coconut
1 cup chopped almonds
1¹/₂ teaspoons almond extract
3 cups chopped fresh fruit

Soften gelatin in water in saucepan. Heat over low heat until gelatin is dissolved. Beat next 6 ingredients in mixer bowl. Stir in gelatin. Chill until slightly thickened; mix well. Spoon into lightly oiled 1¹/₂-quart mold. Chill until firm. Invert onto serving plate. Serve with fruit.

Approx Per Serving: Cal 306; T Fat 16 g; 45% Calories from Fat;
    Prot 14 g; Carbo 30 g; Fiber 3 g; Chol 27 mg; Sod 296 mg.

Horatio's Restaurant Burnt Cream

Yield: 6 servings

4 egg yolks
¹/₂ cup sugar
2 cups whipping cream, scalded

1 tablespoon vanilla extract
¹/₄ cup sugar
1 teaspoon brown sugar

Beat egg yolks and ¹/₂ cup sugar in mixer bowl for 3 minutes. Beat in scalded cream gradually. Stir in vanilla. Pour into six 6-ounce custard cups. Place in baking pan with ¹/₂ inch water. Bake at 350 degrees for 45 minutes or until set. Chill in refrigerator. Sprinkle mixture of ¹/₄ cup sugar and brown sugar over custards. Place under broiler. Broil until medium brown. Chill until serving time.

Approx Per Serving: Cal 422; T Fat 33 g; 70% Calories from Fat;
    Prot 3 g; Carbo 29 g; Fiber 0 g; Chol 251 mg; Sod 36 mg.

Boiled Custard

Yield: 8 servings

1 14-ounce can sweetened
    condensed milk
2 eggs

4 egg yolks
2 teaspoons vanilla extract

Blend condensed milk with enough hot water to measure 4 cups in bowl. Beat eggs and egg yolks in double boiler. Add milk. Cook over hot water for 30 minutes or until mixture coats silver spoon; remove from heat. Cool to room temperature, stirring frequently. Add vanilla.

Approx Per Serving: Cal 214; T Fat 9 g; 36% Calories from Fat;
    Prot 7 g; Carbo 27 g; Fiber 0 g; Chol 177 mg; Sod 84 mg.

Flan de Coco

Yield: 12 servings

1 cup sugar
1 tablespoon water
1 14-ounce can sweetened
    condensed milk

1 15-ounce can evaporated
    milk
Grated meat of 1 coconut
6 eggs

Sprinkle sugar in heavy skillet. Stir in water. Cook over low heat for 8 to 10 minutes or until medium brown, stirring constantly with long-handled spoon. Pour into tube pan. Combine condensed milk, evaporated milk, coconut and eggs in blender container. Process until smooth. Spoon carefully into prepared pan. Bake at 325 degrees for 1 hour. Invert immediately onto serving plate.

Approx Per Serving: Cal 352; T Fat 17 g; 43% Calories from Fat;
    Prot 9 g; Carbo 43 g; Fiber 3 g; Chol 128 mg; Sod 120 mg.

Haupia

Yield: 16 servings

6 tablespoons sugar
6 tablespoons cornstarch
Salt to taste

2 cups coconut milk
1 cup milk

Blend sugar, cornstarch, salt and 1 cup coconut milk in bowl. Combine remaining 1 cup coconut milk with milk in saucepan. Heat until heated through. Add cornstarch mixture. Cook until thickened, stirring constantly. Spoon into 9x9-inch pan. Cool to room temperature. Chill for several hours to overnight. Cut into squares. Serve on ivy, geranium, philodendron, magnolia or Ti leaves.

Approx Per Serving: Cal 107; T Fat 8 g; 61% Calories from Fat;
    Prot 1 g; Carbo 10 g; Fiber <1 g; Chol 2 mg; Sod 11 mg.

Chocolate Pain Perdu

Yield: 12 servings

5 tablespoons butter, softened
12 slices French bread
1 cup semisweet chocolate chips
2½ cups milk
¼ cup dry milk powder

3 eggs
¼ cup sugar
1 teaspoon cinnamon
2 tablespoons confectioners'
  sugar

Butter bread on both sides. Place on baking sheet. Bake at 375 degrees until golden brown on both sides, turning once. Arrange in 9x13-inch baking dish. Melt chocolate chips with ½ cup milk in saucepan. Scald remaining 2 cups milk with milk powder in saucepan. Stir in chocolate mixture. Beat eggs with sugar and cinnamon in mixer bowl. Stir in milk mixture. Pour over bread. Bake at 350 degrees for 40 minutes or until set. Sprinkle with confectioners' sugar. Serve warm with cream.

Approx Per Serving: Cal 291; T Fat 14 g; 43% Calories from Fat;
  Prot 7 g; Carbo 34 g; Fiber 1 g; Chol 73 mg; Sod 292 mg.

Flour Tortilla Torte

Yield: 8 servings

1 cup semisweet chocolate chips
1 cup sour cream
1 tablespoon confectioners' sugar

4 flour tortillas
1 cup sour cream
2 tablespoons confectioners' sugar

Heat first 3 ingredients in double boiler until chocolate chips melt; mix well. Cool in pan of cold water; stir occasionally. Spread mixture between tortillas. Spread mixture of 1 cup sour cream and 2 tablespoons confectioners' sugar over top and side of torte. Invert bowl over torte. Chill for 8 hours to overnight. Garnish with chocolate curls. Cut into wedges.

Approx Per Serving: Cal 294; T Fat 21 g; 60% Calories from Fat;
  Prot 4 g; Carbo 27 g; Fiber 1 g; Chol 26 mg; Sod 101 mg.

Ambrosia Ice Cream

Yield: 16 servings

2 cups whipping cream
4 cups half and half
3 cups sugar
Juice of 3 oranges

2 bananas, mashed
1 10-ounce package frozen
  strawberries, thawed
Juice of 2 lemons

Mix all ingredients in bowl. Spoon into ice cream freezer container. Freeze using manufacturer's instructions. Ripen in freezer for 1 hour or longer.

Approx Per Serving: Cal 353; T Fat 18 g; 45% Calories from Fat;
  Prot 3 g; Carbo 48 g; Fiber 1 g; Chol 63 mg; Sod 37 mg.

Frozen Creole Cream Cheese
Yield: 30 servings

*Creole cream cheese is a New Orleans specialty. You may
substitute milk clabber if desired.*

66 ounces Creole cream cheese,
  softened
1 14-ounce can sweetened
  condensed milk

2 12-ounce cans evaporated
  milk
1 tablespoon vanilla extract
1 cup sugar

Combine all ingredients in mixer bowl; mix until smooth. Spoon into ice
cream freezer container. Add water to fill line. Freeze using manufacturer's instructions.

Approx Per Serving: Cal 317; T Fat 24 g; 69% Calories from Fat;
    Prot 7 g; Carbo 16 g; Fiber 0 g; Chol 79 mg; Sod 226 mg.

Lemon Sorbet
Yield: 4 servings

1¹/₂ cups water
³/₄ cup sugar
20 fresh lemon balm leaves

20 fresh lemon verbena leaves
³/₄ cup fresh lemon juice or
  orange juice

Combine water, sugar, lemon balm and lemon verbena in saucepan.
Bring to a boil; reduce heat. Simmer for 5 minutes. Stir in lemon juice.
Strain into sorbet maker. Freeze using manufacturer's instructions until
firm but not hard. Garnish with lemon balm leaves. Serve as dessert or
to cleanse palate between courses.

Approx Per Serving: Cal 156; T Fat <1 g; 1% Calories from Fat;
    Prot <1 g; Carbo 41 g; Fiber <1 g; Chol 0 mg; Sod 1 mg.

Sugar on Snow
Yield: variable

Snow   **Vermont maple syrup**

Send the children or willing adults to bring in pie plates of "clean snow."
(This is sometimes hard to find in this day and age!) You will need 1 pan
of snow per guest and 1 pan of snow for testing. Bring Vermont maple
syrup to a simmer over low heat. (You may want to butter the rim of the
pot to prevent "boil over.") When syrup begins to thicken, drop by
teaspoonful on testing snow. When it sits in a little golden disc that
droops when picked up with a fork it is done. Remove from heat and
pour into warm pitchers to pass and drizzle over the "clean snow." Some
like little puddles and some like long spirals that wind around a fork.

Nutritional information for this recipe is not available.

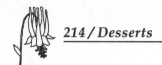

Double Mocha Puff

Yield: 10 servings

2 cups semisweet chocolate chips
2 cups whipping cream
2 tablespoons coffee liqueur
2 teaspoons vanilla extract
3/4 cup water
1/2 cup butter
2 teaspoons sugar
1 teaspoon instant coffee
Salt to taste
3/4 cup flour

1/4 cup baking cocoa
1 teaspoon vanilla extract
4 eggs
1 cup confectioners' sugar
1 tablespoon coffee liqueur
2 teaspoons milk
1 teaspoon butter, softened
1 ounce semisweet chocolate,
    cut into curls
1/2 cup confectioners' sugar

Melt chocolate chips with cream in medium saucepan, stirring until smooth. Pour into bowl. Chill for 3 hours or until firm. Beat until stiff peaks form. Beat in 2 tablespoons coffee liqueur and 2 teaspoons vanilla. Chill in refrigerator. Combine water, 1/2 cup butter, sugar, instant coffee and salt in saucepan. Heat just to the boiling point. Add mixture of flour and cocoa all at once. Cook until mixture leaves side of saucepan, stirring constantly. Cool for 5 minutes. Add 1 teaspoon vanilla. Beat in eggs 1 at a time. Spread or pipe into 4 1/2x11-inch rectangle on buttered baking sheet. Bake at 425 degrees for 20 minutes. Reduce oven temperature to 350 degrees. Bake for 15 to 20 minutes longer or until firm to touch. Cut slit in side of puff. Return to oven. Turn off heat; let puff stand in open oven for 10 minutes. Split puff horizontally; remove top. Discard any uncooked dough. Fill with chocolate filling; replace top. Beat 1 cup confectioners' sugar, 1 tablespoon coffee liqueur, milk and 1 teaspoon butter in mixer bowl until smooth. Drizzle over top of puff allowing to run down sides. Sprinkle with chocolate curls and 1/2 cup confectioners' sugar.

Approx Per Serving: Cal 601; T Fat 43 g; 62% Calories from Fat;
    Prot 6 g; Carbo 52 g; Fiber 2 g; Chol 176 mg; Sod 133 mg.

Chocolate Mousse

Yield: 4 servings

8 ounces dark chocolate
4 egg yolks, beaten
4 egg whites

1/4 cup rum
1/2 cup whipping cream,
    whipped

Melt chocolate in double boiler over simmering water. Combine with egg yolks in bowl; beat until smooth. Cool for 30 minutes. Whip egg whites in mixer bowl until soft peaks form. Fold into chocolate mixture. Spoon into glass bowl or 4 individual dishes. Spoon rum over mousse. Top servings with whipped cream; garnish with grated chocolate.

Approx Per Serving: Cal 513; T Fat 37 g; 66% Calories from Fat;
    Prot 9 g; Carbo 33 g; Fiber 2 g; Chol 254 mg; Sod 79 mg.

Microwave Peach-a-Berry Cobbler   *Yield: 6 servings*

2 cups sliced fresh peaches
½ cup sugar
1 tablespoon cornstarch
¼ cup packed brown sugar
⅓ cup cold water
1 cup fresh or frozen
   blueberries
1 tablespoon butter

1 cup flour
½ cup sugar
1½ teaspoons baking powder
½ teaspoon salt
½ cup milk
¼ cup butter, softened
¼ teaspoon nutmeg
2 tablespoons sugar

Mix peaches with ½ cup sugar in bowl. Blend cornstarch, brown sugar and cold water in bowl. Stir in peaches, blueberries and 1 tablespoon butter. Spoon into round 8-inch glass dish. Microwave for 7 to 9 minutes or until fruit is tender, stirring every 2 to 3 minutes. Sift flour, ½ cup sugar, baking powder and salt into bowl. Add milk and ¼ cup butter; mix well. Spoon over fruit. Sprinkle with mixture of nutmeg and 2 tablespoons sugar. Microwave on High for 3 minutes, turning every minute. May broil until top is brown if desired.

Approx Per Serving: Cal 404; T Fat 11 g; 23% Calories from Fat;
    Prot 4 g; Carbo 76 g; Fiber 2 g; Chol 29 mg; Sod 357 mg.

Alaska Igloos   *Yield: 8 servings*

⅓ cup sifted flour
1 cup quick-cooking oats
½ cup packed brown sugar
½ teaspoon salt
⅓ cup margarine
2 squares chocolate
1 teaspoon vanilla extract

4 egg whites
¼ teaspoon salt
½ cup sugar
½ teaspoon vanilla extract
1 quart vanilla ice cream
½ cup coconut

Mix flour, oats, brown sugar and ½ teaspoon salt in bowl. Melt margarine and chocolate in double boiler. Add to dry ingredients; mix well. Mix in 1 teaspoon vanilla. Press over bottom and ½ inch up sides of 8 greased muffin cups. Bake at 375 degrees for 12 minutes. Cool in pan. Remove to baking sheet lined with heavy paper. Beat egg whites with ¼ teaspoon salt in mixer bowl until frothy. Add ½ cup sugar 1 teaspoon at a time, beating constantly. Add ½ teaspoon vanilla, beating until stiff peaks form. Scoop ice cream into baked cups. Spread with meringue. Sprinkle with coconut. Broil just until light brown.

Approx Per Serving: Cal 439; T Fat 21 g; 41% Calories from Fat;
    Prot 7 g; Carbo 60 g; Fiber 3 g; Chol 30 mg; Sod 391 mg.

Ginger Pear Dessert

Yield: 8 servings

4 medium pears
1/4 cup orange juice
1 cup finely crushed
gingersnaps

1/2 cup sugar
1/4 cup chopped walnuts
1/4 cup melted butter

Peel pears; cut into halves, discarding core. Place cut side up in 6x10-inch baking dish. Drizzle with orange juice. Combine cookie crumbs, sugar, walnuts and butter in bowl. Sprinkle over pears. Bake at 350 degrees for 20 to 25 minutes or until pears are tender. Serve with scoops of ice cream; garnish with mint jelly.

Approx Per Serving: Cal 256; T Fat 10 g; 35% Calories from Fat;
Prot 2 g; Carbo 41 g; Fiber 3 g; Chol 16 mg; Sod 159 mg.

Pineapple-Filled Pastry

Yield: 25 servings

1 tablespoon sugar
1 envelope or cake yeast
2/3 cup milk, scalded, cooled to
lukewarm
3 egg yolks
1 cup butter
2 1/2 cups flour
1 21-ounce can pineapple pie
filling

1 egg yolk
1 egg
2 1/3 cups confectioners' sugar
2 tablespoons water
4 1/2 tablespoons sugar
2/3 cup shortening
1 teaspoon vanilla extract
1 cup chopped pecans

Dissolve 1 tablespoon sugar and yeast in milk in bowl. Add 3 egg yolks; mix well. Cut butter into flour with pastry blender in bowl. Add to yeast mixture; mix well. Divide into 2 portions. Roll 1 portion to fit 12x15-inch baking sheet. Combine pie filling and 1 egg yolk in bowl; mix well. Spread over pastry. Roll remaining dough between waxed paper. Place over filling; peel off waxed paper. Press edges to seal. Let rise in warm place for 1 hour or until light. Bake at 350 degrees for 45 minutes. Cool to room temperature. Beat 1 egg with confectioners' sugar in mixer bowl until smooth. Bring water and 4 1/2 tablespoons sugar to a boil in saucepan. Add to confectioners' sugar mixture; mix well. Beat in shortening and vanilla. Spread over pastry; sprinkle with pecans.

Approx Per Serving: Cal 285; T Fat 18 g; 54% Calories from Fat;
Prot 3 g; Carbo 31 g; Fiber 1 g; Chol 63 mg; Sod 76 mg.

Indian Pudding

Yield: 6 servings

3 cups milk
3 tablespoons cornmeal
1/3 cup dark molasses
1/2 cup sugar
1 tablespoon butter

1/2 teaspoon ginger
1/2 teaspoon cinnamon
1/4 teaspoon salt
1 egg, beaten
1/2 cup milk

Scald 3 cups milk in saucepan. Stir in mixture of cornmeal and molasses. Cook until thickened, stirring constantly; remove from heat. Add sugar, butter, ginger, cinnamon, salt and egg; mix well. Pour into buttered deep baking dish. Bake at 300 degrees for 30 minutes. Pour 1/2 cup milk over top. Bake for 2 hours longer. Serve with whipped cream or ice cream.

Approx Per Serving: Cal 235; T Fat 8 g; 29% Calories from Fat;
Prot 6 g; Carbo 36 g; Fiber <1 g; Chol 60 mg; Sod 193 mg.

Old English Plum Pudding

Yield: 40 servings

3 cups rolled bread crumbs
2 cups flour
1 cup sugar
1 1/2 teaspoons cinnamon
1 teaspoon nutmeg
1/2 teaspoon salt
1 pound suet, finely chopped
1 pound currants
1 pound seedless raisins

1 cup chopped peeled apple
8 ounces candied fruit, chopped
6 eggs
Grated rind and juice of 1
    lemon
1/4 cup brandy
1/2 cup rum
1/2 cup brandy

Mix bread crumbs, flour, sugar, cinnamon, nutmeg and salt in bowl. Stir in suet, currants, raisins, apple and candied fruit. Beat eggs with lemon rind, lemon juice, 1/4 cup brandy and rum in bowl; mix well. Add to fruit mixture; mix well. Fill 1 large greased mold and 3 small greased molds 2/3 full. Cover with baking parchment, buttered muslin or doubled waxed paper; tie securely. Steam, covered, for 3 hours. Heat 1/2 cup brandy in small saucepan. Pour over hot pudding. Ignite brandy. Let stand until flames die down.

Approx Per Serving: Cal 284; T Fat 12 g; 39% Calories from Fat;
Prot 4 g; Carbo 40 g; Fiber 2 g; Chol 40 mg; Sod 95 mg.

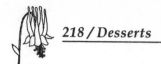

Shortcake

Yield: 8 servings

3 cups flour
1/4 cup sugar
2 tablespoons baking powder
1 teaspoon salt

1/2 cup milk
2 tablespoons butter, softened
3 cups strawberries, sliced
1/4 cup sugar

Sift flour, 1/4 cup sugar, baking powder and salt into bowl. Add milk; mix well. Roll 1 inch thick on floured surface. Place in pie plate; cover with waxed paper. Chill until baking time. Bake at 450 degrees for 15 minutes or until light brown. Cool slightly. Remove from pan. Split into halves; spread with butter. Place bottom half on serving dish. Top with mixture of strawberries and 1/4 cup sugar; replace top. Serve with whipped cream.

Approx Per Serving: Cal 274; T Fat 4 g; 13% Calories from Fat;
Prot 6 g; Carbo 54 g; Fiber 3 g; Chol 10 mg; Sod 546 mg.

Soufflé au Chocolat

Yield: 8 servings

1 envelope unflavored gelatin
3 tablespoons cold water
2 ounces baking chocolate
1/2 cup confectioners' sugar
1 cup warm milk

3/4 cup sugar
1 teaspoon vanilla extract
1/4 teaspoon salt
2 cups whipping cream,
  whipped

Soften gelatin in cold water in bowl. Melt chocolate in saucepan over low heat. Blend in confectioners' sugar. Stir in warm milk gradually. Bring to a boil over low heat, stirring constantly; remove from heat. Stir in gelatin, sugar, vanilla and salt. Chill until slightly thickened. Beat with rotary beater until light and fluffy. Fold in whipped cream. Spoon into 2-quart serving dish. Chill for 2 hours or longer.

Approx Per Serving: Cal 366; T Fat 27 g; 63% Calories from Fat;
Prot 4 g; Carbo 31 g; Fiber 1 g; Chol 86 mg; Sod 103 mg.

 To dry flowers, use a mixture of 3 parts borax to 10 parts cornmeal in a container with a lid. Pick flowers before they are fully opened and cover completely with drying mix for 3 to 10 days. Remove carefully, dust off excess mix, and store in covered containers.

English Trifle

Yield: 30 servings

6 egg yolks
2 ounces castor sugar
2 teaspoons cornstarch
2 pints whipping cream
1 sponge cake
1 cup raspberry jam
1/4 cup sherry

2 tablespoons raspberry jelly
2 bananas, sliced
2 cups raspberries
2 cups strawberries
1/2 cup whipping cream
1/4 cup toasted sliced almonds

Combine egg yolks, sugar and cornstarch in bowl; mix well. Heat 2 pints whipping cream in saucepan. Add a small amount of hot cream to egg yolk mixture; stir egg yolks into hot cream. Cook until thickened, stirring constantly. Cool to room temperature. Split cake into several layers. Spread 1 cup raspberry jam between layers. Cut cake into thin slices. Line glass bowl with slices. Drizzle with sherry and 2 tablespoons jelly. Chill in refrigerator. Layer bananas, raspberries and strawberries in prepared bowl. Top with custard. Chill until serving time. Whip 1/2 cup whipping cream in mixer bowl until soft peaks form. Spread over trifle; top with almonds.

Approx Per Serving: Cal 275; T Fat 16 g; 52% Calories from Fat;
    Prot 4 g; Carbo 30 g; Fiber 2 g; Chol 146 mg; Sod 101 mg.

Peach Trifle

Yield: 14 servings

1   14-ounce can sweetened
    condensed milk
1 1/2 cups cold water
1   4-ounce package vanilla
    instant pudding mix
2 cups whipped topping
1/4 cup orange juice

1 1/2 pounds fresh or frozen
    peaches, sliced
1   10-ounce angel food cake,
    torn into bite-sized pieces
1/2 cup toasted sliced almonds
1/4 cup raspberry preserves

Mix condensed milk and water in large mixer bowl. Add pudding mix; beat until smooth. Chill for 5 minutes. Fold in whipped topping and 1 teaspoon of the orange juice. Toss remaining orange juice with peaches in bowl. Layer cake, peaches, almonds and pudding 1/2 at a time in 2-quart trifle bowl. Top with preserves. Chill until serving time.

Approx Per Serving: Cal 266; T Fat 8 g; 24% Calories from Fat;
    Prot 5 g; Carbo 47 g; Fiber 2 g; Chol 10 mg; Sod 197 mg.

Cakes

Fresh Apple Cake

Yield: 16 servings

5 cooking apples, peeled
5 tablespoons sugar
2 teaspoons cinnamon
3 cups flour
2¹/2 cups sugar
¹/2 teaspoon salt
1¹/2 teaspoons baking soda
1¹/2 teaspoons baking powder

4 eggs
1 cup oil
2 teaspoons vanilla extract
¹/2 cup orange juice
1¹/2 cups confectioners' sugar
2 tablespoons butter, softened
1¹/2 teaspoons vanilla extract
1 to 2 tablespoons water

Core and cut apples into thin slices. Combine with 5 tablespoons sugar and cinnamon in bowl; toss to coat. Combine flour, 2¹/2 cups sugar, salt, baking soda, baking powder, eggs, oil, 2 teaspoons vanilla and orange juice in large mixer bowl. Beat at low speed for 1 minute. Beat at medium speed for 3 minutes. Batter will be very thick. Alternate layers of batter and apple mixture in greased and floured 10-inch tube pan, beginning and ending with batter. Bake at 350 degrees for 1¹/2 hours or until cake tests done. Cool on wire rack for 10 minutes. Invert onto wire rack to cool completely. Blend confectioners' sugar, butter, 1¹/2 teaspoons vanilla and enough water to make of glaze consistency. Drizzle over cooled cake.

Approx Per Serving: Cal 443; T Fat 17 g; 34% Calories from Fat;
Prot 4 g; Carbo 71 g; Fiber 2 g; Chol 57 mg; Sod 205 mg.

Sour Cream Banana Nut Cake

Yield: 15 servings

2 eggs, beaten
1 cup sour cream
1/2 teaspoon baking soda
1 cup sugar
2 bananas, mashed
1 1/2 cups sifted flour
1 teaspoon baking powder
1/2 teaspoon salt

1 teaspoon vanilla extract
1/2 cup chopped pecans
1 1/2 cups packed brown sugar
1/2 cup sugar
2 tablespoons light corn syrup
1/2 teaspoon salt
3/4 cup sour cream

Beat eggs with sour cream and baking soda in mixer bowl. Add 1 cup sugar and bananas; mix well. Sift flour, baking powder and 1/2 teaspoon salt together 3 times. Add to sour cream mixture; mix well. Stir in vanilla and pecans. Pour into greased and floured 9x13-inch cake pan. Bake at 350 degrees for 30 to 35 minutes or until cake tests done. Mix brown sugar and 1/2 cup sugar in saucepan. Add corn syrup, 1/2 teaspoon salt and 3/4 cup sour cream; mix well. Cook over low heat to soft-ball stage, stirring frequently. Cool. Beat until smooth. Frost cooled cake. May add enough confectioners' sugar to make of spreading consistency if frosting fails to thicken.

Approx Per Serving: Cal 338; T Fat 9 g; 24% Calories from Fat;
Prot 3 g; Carbo 63 g; Fiber 1 g; Chol 40 mg; Sod 229 mg.

Carrot Cake with Orange Sauce

Yield: 15 servings

3 eggs
1 1/2 cups vegetable oil
2 teaspoons vanilla extract
1 3/4 cups sugar
2 1/2 cups flour
2 teaspoons baking soda
2 teaspoons cinnamon
1/2 teaspoon salt

2 cups grated carrots
1 cup drained crushed pineapple
3/4 cup chopped walnuts
3/4 cup flaked coconut
2 eggs, beaten
1/2 cup margarine
2 cups packed brown sugar
1 cup orange juice

Combine 3 eggs, oil, vanilla and sugar in mixer bowl; beat until blended. Sift in flour, baking soda, cinnamon and salt; mix well. Stir in carrots, pineapple, walnuts and coconut. Pour into greased 9x13-inch cake pan. Bake at 350 degrees for 1 hour or until cake tests done. Cool. Combine remaining 2 eggs, margarine, brown sugar and orange juice in saucepan; mix well. Cook over low heat until thickened, stirring constantly. Cool. Chill until serving time. Reheat over low heat or in microwave, stirring constantly. Pour over cake just before serving.

Approx Per Serving: Cal 653; T Fat 35 g; 47% Calories from Fat;
Prot 5 g; Carbo 83 g; Fiber 2 g; Chol 71 mg; Sod 298 mg.

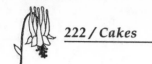

Cherry Nectar Cake

Yield: 16 servings

1 cup shortening
2 cups sugar
4 eggs
3 cups flour
1 tablespoon baking powder
1 teaspoon salt
1 cup (scant) milk
1 teaspoon almond extract
1/2 cup chopped maraschino
   cherries

1/4 cup maraschino cherry juice
1/2 cup chopped pecans
1/2 cup butter, softened
1/2 cup shortening
1 teaspoon almond extract
1 1-pound package
   confectioners' sugar
1/2 cup chopped maraschino
   cherries
1/4 cup chopped pecans

Cream 1 cup shortening and sugar in mixer bowl until light and fluffy. Beat in eggs 1 at a time. Sift in flour, baking powder and salt; mix well. Beat in milk and 1 teaspoon almond extract. Stir in 1/2 cup cherries, cherry juice and 1/2 cup pecans. Pour into 4 greased and floured 8-inch cake pans. Bake at 350 degrees for 15 minutes or until layers test done. Cool on wire rack. Cream butter and 1/2 cup shortening in mixer bowl. Add 1 teaspoon almond extract and confectioners' sugar; beat until of spreading consistency. Stir in 1/2 cup cherries and 1/4 cup chopped pecans. Spread between layers and over top and side of cake.

Approx Per Serving: Cal 619; T Fat 31 g; 44% Calories from Fat;
    Prot 5 g; Carbo 83 g; Fiber 1 g; Chol 71 mg; Sod 269 mg.

Chocolate Mousse Cake

Yield: 10 servings

7 ounces semisweet chocolate
1/2 cup butter

1 cup sugar
7 eggs, separated

Melt chocolate and butter in saucepan over low heat, stirring constantly. Pour into mixer bowl. Add sugar gradually, beating constantly. Add egg yolks 1 at a time, beating well after each addition. Beat egg whites in mixer bowl until stiff peaks form. Fold into chocolate mixture gently. Pour 3/4 of the batter into ungreased 8-inch springform pan. Bake at 325 degrees for 35 minutes. Let stand until cool; cake will fall. Loosen cake from side of pan with knife. Remove side of pan. Spoon remaining batter over top. Chill until serving time. Garnish with whipped cream and chocolate shavings.

Approx Per Serving: Cal 314; T Fat 20 g; 55% Calories from Fat;
    Prot 5 g; Carbo 32 g; Fiber 1 g; Chol 174 mg; Sod 129 mg.

Texas Chocolate Sheath Cake

Yield: 18 servings

2 cups flour
2 cups sugar
1/4 teaspoon salt
1 cup margarine
1/4 cup baking cocoa
1 cup water
1/2 cup buttermilk
2 eggs, slightly beaten
1 teaspoon baking soda

1 tablespoon cinnamon
1 tablespoon vanilla extract
1/2 cup margarine
1/4 cup baking cocoa
6 tablespoons milk
1 teaspoon vanilla extract
1 cup chopped pecans
1 1-pound package
   confectioners' sugar, sifted

Sift flour, sugar and salt into large bowl. Combine 1 cup margarine, 1/4 cup cocoa and 1 cup water in saucepan. Bring to a full rolling boil, stirring frequently. Add to flour mixture; mix well. Add buttermilk, eggs, baking soda, cinnamon and 1 tablespoon vanilla; mix well. Pour into greased and floured 9x13-inch cake pan. Bake at 400 degrees for 20 minutes. Let stand for 10 minutes. Combine 1/2 cup margarine, 1/4 cup cocoa and milk in saucepan. Heat until well blended, stirring constantly. Bring to a boil; remove from heat. Add 1 teaspoon vanilla, pecans and confectioners' sugar; beat until well mixed. Spread over hot cake. Garnish with additional pecans.

Approx Per Serving: Cal 453; T Fat 21 g; 41% Calories from Fat;
   Prot 4 g; Carbo 66 g; Fiber 2 g; Chol 25 mg; Sod 272 mg.

Hershey Bar Cake

Yield: 16 servings

This rich delicious cake requires no frosting.

1 cup margarine, softened
2 cups sugar
4 eggs
2 1/2 cups flour
1/4 teaspoon baking soda
1/2 teaspoon salt

1 cup buttermilk
7 1.65-ounce milk chocolate
   candy bars
1 16-ounce can chocolate syrup
1 cup chopped pecans

Cream margarine and sugar in mixer bowl. Beat in eggs 1 at a time. Add dry ingredients alternately with buttermilk, mixing well after each addition. Melt candy bars in chocolate syrup in double boiler; blend well. Add to batter. Mix in pecans. Pour into greased tube pan. Bake at 350 degrees for 1 hour.

Approx Per Serving: Cal 514; T Fat 25 g; 42% Calories from Fat;
   Prot 7 g; Carbo 70 g; Fiber 2 g; Chol 58 mg; Sod 288 mg.

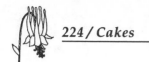

Orange Chocolate Cake

Yield: 20 servings

1 cup quick-cooking oats
1½ cups boiling water
2 cups flour
1 teaspoon baking powder
1 teaspoon baking soda
2 teaspoons cinnamon
¼ cup baking cocoa
⅓ cup canola oil
½ cup sugar
¾ cup packed brown sugar

3 egg whites
¼ cup frozen orange juice
    concentrate, thawed
2 teaspoons vanilla extract
1 cup chocolate chips
¼ cup margarine
¾ cup packed brown sugar
2 tablespoons frozen orange
    juice concentrate, thawed

Combine oats and boiling water in bowl; set aside. Mix flour with baking powder, baking soda, cinnamon and baking cocoa; set aside. Beat canola oil, sugar and ¾ cup brown sugar in mixer bowl until light and fluffy. Beat egg whites with ¼ cup orange juice concentrate and vanilla. Add to sugar mixture alternately with flour mixture and oats, mixing well after each addition. Stir in chocolate chips. Pour into 9x13-inch cake pan sprayed with nonstick cooking spray. Bake at 350 degrees for 25 to 30 minutes or until cake tests done. Combine margarine, ¾ cup brown sugar and 2 tablespoons orange juice concentrate in small saucepan. Bring to a boil. Boil for 1 minute. Spread over cake. Broil for 1 minute or until bubbly; watch carefully. Cool before cutting.

Approx Per Serving: Cal 265; T Fat 10 g; 31% Calories from Fat;
    Prot 3 g; Carbo 44 g; Fiber 1 g; Chol 0 mg; Sod 103 mg.

Pistachio Chocolate Bundt Cake

Yield: 16 servings

1 2-layer package white cake
   mix
1 4-ounce package pistachio
   instant pudding mix
½ cup orange juice

½ cup water
½ cup vegetable oil
4 eggs
¾ cup chocolate syrup

Combine dry cake mix and pudding mix in large mixer bowl; mix well. Add orange juice, water, oil and eggs. Beat for 5 minutes. Pour ⅔ of the batter into greased and floured bundt pan. Blend chocolate syrup into remaining batter. Pour over batter in pan, spreading to edge. Bake at 350 degrees for 1 hour. Cool in pan for 15 minutes. Invert onto cake plate.

Approx Per Serving: Cal 279; T Fat 11 g; 36% Calories from Fat;
    Prot 4 g; Carbo 42 g; Fiber <1 g; Chol 53 mg; Sod 258 mg.

Perfect Chocolate Cake

Yield: 16 servings

1 cup baking cocoa
2 cups boiling water
1 cup butter, softened
2¹/₂ cups sugar
4 eggs
1¹/₂ teaspoons vanilla extract
2³/₄ cups sifted flour
2 teaspoons baking soda

¹/₂ teaspoon salt
¹/₂ teaspoon baking powder
1 cup whipping cream
2³/₄ cups confectioners' sugar
1 teaspoon vanilla extract
1 cup chocolate chips
¹/₂ cup light cream
1 cup butter

Whisk cocoa and water in bowl. Cool. Combine next 4 ingredients in mixer bowl. Beat at high speed for 5 minutes. Sift flour, baking soda, salt and baking powder together. Add to creamed mixture ¹/₄ at a time alternately with cocoa mixture, mixing well after each addition; do not overbeat. Pour into 3 greased and floured 9-inch cake pans; smooth tops. Bake at 325 degrees for 25 to 30 minutes or until layers test done. Cool in pans for 10 minutes. Remove to wire racks to cool completely. Whip whipping cream with ¹/₄ cup confectioners' sugar and 1 teaspoon vanilla in bowl. Chill in refrigerator. Combine chocolate chips, light cream and 1 cup butter in saucepan. Cook over medium heat until smooth, stirring constantly; remove from heat. Blend in remaining 2¹/₂ cups confectioners' sugar. Place in bowl of ice water. Beat until of spreading consistency. Spread whipped cream between layers. Frost with chocolate frosting. Chill for 1 hour.

Approx Per Serving: Cal 636; T Fat 37 g; 51% Calories from Fat;
Prot 6 g; Carbo 76 g; Fiber 2 g; Chol 144 mg; Sod 402 mg.

Holiday Cranberry Torte

Yield: 16 servings

2¹/₄ cups flour
1 cup sugar
1 teaspoon baking soda
1 teaspoon salt
Grated rind of 2 oranges
2 eggs, beaten
1 cup buttermilk

³/₄ cup vegetable oil
2 cups whole fresh cranberries
1 cup chopped dates
1 cup coarsely chopped pecans
1 cup fresh orange juice
1 cup sugar

Combine first 5 ingredients in bowl. Beat eggs with buttermilk and oil in bowl. Add to flour mixture; mix well. Fold in cranberries, dates and pecans. Pour into greased and floured tube pan. Bake at 350 degrees for 1 hour. Invert on wire rack over tray. Heat orange juice and 1 cup sugar in saucepan until sugar dissolves, stirring constantly. Spoon ¹/₃ at a time over warm cake at 5 minute intervals. Let stand for 24 hours.

Approx Per Serving: Cal 359; T Fat 16 g; 40% Calories from Fat;
Prot 4 g; Carbo 52 g; Fiber 2 g; Chol 27 mg; Sod 211 mg.

Old South Fruitcake

Yield: 25 servings

1 cup butter, softened
1 cup sugar
5 eggs
1½ teaspoons vanilla extract
1 teaspoon almond extract
3 cups flour
2 teaspoons baking powder
¼ cup orange juice

1 tablespoon lemon juice
7½ cups chopped pecans
8 ounces candied orange peel
1 pound candied pineapple
4 ounces candied lemon peel
4 ounces candied cherries
1 15-ounce package golden
    raisins

Cream butter and sugar in mixer bowl until light and fluffy. Beat in eggs 1 at a time. Add vanilla and almond extracts. Add mixture of 2 cups flour and baking powder alternately with orange and lemon juices, mixing well after each addition. Combine pecans, chopped candied fruit, raisins and remaining 1 cup flour in bowl. Stir into batter. Spoon into greased and waxed paper-lined 10-inch tube pan. Bake at 250 degrees for 3 hours or until cake tests done. Cool in pan for 10 minutes. Remove to wire rack to cool completely. Garnish with whole candied cherries.

Approx Per Serving: Cal 574; T Fat 33 g; 49% Calories from Fat;
    Prot 6 g; Carbo 69 g; Fiber 4 g; Chol 63 mg; Sod 105 mg.

Macadamia Fudge Cake

Yield: 16 servings

1 cup flour
¾ cup sugar
¾ cup sour cream
1 egg
½ cup butter, softened
¼ cup baking cocoa
1½ teaspoons instant coffee
    powder
½ teaspoon baking soda
½ teaspoon baking powder

¼ teaspoon salt
½ teaspoon vanilla extract
1 cup whipping cream
½ cup sugar
2 tablespoons butter
1 tablespoon corn syrup
4 ounces semisweet chocolate
½ teaspoon vanilla extract
1 7-ounce jar macadamia nuts

Combine first 11 ingredients in large mixer bowl. Beat at low speed until blended. Pour into 9-inch springform pan greased and lined with greased waxed paper. Bake at 350 degrees for 30 minutes or until cake tests done. Cool in pan on wire rack for 10 minutes. Remove to wire rack to cool completely. Combine cream and next 4 ingredients in saucepan. Bring to a boil over medium-high heat, stirring constantly. Cook over medium heat for 5 minutes, stirring constantly. Blend in ½ teaspoon vanilla. Let stand for 10 minutes. Stir in macadamia nuts. Pour evenly over cake. Chill for 1 hour.

Approx Per Serving: Cal 368; T Fat 27 g; 63% Calories from Fat;
    Prot 4 g; Carbo 32 g; Fiber 2 g; Chol 58 mg; Sod 151 mg.

White Fudge Cake

Yield: 16 servings

2¹/2 cups flour
1¹/2 cups sugar
1 teaspoon baking soda
¹/2 teaspoon baking powder
¹/2 teaspoon salt
1 cup butter, softened
1 cup buttermilk
3 eggs
³/4 cup chopped white
   chocolate, melted

1 teaspoon vanilla extract
¹/2 cup chopped pecans
¹/2 cup flaked coconut
³/4 cup chopped white chocolate
2¹/2 tablespoons flour
1 cup milk
1 cup butter
1 cup sugar
1¹/2 teaspoons vanilla extract

Combine first 7 ingredients in mixer bowl. Beat at low speed until moistened. Beat at medium speed for 1 minute. Add eggs, melted chocolate and vanilla. Beat for 1 minute. Stir in pecans and coconut. Pour into 9x13-inch cake pan greased and floured on bottom only. Bake at 350 degrees for 35 minutes or until cake tests done. Cool. Combine ³/4 cup chocolate, 2¹/2 tablespoons flour and 1 cup milk in saucepan. Cook over medium heat until very thick, stirring constantly. Cool. Cream 1 cup butter, 1 cup sugar and 1¹/2 teaspoons vanilla in mixer bowl for 3 minutes or until light and fluffy. Add cooled chocolate mixture gradually. Beat at high speed until consistency of whipped cream. Spread over top of cake.

Approx Per Serving: Cal 574; T Fat 35 g; 53% Calories from Fat;
    Prot 6 g; Carbo 62 g; Fiber 2 g; Chol 109 mg; Sod 376 mg.

Harvey Wallbanger Cake

Yield: 16 servings

1 2-layer package orange cake
    mix
1 4-ounce package vanilla
    instant pudding mix
4 eggs
¹/2 cup vegetable oil
¹/2 cup orange juice

¹/2 cup Galliano
2 tablespoons vodka
1 cup sifted confectioners' sugar
1 tablespoon orange juice
1 tablespoon Galliano
1 teaspoon vodka

Combine cake mix and pudding mix in large mixer bowl. Add eggs, oil, ¹/2 cup orange juice, ¹/2 cup Galliano and 2 tablespoons vodka. Beat at low speed for 30 seconds. Beat at medium speed for 5 minutes. Pour into greased and floured 10-inch tube pan. Bake at 350 degrees for 45 minutes. Cool in pan for 10 minutes. Remove to wire rack. Blend confectioners' sugar and remaining ingredients in small bowl. Spoon over hot cake.

Approx Per Serving: Cal 311; T Fat 11 g; 32% Calories from Fat;
    Prot 3 g; Carbo 45 g; Fiber <1 g; Chol 53 mg; Sod 262 mg.

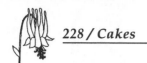

Highland Cake

Yield: 15 servings

1 cup quick-cooking oats
1 cup boiling water
½ cup margarine, softened
1 cup packed brown sugar
½ cup sugar
2 eggs
½ teaspoon vanilla extract
1½ cups flour

1 teaspoon baking soda
1 teaspoon cinnamon
½ teaspoon cloves
⅛ teaspoon salt
3 tablespoons butter
½ cup pecans
½ cup coconut
⅔ cup packed brown sugar

Combine oats and boiling water in bowl. Let stand until cool. Cream margarine with 1 cup brown sugar, sugar, eggs and vanilla in bowl until light and fluffy. Add flour, baking soda, cinnamon, cloves and salt; mix well. Pour into greased 9x13-inch cake pan. Mix remaining ingredients in small bowl until crumbly. Sprinkle over batter. Bake at 350 degrees for 35 minutes. Serve with whipped topping.

Approx Per Serving: Cal 328; T Fat 13 g; 35% Calories from Fat;
    Prot 3 g; Carbo 51 g; Fiber 1 g; Chol 35 mg; Sod 187 mg.

Italian Cream Cake

Yield: 16 servings

½ cup margarine, softened
½ cup shortening
2 cups sugar
5 egg yolks
2 cups flour
1 teaspoon baking soda
1 cup buttermilk
1 teaspoon vanilla extract
8 ounces coconut

1 cup chopped pecans
5 egg whites, stiffly beaten
8 ounces cream cheese, softened
¼ cup margarine, softened
1   1-pound package
    confectioners' sugar
1 teaspoon vanilla extract
3 bananas, sliced
1 cup chopped pecans

Cream ½ cup margarine, shortening and sugar in mixer bowl until light and fluffy. Beat in egg yolks. Add mixture of flour and baking soda alternately with buttermilk and 1 teaspoon vanilla, mixing well after each addition. Mix in coconut and 1 cup pecans. Fold in stiffly beaten egg whites gently. Pour into 3 greased and wax paper-lined 9-inch cake pans. Bake at 350 degrees for 40 minutes or until cake tests done. Beat cream cheese and ¼ cup margarine in mixer bowl until creamy. Add confectioners' sugar and 1 teaspoon vanilla; beat until of spreading consistency, adding a small amount of cream or milk if necessary. Spread layers with frosting. Stack cake, with bananas and 1 cup pecans between layers. Spread remaining frosting over side; sprinkle with remaining pecans.

Approx Per Serving: Cal 679; T Fat 37 g; 47% Calories from Fat;
    Prot 7 g; Carbo 85 g; Fiber 4 g; Chol 83 mg; Sod 232 mg.

Maple Pecan Chiffon Cake

Yield: 16 servings

1 cup egg whites, at room
   temperature
1/2 teaspoon cream of tartar
2¼ cups sifted cake flour
3/4 cup sugar
1 tablespoon baking powder
1 teaspoon salt
3/4 cup packed brown sugar
1/2 cup vegetable oil
5 egg yolks

3/4 cup cold water
2 teaspoons maple extract
1 cup very finely chopped
   pecans
1/4 cup butter
2 cups sifted confectioners'
   sugar
2 tablespoons cream
1 teaspoon vegetable oil
1½ teaspoons vanilla extract

Beat egg whites with cream of tartar in large mixer bowl at high speed for 3 to 5 minutes or until very stiff peaks form; set aside. Sift cake flour, sugar, baking powder and salt into medium mixer bowl. Mix in brown sugar. Make well in center. Add oil, egg yolks, cold water and maple extract. Beat at medium speed for 1 minute. Fold into stiffly beaten egg whites gently just until mixed. Sprinkle with pecans; fold in gently. Pour into ungreased 10-inch tube pan. Bake at 325 degrees for 55 minutes. Increase temperature to 350 degrees. Bake for 10 to 15 minutes longer or until top springs back when lightly touched. Turn pan upside down over bottle or funnel. Let hang until completely cooled. Loosen from side of pan. Remove to cake plate. Heat butter in saucepan over low heat until golden brown; remove from heat. Add confectioners' sugar, cream, 1 teaspoon oil and 1½ teaspoons vanilla; beat until of spreading consistency, adding a small amount of hot water if necessary. May double frosting if desired. Frost cooled cake.

Approx Per Serving: Cal 352; T Fat 18 g; 44% Calories from Fat;
   Prot 4 g; Carbo 47 g; Fiber 1 g; Chol 77 mg; Sod 248 mg.

Rhubarb Upside-Down Cake

Yield: 12 servings

1/4 cup butter
1½ cups packed brown sugar
1/2 teaspoon cinnamon
2 cups chopped rhubarb
1 cup flour
1/2 cup whole wheat flour

1 cup sugar
2½ teaspoons baking powder
1/3 cup melted butter
2/3 cup milk
2 eggs
1/2 teaspoon vanilla extract

Melt 1/4 cup butter in 9x9-inch cake pan. Mix in brown sugar, cinnamon and rhubarb; pat evenly into pan. Combine remaining ingredients in bowl; mix well. Pour over rhubarb mixture. Bake at 350 degrees for 1 hour. Let stand for 10 minutes. Invert onto serving plate.

Approx Per Serving: Cal 352; T Fat 11 g; 26% Calories from Fat;
   Prot 3 g; Carbo 63 g; Fiber 1 g; Chol 61 mg; Sod 177 mg.

Sunshine Sherry Cake

Yield: 16 servings

1 2-layer package lemon cake mix
1 4-ounce package lemon instant pudding mix
½ cup vegetable oil
1 cup sherry brandy
4 eggs
1 tablespoon freshly grated orange rind

1 16-ounce jar orange marmalade
3 tablespoons sherry brandy
1 11-ounce can mandarin orange slices, drained
1 cup whipping cream
2 tablespoons sugar
1 tablespoon sherry brandy

Combine first 6 ingredients in mixer bowl. Beat at low speed for 1 minute. Beat at medium speed for 4 minutes. Pour into greased 10-inch tube pan. Bake at 350 degrees for 45 minutes or until cake tests done. Cool in pan on wire rack for 15 minutes. Invert onto wire rack to cool completely. Bring marmalade and 3 tablespoons sherry to a boil in saucepan, stirring constantly. Simmer for 5 minutes. Cool. Split cake into 2 layers. Spoon marmalade mixture between layers and over top, allowing mixture to drip down side of cake. Arrange orange slices on cake. Whip cream with sugar and 1 tablespoon sherry in bowl until soft peaks form. Dollop on cake. Serve immediately or chill for up to 4 hours.

Approx Per Serving: Cal 429; T Fat 16 g; 35% Calories from Fat;
    Prot 3 g; Carbo 65 g; Fiber <1 g; Chol 74 mg; Sod 274 mg.

Tennessee Black Walnut Cake

Yield: 16 servings

½ cup butter, softened
½ cup shortening
2 cups sugar
5 egg yolks
2 cups flour
1 teaspoon baking soda
1 cup buttermilk
1½ teaspoons vanilla extract

5 egg whites, stiffly beaten
1 cup chopped black walnuts
1 cup coconut
8 ounces cream cheese, softened
¼ cup butter, softened
1 1-pound package confectioners' sugar
1 teaspoon vanilla extract

Cream butter, shortening and sugar in bowl until light and fluffy. Beat in egg yolks. Add flour alternately with baking soda dissolved in buttermilk, mixing well after each addition. Beat in 1½ teaspoons vanilla. Fold in egg whites gently. Fold in walnuts and coconut. Pour into 3 greased and floured 8-inch cake pans. Bake at 350 degrees for 30 minutes. Beat cream cheese and ¼ cup butter in mixer bowl. Add confectioners' sugar and 1 teaspoon vanilla; beat until of spreading consistency. Spread between layers and over top and side of cake.

Approx Per Serving: Cal 566; T Fat 28 g; 43% Calories from Fat;
    Prot 7 g; Carbo 75 g; Fiber 1 g; Chol 106 mg; Sod 202 mg.

Pies

Applesauce Cheese Pie

Yield: 6 servings

1½ cups gingersnap crumbs
5 tablespoons melted margarine
2 cups low-fat cottage cheese
2 eggs
½ cup sugar

¼ cup flour
2 tablespoons lemon juice
1 cup applesauce
1 cup whipped topping
1 teaspoon nutmeg

Mix crumbs and margarine in bowl. Press into 9-inch pie plate. Beat cottage cheese in bowl. Beat in eggs, sugar, flour, lemon juice and applesauce. Pour into prepared pie plate. Bake at 325 degrees for 1 hour and 10 minutes or until set; cool. Top with whipped topping and nutmeg.

Approx Per Serving: Cal 499; T Fat 19 g; 35% Calories from Fat;
Prot 16 g; Carbo 66 g; Fiber 1 g; Chol 77 mg; Sod 666 mg.

Fried Apple Pies

Yield: 24 servings

8 ounces dried apples
1 cup water
2 tablespoons melted margarine
¾ cup sugar

1 teaspoon cinnamon
¼ teaspoon nutmeg
2 tablespoons lemon juice
24 uncooked canned biscuits

Simmer apples in water in saucepan for 30 minutes or until tender; cool. Add margarine, sugar, spices and lemon juice; mash well. Roll each biscuit into 4-inch circle. Spoon 1 tablespoon apple mixture onto each circle; moisten edges. Fold over, sealing edges with fork. Fry in hot oil in large skillet over medium heat until brown; drain.

Approx Per Serving: Cal 121; T Fat 3 g; 23% Calories from Fat;
Prot 2 g; Carbo 22 g; Fiber 2 g; Chol 1 mg; Sod 269 mg.
Nutritional information does not include oil for frying.

Amaretto Banana-Coconut Pie

Yield: 6 servings

19 graham crackers, crushed
6 tablespoons melted margarine
2 4-ounce packages coconut
   cream instant pudding mix

1/2 cup Amaretto
3 1/2 cups milk
2 bananas, sliced
1/4 cup flaked coconut, toasted

Combine graham cracker crumbs and margarine in bowl; mix well. Press over bottom and side of 9-inch pie plate. Bake at 350 degrees for 10 minutes. Let stand until cool. Combine pudding mix, 1/2 cup Amaretto and 3 1/2 cups milk in bowl; mix well. Layer 1/4 of the pudding, bananas and remaining pudding in prepared pie plate. Sprinkle with toasted coconut. Chill in refrigerator. Serve with whipped topping.

Approx Per Serving: Cal 551; T Fat 20 g; 34% Calories from Fat;
    Prot 7 g; Carbo 81 g; Fiber 2 g; Chol 19 mg; Sod 585 mg.

Ambrosia Yum-Yum Pie

Yield: 8 servings

1 11-ounce can mandarin
   oranges
1 tablespoon cornstarch
8 ounces cream cheese, softened
1 14-ounce can sweetened
   condensed milk

1/3 cup lemon juice
1 teaspoon vanilla extract
1 9-inch graham cracker pie
   shell
1/2 cup coconut, toasted

Drain mandarin oranges, reserving 1/2 cup juice. Pat orange sections dry; cut into halves. Mix reserved juice with cornstarch in saucepan. Cook until thickened, stirring constantly. Beat cream cheese in mixer bowl until light and fluffy. Add condensed milk gradually, beating constantly after each addition. Beat in lemon juice and vanilla. Spoon half the cream cheese mixture into pie shell. Layer oranges, orange sauce and remaining cream cheese mixture on top. Sprinkle with toasted coconut. Chill for 3 hours. Garnish with additional mandarin orange slices and fresh mint.

Approx Per Serving: Cal 531; T Fat 28 g; 46% Calories from Fat;
    Prot 8 g; Carbo 64 g; Fiber 2 g; Chol 48 mg; Sod 390 mg.

Artichoke

Chocolate Amaretto Pie

Yield: 8 servings

1/4 cup unsalted butter
1/2 cup baking cocoa
1 cup unsalted butter, softened
1 1/2 cups superfine sugar

1/4 cup Amaretto
4 eggs, at room temperature
1 baked 9-inch deep-dish pie
  shell

Melt 1/4 cup butter in small heavy saucepan. Remove from heat. Stir in baking cocoa. Cream 1 cup butter, sugar and Amaretto in large mixer bowl. Beat in chocolate mixture gradually. Add eggs 1 at a time, beating for 3 minutes after each addition. Beat until sugar is completely dissolved. Pour into pie shell. Chill, covered, for 4 hours or until firm.

Approx Per Serving: Cal 605; T Fat 41 g; 60% Calories from Fat;
    Prot 6 g; Carbo 55 g; Fiber 2 g; Chol 184 mg; Sod 192 mg.

Chocolate Mousse Pie

Yield: 6 servings

4 egg whites
1 cup sugar
1/4 teaspoon cream of tartar
1 egg
2 egg yolks
1 cup chocolate chips, melted

1 teaspoon rum extract
1 cup whipping cream, whipped
2 egg whites, stiffly beaten
1 cup whipping cream
2 tablespoons sugar

Beat 4 egg whites in mixer bowl until soft peaks form. Add mixture of 1 cup sugar and cream of tartar gradually, beating until stiff. Spoon into greased and lightly floured 9-inch pie plate; shape into shell. Bake at 275 degrees until light brown and dry. Beat 1 egg and 2 egg yolks in mixer bowl. Add melted chocolate; mix well. Stir in rum extract. Fold whipped cream and stiffly beaten egg whites gently into chocolate mixture. Spoon into cooled meringue shell. Whip 1 cup whipping cream in mixer bowl until frothy. Add 2 tablespoons sugar gradually, beating until soft peaks form. Spread on pie, sealing to edge. Garnish with grated semisweet or sweet chocolate. Chill in refrigerator. May substitute vanilla extract for rum extract.

Approx Per Serving: Cal 614; T Fat 42 g; 60% Calories from Fat;
    Prot 8 g; Carbo 57 g; Fiber 1 g; Chol 215 mg; Sod 99 mg.

The pastel blossoms of hollyhocks have a slightly sweet flavor. They are especially good stuffed.

Coffee Toffee Pie

Yield: 8 servings

1½ cups flour
6 tablespoons butter, softened
¼ cup packed brown sugar
¾ cup finely chopped pecans
1 ounce unsweetened
   chocolate, grated
1 teaspoon vanilla extract
1 tablespoon water
¾ cup butter, softened

1 cup sugar
1½ ounces unsweetened
   chocolate, melted
1 tablespoon instant coffee
3 eggs
2 cups whipping cream
½ cup confectioners' sugar
2 tablespoons instant coffee
2 tablespoons Kahlua

Combine flour, 6 tablespoons butter, brown sugar, pecans, grated chocolate, vanilla and water in bowl; mix well. Press over bottom and side of buttered 10-inch pie plate. Bake at 350 degrees for 15 minutes. Let stand until cool. Cream ¾ cup butter in mixer bowl. Add sugar gradually, beating until light and fluffy. Stir in cooled melted chocolate and 1 tablespoon instant coffee powder. Beat in eggs 1 at a time. Spoon into prepared pie plate. Beat whipping cream in mixer bowl until frothy. Add confectioners' sugar, 2 tablespoons coffee powder and Kahlua gradually, beating until soft peaks form. Spread on pie, sealing to edge. Chill for 2 hours. Garnish with chocolate curls. May freeze and defrost pie before serving if desired.

Approx Per Serving: Cal 843; T Fat 62 g; 65% Calories from Fat;
   Prot 8 g; Carbo 68 g; Fiber 3 g; Chol 231 mg; Sod 272 mg.

Ice Cream Pie

Yield: 6 servings

1½ cups cornflakes, crushed
¼ cup melted butter
½ cup packed brown sugar
½ cup coconut, toasted
½ cup chopped pecans

½ gallon vanilla ice cream,
   softened
1 6-ounce can frozen
   lemonade concentrate,
   thawed

Mix crushed cornflakes, butter, brown sugar, coconut and pecans in bowl. Press over bottom and side of 9-inch pie plate. Combine softened ice cream with lemonade concentrate in bowl; mix well. Spoon into prepared pie plate. Freeze until firm. Garnish with lemon rind and fresh mint. May double crust recipe and fill second pie shell with ½ gallon softened coffee ice cream; drizzle with chocolate or fudge sauce before serving.

Approx Per Serving: Cal 724; T Fat 36 g; 43% Calories from Fat;
   Prot 9 g; Carbo 97 g; Fiber 2 g; Chol 99 mg; Sod 442 mg.

Florida Key Lime Pie

Yield: 6 servings

1¼ cups vanilla wafer crumbs
1¼ cups graham cracker crumbs
3 tablespoons sugar
1 teaspoon cinnamon
¹⁄₃ cup melted margarine
3 egg yolks

1 14-ounce can sweetened
   condensed milk
2 tablespoons sour cream
¹⁄₂ cup Key lime juice
1 teaspoon grated lime rind

Mix vanilla wafer crumbs, graham cracker crumbs, sugar and cinnamon in bowl. Add melted margarine; mix well. Press over bottom and side of 9-inch pie plate. Bake at 325 degrees for 8 minutes. Chill in refrigerator. Beat egg yolks in mixer bowl. Add condensed milk and sour cream; mix well. Add lime juice and lime rind gradually, beating well after each addition. Spoon into prepared pie plate. Chill in refrigerator for 24 hours. May top with meringue if preferred.

Approx Per Serving: Cal 651; T Fat 36 g; 49% Calories from Fat;
    Prot 10 g; Carbo 77 g; Fiber 1 g; Chol 143 mg; Sod 549 mg.

Raspberry Cream Cheese Pie

Yield: 6 servings

4 ounces cream cheese, softened
¹⁄₄ cup confectioners' sugar
¹⁄₂ teaspoon vanilla extract
¹⁄₄ cup whipped topping
1 baked 10-inch pie shell
1 cup sugar

¹⁄₄ cup dry raspberry gelatin
¹⁄₄ cup cornstarch
1 cup water
4 cups fresh raspberries
2 cups whipped topping

Beat cream cheese, confectioners' sugar and vanilla in mixer bowl until smooth. Stir in ¹⁄₄ cup whipped topping. Spread in pie shell. Chill in refrigerator. Mix sugar, gelatin and cornstarch in saucepan. Stir in water. Bring to a boil. Cook for 1 minute, stirring constantly. Pour over raspberries in bowl; mix gently. Spoon into prepared pie shell. Chill overnight. Spread with 2 cups whipped topping before serving.

Approx Per Serving: Cal 546; T Fat 25 g; 41% Calories from Fat;
    Prot 5 g; Carbo 78 g; Fiber 6 g; Chol 21 mg; Sod 280 mg.

Squash Blossoms

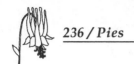

Macadamia Nut Pie

Yield: 6 servings

1¹/₂ teaspoons unflavored
    gelatin
¹/₄ cup cold water
1 cup roasted unsalted
    macadamia nuts
1 tablespoon sugar
3 egg yolks

¹/₂ cup sugar
¹/₄ teaspoon salt
1 cup whipping cream, whipped
1 teaspoon vanilla extract
1 baked 9-inch pie shell
1 cup whipping cream
1 tablespoon sugar

Soften unflavored gelatin in cold water in small bowl for 10 minutes. Place small bowl in large bowl of simmering water; stir until gelatin is completely dissolved. Let stand until cool and syrupy. Combine macadamia nuts and 1 tablespoon sugar in food processor container. Process with steel blade for 30 seconds. Beat egg yolks, ¹/₂ cup sugar and salt in mixer bowl until thick and lemon-colored. Stir in gelatin and macadamia nuts. Fold in whipped cream and vanilla. Spoon into cooled pie shell. Chill for 4 hours or until set. Whip 1 cup whipping cream in mixer bowl until frothy. Add 1 tablespoon sugar gradually, beating until soft peaks form. Spread on pie, sealing to edge.

Approx Per Serving: Cal 702; T Fat 59 g; 74% Calories from Fat;
    Prot 7 g; Carbo 39 g; Fiber 2 g; Chol 215 mg; Sod 309 mg.

Dried Peach Custard Pie

Yield: 6 servings

¹/₂ cup dried peaches
1 cup (or more) water
1¹/₂ cups plus 2 tablespoons
    sugar
2 tablespoons butter, softened
2 tablespoons flour
3 egg yolks, beaten

1 cup milk
1 teaspoon vanilla extract
¹/₈ teaspoon salt
1 unbaked 9-inch pie shell
5 egg whites
6 tablespoons sugar
¹/₈ teaspoon salt

Cook peaches in water in saucepan until tender. Drain and mash well. Add ¹/₂ cup plus 2 tablespoons sugar; mix well. Let stand until cool. Cream remaining 1 cup sugar, butter and flour in mixer bowl. Add egg yolks, milk, vanilla and ¹/₈ teaspoon salt. Add peaches; mix well. Spoon into pie shell. Bake at 350 degrees until set. Let stand until cool. Beat egg whites until soft peaks form. Add 6 tablespoons sugar and ¹/₈ teaspoon salt gradually, beating until stiff. Spread on cooled pie, sealing to edge. Bake until lightly browned.

Approx Per Serving: Cal 543; T Fat 18 g; 29% Calories from Fat;
    Prot 8 g; Carbo 89 g; Fiber 1 g; Chol 122 mg; Sod 369 mg.

Paradise Pumpkin Pie

Yield: 6 servings

8 ounces cream cheese, softened
1/4 cup sugar
1/2 teaspoon vanilla extract
1 egg, slightly beaten
1 unbaked 9-inch pie shell
1 1/4 cups canned pumpkin
1 cup evaporated milk

2 eggs, slightly beaten
1/2 cup sugar
1 teaspoon cinnamon
1/4 teaspoon ginger
1/4 teaspoon nutmeg
1/4 teaspoon salt
1 tablespoon maple syrup

Beat cream cheese and 1/4 cup sugar in mixer bowl until smooth. Add vanilla and 1 egg; mix well. Spoon into pie shell. Combine pumpkin, evaporated milk, 2 eggs, 1/2 cup sugar, cinnamon, ginger, nutmeg and salt in mixer bowl; mix well. Pour carefully over cream cheese layer. Bake at 350 degrees for 1 hour or until set. Let stand until cool. Brush top with maple syrup.

Approx Per Serving: Cal 501; T Fat 29 g; 52% Calories from Fat;
Prot 11 g; Carbo 50 g; Fiber 2 g; Chol 160 mg; Sod 467 mg.

Strawberry Glaze Pie

Yield: 6 servings

1 cup water
3 tablespoons light corn syrup
1 cup sugar
3 tablespoons cornstarch
3 tablespoons strawberry
    gelatin

Several drops of red food
    coloring
1 quart strawberries, hulled
1 baked 9-inch pie shell

Combine water, corn syrup, sugar and cornstarch in heavy saucepan; mix well. Bring to a boil over low heat, stirring constantly; reduce heat. Simmer until syrup is transparent. Add gelatin and food coloring. Cook until gelatin is dissolved, stirring constantly. Arrange strawberries in pie shell starting at outer edge. Pour syrup over strawberries. Chill in refrigerator.

Approx Per Serving: Cal 364; T Fat 10 g; 25% Calories from Fat;
Prot 3 g; Carbo 68 g; Fiber 3 g; Chol 0 mg; Sod 201 mg.

Remove a few scales from the base of expensive bulbs such as the genus lilium. Keep scales in slightly moistened peat moss for several months to grow a number of small bulblets exactly like the parent bulb.

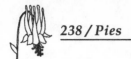

Frozen Strawberry Margarita Pie   *Yield: 8 servings*

½ cup butter
1¼ cups crushed salted pretzels
½ cup sugar
1 14-ounce can sweetened
   condensed milk
¼ cup lime juice

3 tablespoons Tequila
3 tablespoons Triple Sec
½ cup thawed frozen
   strawberries with syrup
2 cups whipping cream,
   whipped

Melt butter in saucepan over low heat. Remove from heat. Add pretzel crumbs and sugar; mix well. Press mixture over bottom and side of greased 9-inch pie plate. Freeze until firm. Combine condensed milk, lime juice, Tequila and Triple Sec in large mixer bowl. Beat at medium speed for 3 minutes or until smooth. Add strawberries with syrup. Beat at low speed for 30 seconds. Fold whipped cream gently into strawberry mixture. Spoon into prepared pie plate mounding filling in center. Freeze for 2 hours. Remove from freezer; wrap airtight. Freeze overnight. Transfer to refrigerator 30 minutes before serving. Garnish with 3 thin pretzel sticks or 3 strawberry slices shaped into a fan.

Approx Per Serving: Cal 621; T Fat 38 g; 57% Calories from Fat;
    Prot 7 g; Carbo 59 g; Fiber 1 g; Chol 129 mg; Sod 398 mg.

Real Food Heart Healthy Pie Crust   *Yield: 8 servings*

*This pie crust is best when the filling is allowed to "marry" the crust.
Chill filling in pie shell overnight and serve the following day.*

1 to 2 cups ground roasted
   almonds

3 to 6 tablespoons rolled barley
2 to 4 tablespoons water

Process almonds and barley in food processor until smooth. Add water gradually, processing until soft ball forms. Press over bottom and side of 10-inch pie plate; flute edge. Bake at 350 degrees for 30 to 40 minutes. Do not overbake. May substitute baby oats or wheat flour for barley. May make 2 smaller pie shells, if desired.

Approx Per Serving: Cal 438; T Fat 36 g; 69% Calories from Fat;
    Prot 12 g; Carbo 24 g; Fiber 11 g; Chol 0 mg; Sod 8 mg.

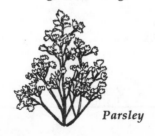

Parsley

Cookies & Candies

Fly With the Birds

Pacific Region

Alaska • Arizona • California • Hawaii • Idaho
Nevada • Oregon • Washington

*T*ruly a region of contrasts, from North America's highest spot at Mt. McKinley to the lowest in Death Valley; from heating homes in Idaho with underground hot springs to constructing "moose" fences in Alaska to protect community gardens. With thousands of acres of forest land, fertile valleys, coastlines, mountains, volcanoes and deserts, it is natural that members have been in the forefront of environmental concerns to protect the beauty and grandeur of the region.

Basque Lamb Barbecue

The Basque people came to Umatilla County in Oregon during the early pioneer days. Many of the men became shepherds and, dressed in their native garb, they were colorful, happy people lending special character to the hillsides in this noted sheep country.

Basque Lamb Chops*   Layered Egg and Potato Salad*
Buttered Corn on the Cob
Garlic Bread or Shepherd's Bread*

Delicious Alaskan Dinner

Halibut au Gratin*   Parslied Potatoes
Fiddlehead Fern Stir-Fry*   Cabbage Carrot Salad
Raspberry Cream Cheese Pie*

Luau Hawaiian-Style

Hawaiian Sesame Shrimp*
Stuffed Lychee*   Lomi Salmon*
Kalua Pig Mainland-Style*   Sweet Potatoes
Rice   Chicken Luau*
Mixed Fruit Platter   Haupia*
*See index for recipes.

Cookies

Almond Swedish Brownies

Yield: 24 servings

1 cup melted butter
2 teaspoons almond extract
4 eggs, slightly beaten
2 cups sugar
2¹/₂ cups flour

¹/₂ teaspoon salt
4 ounces sliced almonds
3 tablespoons sugar
¹/₄ teaspoon cinnamon

Beat first 6 ingredients in mixer bowl. Spoon into 10x15-inch baking pan. Sprinkle with almonds, 3 tablespoons sugar and cinnamon. Bake at 325 degrees for 30 minutes or until edges pull from side of pan. Cool and cut into squares.

Approx Per Serving: Cal 228; T Fat 11 g; 44% Calories from Fat;
    Prot 3 g; Carbo 29 g; Fiber 1 g; Chol 56 mg; Sod 122 mg.

Almond Madeleines

Yield: 24 servings

6 tablespoons unsalted butter,
    softened
2 tablespoons toasted almond
    oil
2 egg yolks

²/₃ cup sugar
1 cup sifted flour
1 teaspoon baking powder
2 egg whites, stiffly beaten
¹/₄ cup ground toasted almonds

Cream butter and almond oil in bowl. Beat egg yolks and sugar in mixer bowl. Add butter mixture and mixture of flour and baking powder. Fold egg whites into batter with ground almonds. Fill 24 buttered and floured madeleine molds ¹/₂ full. Bake at 400 degrees for 10 to 15 minutes or until golden brown. Cool on wire rack.

Approx Per Serving: Cal 88; T Fat 5 g; 52% Calories from Fat;
    Prot 1 g; Carbo 9 g; Fiber <1 g; Chol 26 mg; Sod 19 mg.

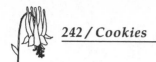

Biscochitos

Yield: 48 servings

1 cup lard
1/2 cup sugar
1 egg
3 cups flour
1 1/2 teaspoons baking powder

1/2 teaspoon salt
3 tablespoons sweet wine
1 teaspoon aniseed
1/4 cup sugar
1 tablespoon cinnamon

Cream lard and 1/2 cup sugar in mixer bowl until light. Beat in egg until fluffy. Sift flour, baking powder and salt together. Add to creamed mixture. Stir in wine and aniseed. Roll dough 1/4 inch thick on floured surface. Cut into squares. Sprinkle mixture of 1/4 cup sugar and cinnamon on top. Place on baking sheet. Bake at 350 degrees for 15 to 20 minutes or until golden brown. Remove to wire rack to cool. May substitute shortening for lard.

Approx Per Serving: Cal 82; T Fat 4 g; 50% Calories from Fat;
Prot 1 g; Carbo 9 g; Fiber <1 g; Chol 9 mg; Sod 34 mg.

Choco-Mint Cookies

Yield: 48 servings

3/4 cup margarine
1 1/2 cups packed dark brown
sugar
2 tablespoons water
2 cups semisweet chocolate
chips

2 eggs
1 1/2 cups flour
1 1/4 teaspoons baking soda
1/2 teaspoon salt
24 (or more) Andes mints, cut
into halves

Combine margarine, brown sugar and water in glass bowl. Microwave on High until melted. Add chocolate chips; stir until melted. Spoon mixture into mixer bowl. Let stand for 10 minutes or until cool. Add eggs 1 at a time, beating well at high speed after each addition. Add flour, baking soda and salt; beat at low speed until blended. Chill dough for 1 hour. Shape dough into small balls. Place on nonstick cookie sheet. Bake at 350 degrees for 8 to 10 minutes or until firm. Place 1/2 mint on top of each cookie. Let stand until softened. Swirl softened candy on top of each cookie. Remove to wire rack to cool.

Approx Per Serving: Cal 134; T Fat 6 g; 40% Calories from Fat;
Prot 1 g; Carbo 20 g; Fiber <1 g; Chol 9 mg; Sod 95 mg.

*Early spring flowering shrubs should be pruned
after they have finished blooming to remove
blossoms of buds formed in the fall
of the year before.*

Crème de Menthe Squares

Yield: 16 servings

1/2 cup butter, softened
1 cup sugar
4 eggs
1 cup flour
1/2 teaspoon salt
1 16-ounce can chocolate syrup

1 teaspoon vanilla extract
2 cups confectioners' sugar
1/2 cup butter, softened
3 tablespoons Crème de Menthe
1 cup chocolate chips
6 tablespoons butter

Cream 1/2 cup butter and sugar in mixer bowl until light and fluffy. Beat in eggs. Add flour, salt, chocolate syrup and vanilla; mix well. Spoon into greased 9x13-inch baking pan. Bake at 350 degrees for 30 to 35 minutes or until layer tests done. Let stand until cool. Beat confectioners' sugar, 1/2 cup butter and Crème de Menthe in mixer bowl until smooth. Frost cooled baked layer. Let stand for 20 minutes. Melt chocolate chips and 6 tablespoons butter in double boiler, stirring until smooth. Spread over layers. Cut into squares before chocolate becomes firm.

Approx Per Serving: Cal 424; T Fat 22 g; 44% Calories from Fat;
    Prot 4 g; Carbo 58 g; Fiber 1 g; Chol 96 mg; Sod 243 mg.

Chocolate Revel Bars

Yield: 75 servings

1 cup margarine, softened
2 cups packed brown sugar
2 eggs
2 teaspoons vanilla extract
2 1/2 cups flour
1 teaspoon baking soda
1 teaspoon salt
3 cups oats

1 14-ounce can sweetened
    condensed milk
2 cups chocolate chips
2 tablespoons butter
1/2 teaspoon salt
1 cup chopped walnuts
2 teaspoons vanilla extract

Cream margarine and brown sugar in mixer bowl until light and fluffy. Beat in eggs and 2 teaspoons vanilla. Sift flour, baking soda and salt together in bowl. Stir in oats. Add dry ingredients to creamed mixture; mix well. Combine condensed milk, chocolate chips, butter and 1/2 teaspoon salt in heavy saucepan. Cook over low heat until chocolate chips melt, stirring frequently. Stir in walnuts and 2 teaspoons vanilla. Pat 2/3 of the oat mixture in 10x15-inch baking pan. Spread chocolate mixture over top. Dot with remaining oat mixture. Bake at 350 degrees for 25 to 30 minutes or until light brown. Let stand until cool. Cut into 1x2-inch bars.

Approx Per Serving: Cal 132; T Fat 6 g; 41% Calories from Fat;
    Prot 2 g; Carbo 18 g; Fiber 1 g; Chol 8 mg; Sod 98 mg.

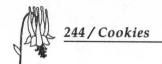

Homemade Fig Bars

Yield: 30 servings

These cookies are "better than store-bought." They ship well, are great on trips, and will keep for several weeks in the refrigerator.

1½ cups whole wheat flour
¾ cup all-purpose flour
½ cup packed brown sugar
¼ cup wheat germ
1 teaspoon baking powder
1 teaspoon cinnamon
½ teaspoon salt
2 eggs, slightly beaten
⅓ cup melted butter

¼ cup honey
¼ cup molasses
1 cup orange juice
1 tablespoon finely chopped
  orange rind
1 teaspoon vanilla extract
1 cup chopped figs
¾ cup chopped raisins
¾ cup (or more) chopped walnuts

Mix whole wheat flour, all-purpose flour, brown sugar, wheat germ, baking powder, cinnamon and salt in large mixer bowl. Combine eggs, butter, honey, molasses, orange juice, orange rind and vanilla in bowl; mix well. Add to dry ingredients; beat until smooth. Stir in figs, raisins and walnuts. Spread in greased 9x13-inch baking pan. Bake at 350 degrees for 35 minutes or until edges pull from side of pan. Cool on wire rack. Cut into bars.

Approx Per Serving: Cal 136; T Fat 5 g; 29% Calories from Fat;
  Prot 3 g; Carbo 23 g; Fiber 2 g; Chol 20 mg; Sod 72 mg.

Ginger Cookies

Yield: 72 servings

These cookies ship well and have been sent to many foreign countries including to troops in Operation Desert Storm.

1½ cups shortening
2 cups sugar
2 eggs
½ cup molasses
4 cups sifted flour

2 teaspoons baking soda
2 teaspoons cinnamon
2 teaspoons ground cloves
2 teaspoons ginger
1 cup (or more) sugar

Cream shortening and 2 cups sugar in mixer bowl until light and fluffy. Beat in eggs and molasses. Add flour, baking soda, cinnamon, cloves and ginger; mix well. Chill dough for several hours to overnight. Shape dough into 1-inch balls; dip in remaining 1 cup sugar. Place on greased cookie sheet. Flatten slightly. Bake at 375 degrees for 8 to 10 minutes or until cookies rise slightly and then flatten. Remove to wire rack to cool. Store in airtight container.

Approx Per Serving: Cal 100; T Fat 4 g; 40% Calories from Fat;
  Prot 1 g; Carbo 14 g; Fiber <1 g; Chol 6 mg; Sod 25 mg.

Oregon Filbert Clouds

Yield: 40 servings

1 cup butter, softened
5 tablespoons sugar
1 teaspoon vanilla extract
2 cups sifted flour

2 cups very finely ground
  filberts
40 whole filberts
1/2 cup confectioners' sugar

Beat butter at high speed in mixer bowl until creamy and almost white. Beat in sugar 1 tablespoonful at a time. Add vanilla; mix well. Add flour gradually, beating well after each addition. Beat in ground filberts 1/2 cupful at a time. Beat at high speed for 3 to 5 minutes or until fluffy. Chill dough for 1 hour. Shape dough into walnut-sized balls. Arrange on greased cookie sheet. Press 1 whole filbert into each cookie. Bake at 325 degrees for 15 to 20 minutes or until golden brown. Cool slightly. Sift confectioners' sugar over tops of cookies. Cool completely. Store cookies in airtight container.

Approx Per Serving: Cal 129; T Fat 10 g; 68% Calories from Fat;
    Prot 2 g; Carbo 9 g; Fiber 1 g; Chol 12 mg; Sod 39 mg.

Italian Filled Cookies

Yield: 72 servings

2 cups chopped dates
1/2 cup butter
2 cups chopped pecans
1 cup raisins
1/2 cup grated orange rind
1/2 cup sugar
2 tablespoons rum flavoring

5 eggs, slightly beaten
2/3 cup vegetable oil
1 cup sugar
2 tablespoons baking powder
1/2 teaspoon vanilla extract
4 cups flour
1 cup confectioners' sugar

Combine dates, butter, pecans, raisins, orange rind, 1/2 cup sugar and rum flavoring in saucepan. Bring to a boil; reduce heat. Cook until thickened, stirring constantly. Let stand until cool. Combine eggs, oil, 1 cup sugar, baking powder and vanilla in mixer bowl; mix well. Add flour; mix well. Divide dough into 6 portions. Roll each portion into 5-inch wide rectangle on lightly floured surface. Spread each rectangle with filling. Roll from long side to enclose filling. Place seam side down 2 inches apart on ungreased cookie sheet. Bake at 375 degrees for 15 minutes. Remove to wire racks to cool. Roll in confectioners' sugar. Slice rolls diagonally. May substitute prunes for dates or water for rum flavoring if desired.

Approx Per Serving: Cal 128; T Fat 6 g; 39% Calories from Fat;
    Prot 1 g; Carbo 18 g; Fiber 1 g; Chol 18 mg; Sod 44 mg.

Kifles

Yield: 24 servings

*This old Polish recipe is fun to make and is wonderful
to serve for holidays or teas.*

1 cake compressed yeast
2 cups flour
1/2 cup margarine
2 egg yolks
1/2 cup sour cream

1 cup finely chopped walnuts
1/2 cup sugar
1 teaspoon vanilla extract
2 egg whites, stiffly beaten
1 cup confectioners' sugar

Crumble yeast into flour in large bowl. Cut in margarine with pastry blender. Add egg yolks and sour cream; mix well. Shape into ball and knead. Divide into 3 portions. Wrap each portion individually in waxed paper. Chill for 1 hour. Mix walnuts, sugar and vanilla in bowl. Fold in stiffly beaten egg whites. Roll 1 portion chilled dough into circle on surface sprinkled with confectioners' sugar. Cut each circle into 8 wedges. Place 1 heaping teaspoon walnut filling on wide end of each wedge. Roll up from wide end. Place seam side down on greased 11x14-inch cookie sheet. Bake at 350 degrees for 27 minutes or until golden brown. Remove to wire rack to cool. Store in airtight container.

Approx Per Serving: Cal 158; T Fat 8 g; 48% Calories from Fat;
    Prot 3 g; Carbo 18 g; Fiber 1 g; Chol 20 mg; Sod 53 mg.

White Chocolate Fruit Pizza

Yield: 16 servings

3/4 cup butter, softened
1/2 cup confectioners' sugar
1 1/2 cups flour
10 ounces white chocolate
1/4 cup whipping cream
8 ounces cream cheese, softened
1 cup sliced kiwifruit

1 cup sliced peaches
1 cup strawberries
1 cup blueberries
1/4 cup sugar
1 tablespoon cornstarch
1/2 cup pineapple juice

Cream butter and confectioners' sugar in mixer bowl until light and fluffy. Blend in flour. Press over bottom and side of 12-inch pizza pan. Bake at 300 degrees for 20 to 25 minutes or until light brown. Cool completely. Combine white chocolate and whipping cream in glass bowl. Microwave on High for 1 to 1 1/2 minutes or until melted; mix well. Beat in cream cheese. Spread over crust. Arrange fruit over top. Mix sugar and cornstarch in small saucepan. Blend in pineapple juice. Cook over medium heat until thickened. Cool to room temperature. Spread over fruit.

Approx Per Serving: Cal 324; T Fat 21 g; 56% Calories from Fat;
    Prot 4 g; Carbo 33 g; Fiber 2 g; Chol 48 mg; Sod 132 mg.

Lemon Zephyrs

Yield: 36 servings

1 egg, slightly beaten
1 cup sugar
3 tablespoons lemon juice
Grated rind of 1 lemon
1 cup butter, softened

1 cup confectioners' sugar
1 teaspoon lemon extract
2 cups flour
1/2 teaspoon salt

Combine egg, sugar, lemon juice and lemon rind in heavy saucepan. Cook over low heat until thickened, stirring constantly. Cream butter and confectioners' sugar in mixer bowl until light and fluffy. Add lemon extract, flour and salt; mix well. Chill in refrigerator. Divide dough into 2 portions. Roll each portion 1/4 inch thick on lightly floured surface. Cut with 1 1/4-inch cutter. Place on ungreased cookie sheet. Bake at 400 degrees for 8 to 10 minutes or until golden brown. Remove to wire rack to cool. Spread lemon filling between cookies. Do not substitute margarine for butter in this recipe.

Approx Per Serving: Cal 108; T Fat 5 g; 44% Calories from Fat;
Prot 1 g; Carbo 14 g; Fiber <1 g; Chol 20 mg; Sod 75 mg.

Fat-Free Oatmeal Raisin Cookies

Yield: 30 servings

1 cup flour
1 cup quick-cooking oats
1/2 cup sugar
1/2 teaspoon salt
1/2 teaspoon baking powder
1/2 teaspoon baking soda

1/2 teaspoon cinnamon
2 egg whites
1/3 cup corn syrup
1 teaspoon vanilla extract
1/2 cup raisins

Combine flour, oats, sugar, salt, baking powder, baking soda and cinnamon in large bowl. Stir in egg whites, corn syrup and vanilla. Add raisins; mix well. Batter will be stiff. Drop by rounded teaspoonfuls onto cookie sheet sprayed with nonstick cooking spray. Bake at 375 degrees for 8 minutes or until firm; do not overbake. Remove to wire rack to cool.

Approx Per Serving: Cal 58; T Fat <1 g; 3% Calories from Fat;
Prot 1 g; Carbo 13 g; Fiber 1 g; Chol 0 mg; Sod 60 mg.

Queen Anne's Lace

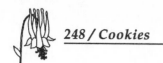

Potato Chip Cookies

Yield: 60 servings

2 cups margarine, softened
1 cup sugar
2 teaspoons vanilla extract

3 cups flour
1 cup chopped black walnuts
1 cup crushed potato chips

Cream margarine and sugar in mixer bowl until light and fluffy. Add vanilla and flour; mix well. Stir in walnuts and potato chips. Chill for 30 minutes. Shape into walnut-sized balls. Place on ungreased cookie sheet. Flatten with bottom of glass dipped in sugar. Bake at 350 degrees for 12 minutes. Remove to wire rack to cool.

Approx Per Serving: Cal 108; T Fat 8 g; 63% Calories from Fat; Prot 1 g; Carbo 9 g; Fiber <1 g; Chol 0 mg; Sod 76 mg.

Shortbread

Yield: 24 servings

1 cup butter, softened
1/2 cup sugar

2 cups flour

Cream butter and sugar in mixer bowl until light and fluffy. Add flour. Beat until smooth. Spread in nonstick 8-inch square baking pan. Prick with fork. Bake at 375 degrees for 35 to 40 minutes or until golden brown. Let stand until cool. Cut into 24 servings.

Approx Per Serving: Cal 122; T Fat 8 g; 57% Calories from Fat; Prot 1 g; Carbo 12 g; Fiber <1 g; Chol 21 mg; Sod 65 mg.

Walnut Chews

Yield: 24 servings

1 cup flour
1/2 cup butter, softened
2 tablespoons sugar
2 eggs
1 1/2 cups packed brown sugar
1 1/2 teaspoons vanilla extract

2 tablespoons flour
1/2 teaspoon baking soda
1/8 teaspoon salt
1 cup chopped maraschino cherries
1 cup chopped English walnuts
1/4 cup coconut

Combine 1 cup flour, butter and sugar in bowl; mix well. Press into 9x13-inch baking pan. Bake at 250 degrees for 20 minutes. Beat eggs, brown sugar and vanilla in mixer bowl. Add 2 tablespoons flour, baking soda and salt; mix well. Stir in cherries, walnuts and coconut. Spoon over baked layer. Increase oven temperature to 350 degrees. Bake for 30 minutes. Let stand until cool. Cut into bars.

Approx Per Serving: Cal 177; T Fat 8 g; 38% Calories from Fat; Prot 2 g; Carbo 26 g; Fiber 1 g; Chol 28 mg; Sod 75 mg.

Candies

Lace

Yield: 72 servings

1 cup oats
3 tablespoons flour
¼ teaspoon baking powder
½ teaspoon salt
1 cup sugar

½ cup finely chopped English
    walnuts
½ cup melted butter
1 tablespoon vanilla extract
1 egg, beaten

Combine oats, flour, baking powder, salt, sugar and walnuts in large bowl. Add melted butter, vanilla and egg; mix well. Chill overnight. Drop by ½ teaspoonfuls 3 inches apart onto foil-lined baking sheet. Bake at 325 degrees for 11 minutes. Lift foil from baking sheet to wire rack to cool. Remove carefully from foil.

Approx Per Serving: Cal 35; T Fat 2 g; 50% Calories from Fat;
    Prot <1 g; Carbo 4 g; Fiber <1 g; Chol 6 mg; Sod 28 mg.

Chocolate Almond Bark

Yield: 15 servings

4 ounces saltine crackers
1 cup butter
¾ cup packed brown sugar

2 cups chocolate chips
3½ ounces slivered almonds

Line 12x15-inch baking sheet with foil. Spray with nonstick cooking spray. Arrange crackers on foil. Melt butter and brown sugar in saucepan. Bring to a boil; reduce heat. Simmer for 5 minutes. Pour over crackers. Bake at 350 degrees for 5 minutes. Cool slightly. Melt chocolate chips in double boiler. Spread over baked layer. Sprinkle with almonds. Chill in refrigerator.

Approx Per Serving: Cal 345; T Fat 25 g; 61% Calories from Fat;
    Prot 3 g; Carbo 33 g; Fiber 2 g; Chol 36 mg; Sod 211 mg.

Bun Bars

Yield: 60 servings

4 cups chocolate chips
2 cups peanut butter
1 16-ounce package blanched
    peanuts
1 cup butter

2 1-pound packages
    confectioners' sugar
½ cup evaporated milk
1 4-ounce package French
    vanilla instant pudding mix

Melt chocolate chips with peanut butter in saucepan, stirring until smooth. Stir in peanuts. Spread half the mixture in greased 10x15-inch pan. Let stand until cool. Melt butter in saucepan. Add next 3 ingredients; stir until smooth. Spread over cooled layer. Spread remaining chocolate mixture over top. Cut into bars.

Approx Per Serving: Cal 258; T Fat 15 g; 50% Calories from Fat;
    Prot 5 g; Carbo 29 g; Fiber 2 g; Chol 9 mg; Sod 78 mg.

Easy Caramels

Yield: 81 servings

1 14-ounce can sweetened
    condensed milk

1 cup light corn syrup
1 teaspoon vanilla extract

Combine condensed milk and corn syrup in 2-quart saucepan. Cook over medium heat to 234 to 240 degrees on candy thermometer, soft-ball stage. Remove from heat. Stir in vanilla. Pour into buttered 9x9-inch dish; do not scrape saucepan. Cool until firm. Cut into 1-inch squares.

Approx Per Serving: Cal 27; T Fat <1 g; 14% Calories from Fat;
    Prot <1 g; Carbo 6 g; Fiber 0 g; Chol 2 mg; Sod 8 mg.

Buttercrunch

Yield: 50 servings

1 cup butter
1 cup sugar
1 tablespoon light corn syrup
3 tablespoons water

1½ cups finely chopped
    walnuts
4 ounces semisweet chocolate,
    chopped

Melt butter in 2-quart saucepan. Add sugar. Bring to a boil over medium heat, stirring constantly. Remove from heat. Add corn syrup and water; mix well. Cook over medium heat to 300 to 310 degrees on candy thermometer, hard-crack stage. Stir in ¾ cup walnuts. Pour into buttered 10x15-inch pan. Let stand until cool, running a spatula under candy 2 or 3 times to loosen. Invert onto tray. Pat remaining walnuts and chocolate on top; chill. Break into pieces. Store in refrigerator or freezer.

Approx Per Serving: Cal 84; T Fat 7 g; 69% Calories from Fat;
    Prot 1 g; Carbo 6 g; Fiber <1 g; Chol 10 mg; Sod 32 mg.

Blue Ribbon Fudge

Yield: 24 servings

This recipe won first place at the West Virginia State Fair.

1 1-pound package confectioners' sugar	6 tablespoons butter 1 tablespoon vanilla extract
1/2 cup baking cocoa	1/4 teaspoon salt
1/4 cup milk	1 cup chopped pecans

Combine first 6 ingredients in double boiler. Cook over simmering water until smooth, stirring constantly. Stir in pecans. Spread in buttered 5x9-inch loaf pan. Cool until firm. Cut into squares.

Approx Per Serving: Cal 154; T Fat 7 g; 37% Calories from Fat;
   Prot 1 g; Carbo 25 g; Fiber 1 g; Chol 8 mg; Sod 48 mg.

Pecan Pralines

Yield: 64 servings

4³/4 cups sugar	1/8 teaspoon salt
4 cups coarsely chopped pecans	3/4 cup sugar
2 cups water	2 tablespoons butter

Combine 4³/4 cups sugar, pecans, water and salt in heavy saucepan. Bring to a boil, stirring constantly. Caramelize 3/4 cup sugar in cast-iron skillet; do not scorch. Pour into pecan mixture. Cook to 240 to 248 degrees on candy thermometer, firm-ball stage. Add butter. Beat until cool. Drop by spoonfuls onto waxed paper. Let stand until cool. Store in airtight container.

Approx Per Serving: Cal 119; T Fat 5 g; 39% Calories from Fat;
   Prot 1 g; Carbo 19 g; Fiber <1 g; Chol 1 mg; Sod 8 mg.

Microwave Peanut Brittle

Yield: 16 servings

1 cup sugar	1 tablespoon butter
1/2 cup light corn syrup	1 teaspoon vanilla extract
1/4 teaspoon salt	1 teaspoon baking soda
1¹/2 cups unsalted dry-roasted peanuts	

Combine sugar, corn syrup and salt in 2-quart glass bowl. Microwave on High for 5 minutes. Stir in peanuts. Microwave for 2 to 6 minutes or until syrup and peanuts are light brown, stirring every 2 minutes. Add butter, vanilla and baking soda; stir until light and foamy. Spread 1/4 inch thick on buttered tray. Let stand until cool. Break into pieces.

Approx Per Serving: Cal 161; T Fat 7 g; 39% Calories from Fat;
   Prot 4 g; Carbo 22 g; Fiber 1 g; Chol 2 mg; Sod 98 mg.

Contributor List

Response by members of the National Council of State Garden Clubs to requests for recipes was overwhelming. Thanks to each and every contributor for being a part of this *Blooming Good* cookbook, and please excuse any errors or omissions in this tremendous list. Regional Directors are followed by an asterisk.

NEW ENGLAND
*Mrs George Saul VT ***
Mrs. William Horton, Pres. CT
Mrs. Thomas Atwell, Pres. ME
Mrs. Stephen Freidberg, Pres. MA
Mrs. Louis Krause, Pres. NH
Mrs. Robert Panoff, Pres. RI
Mrs. Richard Symons, Pres. VT
Frances Ackerman NH
Louise Ackerman NH
Helen Agar MA
Virginia Allen VT
Gladys Apgar NH
Kathy Arment MA
Shirley Barnes NH
Sib Barratt NH
Lee Bauerfeld CT
Alma Benedetti MA
Glenice Boyd MA
Meg Bremer CT
Mildred Broughton MA
Wanda Brown ME
Linda Callahan CT
Elizabeth Carpenter ME
Vicki Coderre MA
Kathleen Congdon RI
Shirley Copeland NH
Mrs. Robert Cormack NH
Jane Cote ME
Ruth Coughlin MA
Marie Crabtree NH
Julie Crocker NH
Mrs. Leslie Crompton NH
Mrs. Carl Dahlgren NH
Emily Dancause NH
Janet Davis-Schultz MA
Ann De Leo RI
Judy Dembsey NH
Penny Dickson MA
Elaine Driscoll MA
Martha Durrance ME
Margaret Dye VT
Jeanette Egan NH
Nancy Erne MA
Mary Rose Fiore CT
Loraine Fischer NH
Doris Flaherty NH
Gertrude Foley MA
Ida Foster NH
Muriel Francoeur NH
Helen Gallant NH
Jolly Gardner NH

Ginny Garland ME
Lois Gough CT
Margaret Grace NH
Mary Gray CT
Connie Gray NH
Joan Hale MA
Jean Hartka MA
Marian Hawkins NH
Alta Jo Hazard RI
Joan Heidelbach NH
Mary Hill NH
Winona Houle NH
Thelma Hutton NH
Brenda Jache NH
Janet Jackson CT
Betty Johnson MA
Irma Jones NH
Gael Ketch ME
Helene Kimball ME
Joan Kovaly MA
Dorothy Krause NH
Doris Lamprey NH
Marilyn Lane MA
Jinny Leonard MA
Madeline Lia VT
Elizabeth Locke NH
Geraldine Lynch MA
Catherine MacDonald MA
Betty MacKay NH
Lucy Magoon NH
Muriel Marsten MA
Kaye McGovern NH
Janet Meryweather ME
Marcia Michel MA
Laura Micklon NH
Betty Millner ME
Barbara Morehouse MA
Dee Mozzochi CT
Judith Niles MA
Christa Oechsle MA
Mabel Pacheco RI
Barbara Pandolfi MA
Jeanne-Marie Parkes MA
Mrs. C. U. Phillips RI
Alexandria Potter MA
Polly Povall MA
Mrs. Fletcher Pyle MA
Judy Richards MA
Judy Roberts CT
Josephine Ross ME
Carol Rumph MA
Gerry Russell MA

Bernice Russo MA
Bessie Sadlier MA
Kathy Schirf MA
Georgia Schlepegrell MA
Simone Schunder CT
E. Sjostrom NH
Lyn Slade MA
Linda Jean Smith MA
Mrs. Donald Somers MA
Southbridge G C MA
Pauline St. Martin NH
Virginia Teel MA
Mrs. H. C. Telfer NH
Carol Tennant MA
Vivan Thelin ME
Marion Thisse MA
Mrs. Theodore Thomas NH
Virginia Thurston MA
Joan Torres NH
Elsie Trull NH
Ruth Van Doren MA
Sandra Vining MA
Wareham G C MA
Mrs. William Webb MA
Mall Weiderpass RI
Mary Welch MA
Rena Wheeler NH
Becky Whitehouse NH
Celeste Wilson MA
Leona Wood VT

CENTRAL ATLANTIC
*Mrs. Frank Coulter MD ***
Mrs. Robert Shepherdson, Pres. DE
Mrs. James Moxley, Jr., Pres. MD
Mrs. Walter Bucher, Pres. NCA
Mrs. Kenneth Clevett, Pres. NJ
Mrs. Richard Corbisiero, Jr., Pres. NY
Mrs. Joseph Celin, Pres. OH
Mrs. Walter Metzger, Pres. PA
Elaine Altmaier OH
Helen Armstrong PA
Vivian Arndt OH
Mrs. John Ashby PA
Joyce Atherton NY
Antoinette Babb NY
Mrs. E. L. Barker NCA
Ethel Barnsbee NY
Betty Barrett PA
Clara Benecki DE
Carol Benn NY
Pauline Berry NJ

Lee Beveridge PA
Camille Beyer PA
Anne Bindus PA
Barbara Bix NCA
Mrs. Myron Blankenburg OH
Joan Bonine DE
Carolyn Bracken MD
Jean Brennan PA
Doris Bryan NJ
Mary Buckley PA
Lenora Bukata PA
Shari Byrne NCA
Mary Ellen Calta NY
Patricia Cargnoni NY
Nancy Carlin PA
Carol Carter NCA
Patrice Cason MD
Mrs. Douglas Cayce MD
Prue Chance DE
Pat Christie DE
Joan Cipra NJ
Iris Clarke OH
Barbara Coates OH
Mrs. Leroy Collins DE
Mary Conaway OH
Dorothy Connor PA
Mrs. Robert Conway NCA
Virginia Cooper NJ
Mary Corley NCA
Helen Cottrell NY
Elvere Cox NCA
Charlotte Cully MD
Dorothy Dailey NY
Alice Davenport NJ
Betty Davis DE
Janice Davis NY
Glenna Davis OH
Mary Ann De Graw DE
Mrs. Henry de Haan NCA
Mrs. John de Veer NY
Carmie de Vito OH
Susan Dean PA
Lyn Decker PA
Elsie Denby PA
Ingrid Dennis NY
Dorothy Dennison PA
Doreen Dew-Kaufman PA
Margaret Dinardo PA
Becky Douglass DE
Edith Duncan PA
Mrs. George Dunn NCA
Janet Eck PA
Susan Emma PA
Carolyn Epple NCA
Judith Eschweiler NY
Mary Ferry PA
Mrs. Francis Fink OH
Midge Fisher PA
Polly Flacco PA
Marcia Fransko PA
Kathy Frazer DE
Virginia Frazier DE
Jean Freedman NY
Joan Frey DE
Phyllis Frey PA

Doris Froning PA
Patricia Fulton PA
Elizabeth Galbraith NY
Doris Galione NJ
Joan Galloway PA
Mrs. John Galvin NCA
Mrs. F. L. Gardner PA
Bert Garino NCA
Patricia Garrabrant NCA
Kitty Genuardi PA
Joyce George PA
Marie Gifford OH
Helen Gilroy NY
Marian Glover OH
Sheila Goeller NY
Allison Goodwin NCA
Sally Gordon MD
Sue Gray MD
Evelyn Guinther OH
Elizabeth Hain NY
Peggy Hallowell PA
Nancy Hammersmith PA
Helen Hanna DE
Mrs. John Hannon PA
Bebe Harrison NY
Phoebe Hauber PA
Ruth Hausman PA
Rosemary Hayes NY
Kay Heasley NY
Maxine Henry DE
Ruth Herbert OH
Muriel Herzig NY
Janet Hewson NCA
Christine Hoffman MD
Margaret Hooker NCA
Kathryn Horst PA
Ellen Huelf OH
Geneva Hunt VA
Mrs. O. L. Igou NY
Virginia Ingram PA
Betsy Jackson PA
Edith Jenkins PA
Ruth Johnson DE
Marian Johnson OH
Roberta Johnson PA
Rita Johnston PA
Claire Jones MD
Jo Jones NY
Charlotte Jones NY
Katherine Kane NCA
Mary Miyares Keener NCA
Catherine Kehoe NY
Laura Kerr PA
Elizabeth Kitch MD
Lillian Koelsch NJ
Frances Kokinda PA
Jean Kolb PA
Dorothy Krape PA
Mary Lou Lachman PA
Elizabeth Lampe PA
Mrs. Milton Lang OH
Jean Lanham NY
Melba Lawless PA
Mary Leach DE
Nickie Lehman PA

Pat Lennon NY
Naomi Liggett OH
Cindy Lininger OH
Penny Lippiatt OH
Marilyn Litvack NJ
Ruth Loew PA
Dora Longway NY
Deb Majer PA
Sandy Manthorpe PA
Beth Marsh PA
Esther Martin DE
Grace Martin PA
Margaret Mask DE
Mary Maybee NY
Jan McClain NCA
Marge McCune PA
Mrs. C. Q. McGee OH
Janet McGee NCA
Louise McGraw PA
Helen McKendrick PA
Jennie McManemy OH
Edith Medina OH
Albina Merhar OH
Mary Michael DE
Gene Miller NCA
Una Miller PA
Joan Moran MD
Ann Morgan NY
Helen Morton NCA
Genevieve Mott DE
Mary Lou Mudrick PA
Charlotte Mueller NY
Flossie Narducci PA
Dorothy Nason OH
Pauline Neal PA
Kitty Newcombe PA
Peg Newill OH
Vera Ann Nichols OH
Shirley Nicolai NCA
Norristown G C PA
Dorothy Nowers NCA
Ardis O'Connor MD
Mary Ellen O'Leary NY
Alma Olson NY
Mrs. E. W. Overdorff, Jr. PA
Marlene Owens PA
Mary Jane Parrish MD
Martha Parvis DE
Patricia Passamonti NCA
Myrtle Pelletier NY
Violet Penner MD
Ann Perry PA
Helen Picciano NY
Georgette Pirkl NY
Ruth Pitts PA
Lorraine Poirier PA
Kitty Pottmeyer PA
Elaine Pringle DE
Marge Purnell OH
Martha Ann Quinn NY
Theodora Raines PA
Helen Read PA
Helen Reed PA
Lenora Reese PA
Bonnie Rehling NCA

Sally Reich NCA
Marie Reiser NY
Bertha Reppert PA
Marianne Rindfleisch NY
Elsie Ritchie NY
Mrs. Tom Ritz OH
Kathryn Riu PA
Louise Rohrbach PA
Pat Roma NY
Marge Rosher OH
Mimi Ruby NCA
Diane Ruma OH
Jean Russell NY
Mrs. J. Russell OH
Christine Russo OH
Eleanor Sable PA
Doris Sadowski NY
Connie Sancetta NY
Mrs. H. J. Sandlas, III NY
Bobbi Sandorf OH
Janice Sands MD
Joyce Schaefer DE
Margery Schriber PA
Frances Schumacher NY
Marilyn Searles NY
Charlyne Segmiller OH
Charlotte Selander OH
Jo Sellers NCA
Genet Sellers PA
Lois Shuster PA
Beatrice Sletto OH
Betty Smalley NCA
Charlotte Smith NY
Jess Smith NY
Roberta Snowberger PA
Beverley Soriano NJ
Mrs. G. F. Sparks, Jr. NJ
Adele Spraver DE
Lena Stadler NY
Phyllis Steen MD
Sharon Storm NY
Nelda Thomas MD
Carole Thompson NY
Naida Thompson NCA
Mary Ellen Timm DE
Angela Trautlein NY
Mary Troiano PA
Kathleen Troncelliti PA
Marie Twitchell NCA
Isadora Ullrich NY
Rosemarie Vassaluzzo PA
June Veronda NCA
Mrs. W. F. Wadsworth, Jr. MD
Doris Wagner PA
Mrs. J. C. Ward PA
Mrs. Reuben Warrell NY
Janet Watson DE
Shirley Wenrich PA
Marie White NCA
Jean White PA
Judith White PA
Lou Whittington MD
Shirley Wilbur NY
Lee Williams MD
Jean Williams PA

LaVerne Williams PA
Carol Wilson NY
Jane Wilson NCA
Roberta Winston OH
Darlene Wolf NCA
Nancy Jane Woolley NY
Betty Wootten DE
Mrs. N. T. Worthington, Jr. MD
Nella Wotherspoon NJ
Bobbie Wright PA
Betty Yerger PA
Mrs. K. E. York PA
Claire Zaragoza DE
Gloria Zimmerman PA

SOUTH ATLANTIC
Mrs. O. O. Van Deusen VA *
Mrs. Ramon Oliver, Pres. KY
Mrs. Kenneth Daber, Pres. NC
Mrs. Gordon Farmer, Pres. SC
Mrs. Raymond Ohmsen, Pres. VA
Mrs. Charles Sampson, Pres. WV
Pat Abercrombie SC
Josephine Abney SC
Virginia Adams VA
Margie Adkins NC
Gaynell Adkins WV
Katherine Akers WV
Mrs. G. A. Allison WV
Opal Anderson WV
Josie Arbogast WV
Georganna Ashford WV
June Ashworth WV
Judy Avampato WV
Roseann Baker NC
Debra Baker WV
Lois Baker WV
Margaret Baylis VA
Macie Beasley SC
Mrs. A. C. Bell WV
Peggy Bischoff SC
Hazel Bissett NC
Madeline Blake WV
Eloise Bland WV
Mrs. W. L. Blankenbaker VA
Geneva Blue KY
Mrs. A. P. Bohannon, Jr. VA
Phyllis Boos VA
Betty Bowman VA
Margie Broadders VA
Sandy Burgess VA
Mildred Burk WV
Mrs. Glenn Burney SC
Clara Burton WV
Mary Butt VA
Mrs. William Calfee WV
Katherine Carrigan WV
Janet Carson WV
Reba Carson WV
Dorothy Caskey KY
Betty Jo Castle NC
Martha Chaire
Elizabeth Chamberlain SC
Virginia Charlton WV
Hazel Christian WV

J. Winn Ciucci VA
Dee Clements VA
Grace Condrey VA
Mary Lynn Corning VA
Mrs. Leonard Cottrill WV
Mary Helen Cox VA
Cecile Coyhran SC
Wanda Crawford WV
Lynn Creger VA
Perrine Crouch SC
Mrs. Hunt Cunningham WV
Marian Danco VA
Elsie Daugherty WV
Wilda Davis VA
Ruth Dean WV
Nancy DeCarlo WV
Helen Decker WV
Mildred Deligne WV
Rosemary Dent WV
Mary Dixon VA
Elizabeth Dunnington VA
Irene Earnest WV
Lutoria Edmundson NC
Patria Ellison WV
Anne Emmert WV
Frances Evans WV
Thelma Everhart NC
Majel Farha WV
Alice Ferguson VA
Maxie Foster WV
Heidi Frazier SC
Shirley Frenia VA
Peggy Fuller SC
Coralee Garrett WV
Anna Gathmann NC
Kelly George WV
Toby Gilkeson WV
Mrs. Percy Gillie WV
Marie Goodlett SC
Mary Gould SC
Ginny Gray KY
Donna Green VA
Maxine Greer SC
Barbara Griffith WV
Sara Grimes SC
Marianne Gross VA
Joan Groves WV
Joan Guthrie WV
Judy Guye WV
Thelma Halsey WV
Marie Hammond SC
Grace Hancock VA
Shirley Hanson KY
Lynn Harding NC
Dot Harmon NC
Virginia Harris WV
Mrs. E. M. Harrison VA
Frances Hart SC
Mary Hawkins VA
Irene Hayes WV
Loreida Hedger WV
Alice Hedrick VA
Bob Henkel VA
Mrs. Woodrow Hinchman WV
Anne Hinnant NC

Sharon Hobbs WV
Yvonne Holt NC
Sally Janney WV
Michelle Jarrell WV
Mary Nick Johns VA
Romanza Johnson KY
Eloise Johnson NC
Jo Ann Johnson SC
Edna Jones VA
Dorothy Jones VA
Emma Jones WV
Joyce Jones WV
Loretta Jordan VA
Lori Kay VA
Mrs. Owen Keller NC
Rene Kelly WV
Mrs J. P. Kent VA
Susan Kent VA
Mrs. N. H. Key VA
Doris Killion VA
Lucy King VA
Catherine Knapp WV
Barbara Kriskovich VA
Liz Kuster KY
Shirley LaGarde SC
Lake Cumberland Garden
 Club KY
Jean Lang WV
Zelia Lawson VA
Jan Lehouck NC
Opal Lively WV
Naomi Long WV
Paul Lynn VA
Donna Marsh SC
Betty Jo Marteney WV
Mrs. Lil Martin
Theresa Martin KY
Margaret Martin KY
Frances Martin WV
Gladys Matheney WV
Helen McCoy WV
Lil McCracken WV
Mary Helen McFadden VA
Betty McGurn NC
Jan McKay VA
Julia McLaurin SC
Mildred Meredith WV
Martha Mergler VA
Mrs. G. B. Midden, Jr. KY
Orene Miller WV
Dorothy Mitchell WV
Mrs. J. Moellendick WV
Barbara Moeller NC
Martha Morgan KY
Mary Morris KY
Kate Morris WV
Sandra Morris WV
Ruth Neal VA
April Nickell WV
Maxine O'Dell WV
Virginia Otto WV
Mrs. Sam Parker VA
Mrs. Jack Peltier VA
Ramona Pennington WV
Pat Perelman WV

Mrs. George Perros KY
Hannah Phelps VA
Genevieve Philips WV
Pine Garden Club WV
Mrs. R. H. Pope WV
Hazel Pritchard WV
Pat Pyles WV
Lindsley Rada SC
Mrs. W. B. Reynolds VA
Emmagene Rhodes SC
Ann Rider WV
Janet Robarr VA
Regina Robbins WV
Annie Mae Robertson VA
Joan Robie VA
Anne Robinson VA
Betty Rogers VA
Carolyn Roof KY
Ann Samson WV
Gail Satterfield WV
Maxine Scarbro WV
Mrs. R. A. Schmitz WV
Shirley Schwenker VA
Shirley Schwork WV
Zelma Scott NC
Barbara Senecal VA
Cammie Sevy WV
Susan Kamer-Shinaberry WV
Diane Shott VA
Marie Shutt VA
Sue Skinner WV
Frances Smith NC
Mrs. Edward Smith VA
Mrs. C. Manning Smith WV
Mrs. E. A. Smith, Jr. VA
Lorene Snodderly NC
Mary Frances Snyder WV
Linda Spencer WV
Brenda Spencer WV
Mrs. Ben Stands SC
Kalliope Stanley WV
Juanita Stehly WV
Emily Stephens SC
Rosa Stephenson WV
Carol Stering WV
Mary Jane Stinson WV
Celia Stone VA
Irene Stuart WV
Richard Surgnier NC
Dot Tanner VA
Thelma Taylor VA
Theanna Tennant WV
Karen Thaxton WV
Mona Thomas WV
Evelyn Thomas WV
Leah Thomas WV
Martha Thomason SC
Gordie Thorpe WV
Mrs. C. V. Townsend WV
Julia Tuggle NC
Jeannie Turner VA
Iydella Unger KY
Barbara Van Dyne WV
Daisy Vaughan NC
Patty Veneri WV

Barbara Volk NC
Betsy Voress WV
Violet Watson VA
Esther Wellons VA
Mrs. H. A. West VA
Dee White KY
Imogene Willard WV
Nannie Williams WV
Joan Wipperman KY
Melba Woodward SC
Lee Wray VA
Martha Wright KY
Dorothy Wulfers WV
Eleanor Yates NC
Judith Young WV
Jacqueline Zacharias VA
Mrs. Aaron Zuckerman VA

DEEP SOUTH
Mrs. Noel Cumbaa MS *
Mrs. O. W. Green, Pres. AL
Mrs. W. Reese Harris, Pres. FL
Mrs. Robert Gibson, Pres. GA
Mrs. W. O. Wissman, Pres. LA
Mrs. L. C. White, Pres. MS
Mrs. Joseph Crane, Pres. TN
Letizia Adams MS
Joy Albright GA
Mrs. Jack Allinder TN
Aurora Plantation Gardeners LA
Jerri Baker MS
Betty Bangs GA
Beverly Barbaree GA
Margaret Bateler MS
Lynn Bernard LA
Mrs. F. C. Black MS
Catherine Bouler AL
Helen Bozzuto FL
Shirley Brock AL
Hazel Brownlee AL
Lillian Brundage FL
Josephine Burgess FL
Dolores Burris AL
May Calico LA
Mrs. M. U. Chambless GA
Marjorie Claybrook GA
Justine Combs GA
Ann Cooksey LA
Anne Cooper MS
Nell Cornwell FL
Janette Crawford MS
Anite Currault LA
Berne Davis FL
Mrs. Arthur Davis TN
Helen Derryberry MS
JoAnn Dollar GA
Mary Jo Dougherty TN
Mrs. E. M. Doyle MS
Linda Edington TN
Jeanne Edwards FL
Martha Evans MS
Tammy Forbus GA
Gail Frier GA
Barbara Gerace LA
Jo Gilliland MS

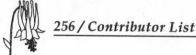

Sylvia Giovingo LA
Dian Goldwire GA
Mary Gosdin FL
Helen Gough MS
Eve Hannahs FL
Elizabeth Harris GA
Mrs. G. A. Harrison MS
Jan Haymore TN
Nancy Hendon MS
Marion Hilliard FL
Thelma Hogan LA
Cherry Horn GA
Jane Hovas MS
Laura Huff GA
Mrs. Harley Irwin TN
Evelyn Isbell AL
Dana Jackson GA
Sally Jaskelainen FL
Epsy Johnson MS
Mrs. W. F. Johnston TN
Alynda Jones GA
Mrs. Casey Jones LA
Alice Jones MS
Helen Kerner LA
Mrs. Fred Kerr TN
Mrs. J. W. King LA
Mary Kirkpatrick FL
Harriet Koella TN
Bertha Kolb MS
Orrie Laing GA
Charlotte Lasater TN
Ronnie LeMay TN
Gladys Lesser FL
Shirley Lewis GA
Mary Helen Lindsey GA
Linda Loewen GA
Nancy Long GA
Mrs. Roy Long MS
Lovely Touch G C AL
Margie Lowry AL
Kate Lynch TN
Sadie Marcello LA
Diana Marler MS
Audrey Marshall FL
Dolores Masson LA
Nedra Mathis GA
Martha McBurney LA
Ruth McKinnon GA
Kathy Merithew MS
Betty Millar TN
Alene Miller AL
Mrs. H. T. Miller MS
Bea Montgomery FL
Becky Moore AL
Jeanette Morring TN
Edna Morris AL
Louise Murray FL
Mrs. Forrest Newman MS
Peggy Newman MS
Marvina Northcutt GA
Peggy Nuse FL
Abbie Owen FL
K. T. Owens AL
Elizabeth Pajerski MS
Roberta Parrish TN

Ellen Partridge GA
Adelle Payne LA
Dorothy Penn TN
Mary Pennington TN
Nonie Post LA
Carolyn Powell MS
Candy Price MS
Alice Randazzo LA
Mrs. W. L. Rawls TN
Regina Remetich LA
Mrs. L. E. Reynolds AL
Charmaine Rini LA
Corine Roberie LA
Nancie Robinson AL
Kathleen Rourke FL
Beth Rush LA
Kathy Rychen TN
Hazel Sammons AL
Mrs. C. E. Sanford AL
Zelma Schutt TN
Sylvia Scott FL
Marion Searcy AL
Frances Seawright MS
Shirley Sharp GA
Aerline Shippey FL
Carmen Shrum FL
Murrelle Smith AL
Lorene Smith AL
Dorothy Smith FL
Lynn Smith GA
Deen Day Smith GA
Paulet Solomon MS
Elsie Stem TN
Margalee Stephenson FL
Mrs. J. R. Stingily MS
Margaret Strickland GA
Joy Stuart GA
Katie Swanson MS
Janice Thetford MS
Bob Thomas FL
Nancy Thompson LA
Ola Mae Thornton LA
Mrs. R. T. Tillman GA
M. H. Tucker LA
Carolyn Vincent FL
Audrey Watson GA
Mrs. George Weesner TN
Mechelle Wheless GA
Louise White TN
Gladys Whitesell FL
Mrs. Vernon Whitlock LA
Marguerite Williams FL
Vorene Williams MS
Louisa Witherington AL
Jo Wittchow FL
Phyllis Wood FL
Peggy Woodham AL
Marie Worley GA
Jane Youell MS
Mrs. James Young MS
Casey Zito GA
Gladys Zoellick FL

CENTRAL REGION
Mrs. Walter Breymann IA *

Mrs. Dale Schafernak, Pres. IL
Mrs. Jean Paul Christy, Pres. IN
Mrs. James Sylvester, Pres. IA
Mrs. John McGoff, Pres. MI
Mrs. Duane Roberts, Pres. MN
Mrs. Margaret Rone, Pres. MO
Mrs. Byron Murken, Pres. WI
Mary Ellen Albanese WI
Winifred Albright MI
Barbara Alexander IN
Judy Armfield MI
Marjorie Armstrong IL
Alexandra Atkin MI
Au Gres Garden Club MI
Marge Backer MO
Christine Baer MI
Jan Baker IN
Joan Ball MO
June Barber MI
Ruby Barry IA
Dottie Barry IL
Iva Baum IA
Martha Baxter MO
Peggy Bee MI
Freda Beebe IA
Joan Behm WI
Reva Bennett IA
Rosemary Benson IL
Helen Berndtson IL
Willie Betts WI
Harriet Betzold MN
Eileen Bevins IA
Linda Biagioni IL
Ruth Blair IL
Lois Blakeslee MI
Carol Blaney MO
Caroline Blochberger MO
Jamie Borrett WI
Marjorie Borror WI
Joan Bourisaw MO
Elaine Boyce WI
Genevieve Boyd IA
Alice Boyle IN
Sally Bradford MI
Hazel Bradle IL
Sophia Bradley MI
Dorothy Brenner MO
Judith Bridges IL
Lorraine Briggs IL
Phyllis Bronson MI
Helen Brostrom MN
Barbara Brott MI
Marjorie Brown IA
Opal Burd IL
Mae Martha Burgess MI
Delores Burkland IA
Mae Butler IA
Lyn Butus MI
Dianne Caliva WI
Beth Campbell IL
Jean Campbell IN
Helen Cedervall IL
Mary Nell Chew IL
Wanda Christensen IA
Beryle Christesen MN

Louise Clark IA
Nina Clausen IA
Jane Clemsen IA
Mabel Clift MO
Gertrude Collins MO
Lucille Condra IN
June Conine IN
Phyllis Connell IA
Maxine Cooper IL
Betty Corr IL
J. Arleen Corson IN
Robin Courtwright MO
Bette Cox IA
Karen Cummins MI
Bernice Curtis IL
Inge Dalbke MI
Pat Dale MI
Lillian Dalman MI
Mrs. R. E. Dalton IN
Miriam Davies IL
Violet Dawson IL
Agnes Degischer IN
Janice Derrig MN
Helen Dicke-Krivacek WI
Janet Dildine MI
Esther Dockstader IA
Jan Dougherty IA
Susan Doyle MI
Deanna Drunasky WI
Rita Drunasky WI
Joan Duncan MI
Bonnie Dunlap MO
Holly Durham MI
Louise Dusenbery MO
Pat Dvorak WI
Maurine Edmond IA
Mrs. Lee Edwards MO
Helen Eiceman MO
Marilyn Ellison IL
Ana Eng IL
Mildred Engel IA
Alice Engerer IN
Joan Eschweiler WI
Judy Eshleman IL
Adeline Evans WI
Patricia Even IA
Evelyn Eyermann WI
Winnie Fadler MO
Fannie Faqua MO
Hertha Fennern IA
Rachel Fennern IA
Diana Fleharty MI
Marcia Fletcher IA
Lucille Frank IA
Madeline Frank MI
Mary Ann Frantz IL
Grayce Friest IA
Allene Fritsch MI
Casey Funk MN
Catherine Gaines MO
Lillian Gale MI
Ethel Gallagher MI
Doris Galonski WI
Helen Garety MI
Karla Geiger WI

Mona Gerstenberger IA
Elayne Gilhausen MN
Norma Gillette MI
Martha Given IL
Carolyn Gleeson IL
Maxine Glosser IA
Bertha Goettler IN
Arlene Grace MO
Margery Graham MI
Caroline Gray MI
Gloria Greene IL
Phyllis Greiber WI
Jeannine Gundle MI
Mary Gustafson IL
Lenore Halac IL
Beatrice Halford IL
Hazel Hall IN
Barbara Hall MI
Phyllis Hall MO
Doris Hamilton MO
Marjorie Hammen MO
Jenny Hannon MO
Nellie Hanold WI
Mary Hansen MI
Myrtle Harper IA
Mrs. George Hart IA
Ruth Hartley IN
Mrs. Vil Hartog IA
Helen Hawkins IL
Rachel Hawkins IN
Agnes Hawley WI
Bernyce Heairet MN
Erie Heermann MI
Vivian Heffran IL
Luella Hein IA
Pat Heisdorf WI
Willa Helwig IA
Diane Hensen WI
Dorothy Herberg MN
Lillian Herbrandson IA
Loquitta Herren MO
Pat Herrington MI
Susan Hetzel IL
Jean Hicks MN
Lola Hill IA
Vera Hilton IA
Laura Hinderaker IA
Nadine Hofstetter MO
Evelyn Holup IL
Mildred Hoover MI
Lauran Howard MI
Maxine Huff IN
Lorraine Hughes MI
Erna Hughes WI
Janet Illston MO
Lorraine Jaeger WI
Bernardine Jagodzinski WI
Elsie Janek IL
Mrs. R. A. Johnson IA
Dolores Johnson IA
Betty Johnson WI
Joanne Kaiser IA
Margaret Kampe IL
Bernice Kaschynyc MI
Betty Jane Keil MI

Mary Keith IL
Dorothy Kelley IA
Catherine Kellogg IL
Joan Kelly IL
Esther Kennedy MN
Florence Kessler MI
Louise Kier IA
Shirlie Klaus MN
Margaret Klinger IA
Diane Knitter WI
Eileen Knox WI
Roberta Koch IL
Patty Koch WI
Dorothy Kramer IL
Jo Anne Krause MI
Barb Krebs WI
Ruth Krulce IN
Despi Kyriazes IL
Janice Lacy IN
Jayne Ladd IL
Blanche Laffey MO
Kitty Larkin WI
Mrs. M. C. Larson IA
Joanne Larson IL
Margery Larson MN
Jeanette Lawrence IA
Leona Lee IL
Jane Lee IL
Annette Lefley MI
Wilma Lesan IL
Mary Lester IL
Shirley Lewis IN
Marie Lippold IA
Genevieve Logsden IL
Lelah Long MO
Anita Luke MI
Jean Mahowald MN
Marie Maiers IA
Frances Mantler MO
Martha Marsh MI
Marilyn Martin IL
Madge Mason IA
Gloria Mather IL
Joanie Matrosic MI
Linda McCafferty IN
Alice McDaniel IL
Carmen McDonald IL
Virginia McDonough IA
Alyce McGowan IL
Genevieve McGrath MI
Lera McManama MO
Mary Ann Meador MO
Jimmie Meinhardt MO
Jane Meyer WI
Lou Milburn IL
Linda Millard WI
Faye Miller MI
Louise Milton IN
Lenore Moe MI
Susan Moesch IL
Phyllis Monte MI
Marlene Moorman IA
Dawn Mozgawa WI
Harriet Mullin IN
Sally Murphy IN

Judy Murray IL
Holly Myers IA
Mrs. C. A. Myers IN
Helen Nagel IL
Betty Nail IA
Mary Neal IL
Donna Nehil MI
Sally Neidinger IL
Mildred Nelson WI
Jean Nethery WI
Judy Newman WI
Bernice Nicolas MO
Diana Nicolas MO
Winifred Nolan IA
Mae Nothstine MO
Mary Jane Nugent IL
Judith Nykamp MI
Carmen O'Brien IN
Margaret Oberender IA
Marion Oldenburg WI
Caroline Olson WI
Margaret Oltmann IL
Gloria Ormerod WI
Ann Ostenson IL
Dorothy Page MO
Marge Parsons MN
Marjorie Patton IL
Dorothy Paulsen IA
Betty Payne IA
Zorah Pender IA
Margaret Pennington IA
Joyce Person IL
Evelyn Petersen IA
Tempest Petovello MI
Marjorie Petrick IL
Theodora Pfister IN
Clarice Phegley IN
Dee Pinski IL
Barbara Pirtle IN
Althea Pogue IN
Jeanne Poll MI
Sally Pore IL
Louise Porter IN
Judy Portz IA
Joan Posejpal IL
Ione Potter MI
Diane Powelka WI
Martha Powell MO
Dee Powers IL
Sue Presley MO
Mabel Prior IA
Jenny Prochaska IA
Marilyn Pulaski IL
Mary Pulick MI
Sandy Quam IA
Mary Jane Quinn WI
Mary Ellen Quintal IL
Carol Rapp IL
Marlene Rasmussen IA
Aliene Ray IL
Norma Reddeman WI
Carolyn Redic IL
Marie Reed IL
Suzanne Reising MI
Stella Rife IA

Kay Roberts IA
Chris Rochman MI
Kathleen Romine MO
Annette Roos IL
Edna Rosenfield MI
Virginia Rosholt IL
Julee Rosso MI
Sara Roth MO
Barbara Rusk IA
Alta Sadow MO
Mary Scanlan IL
Joyce Schick IN
Ruth Schim WI
Leonora Schmidt MO
Audrey Schoenherr WI
Veva Schreiber IL
Joyce Schumann MI
Char Schwan IL
Barbara Schwebel MO
Betsy Schwind WI
Clem Scott MN
Marion Scott MN
JoAnne Searle MI
Hazel Seaver MI
Elaine Seeliger WI
Irene Seener MO
Fran Seymour MI
Phyllis Shade MO
Wanda Shideler MI
Nellie Shmitka MN
Kay Shoemaker MI
Muriel Shurvey WI
Donna Siegner MI
Leah Sinn MO
Laurie Skrzenta IL
Phyllis Slaasted WI
Susan Slivkin IL
Cindy Smit IL
Julie Smith IL
Mable Smith MO
Constance Snell MI
Margaret Spick IA
Gerry St. Peters IN
Rebecca Steinmeier IL
Maryanne Steinmetz IN
Barbara Stephens MO
Julie Stimple IL
Helen Stoltz IL
Eleanor Strait IA
Lillian Strohm IL
Fran Stueck IA
Barbara Stuessy IL
Arlene Sturtz IA
Susie Sullivan MI
Jane Suppes MI
Lucille Swanson IA
James Sylvester IA
Kory Sylvester IA
Mary Taucher WI
Yolanda Taylor MO
Helene Teel MO
Anna Thayer MI
Doris Thomas IA
Florence Thomas IA
Virginia Thomas MO

Lenore Thompson IA
Ruby Thompson IL
Karen Timonen WI
Susie Toenjes WI
Rhea Tracy MI
Hazel Treanor MO
Sally Trimpe IN
Betty Trombetta WI
Ila Tschannen MN
Betty Tucker IL
Jean Turner IA
Alice Ullem IA
Armeline Van Slembrouck MI
Carole Van Vranken MO
Nelda Vanicek WI
Jackie Vastola WI
Phyllis Vinyard IL
Katrina Vollmer IN
Marie Voss IA
Donna Wagner IL
Val Wagner MN
Carole Wahlers IA
Mary Walker IN
Mrs. Lloyd Walton IA
Mary Lou Wangen WI
Helen Wattles MI
Shirley Weersing MI
Gladys Werner IA
Barbara Wesley WI
Janet West-Teskey MI
Elizabeth Whetsell IN
Doris White IA
Sibyl Whitehead IA
Dorothy Wick WI
Constance Wilcox MN
Joyce Wildin IA
Sally Wiley IL
Dolores Wilgenbusch IA
Marcia Wilheim IL
Betty Willasson IA
Mary Wilsberg MI
Jane Wilson MO
Lydia Wirka IA
Crista Wise MI
Mary Ann Wright IL
Edie Wurcer WI
Jane Yantis MI
Barbara Yoder IN
Janie Zieloski WI
Marian Zoller MO

SOUTH CENTRAL
Mrs. J. M. Matthews AR *
Mrs. Floyd Sleeper, Pres. AR
Mrs. Glen Graves, Pres. NM
Mrs. Garold Busse, Pres. OK
Mrs. Kenneth Blaschke, Pres. TX
Elizabeth Allbright TX
Jonni Almoney TX
Loyce Anderson OK
Doris Rae Arens OK
Priscilla Arnold TX
Andy Arnold TX
Pat Atkinson TX
Saralee Attaway TX

Carolyn Baer TX
Betty Baker TX
Mary Louise Barr TX
Kay Barron TX
Janet Barton TX
Beverly Basher TX
Marolyn Bean TX
Ruth Bentley TX
Betty Berchtold NM
Dot Best TX
Olga Bezpalko NM
Eve Billingsley TX
Frances Blades OK
Elizabeth Blevins TX
Mary Lou Boegler TX
Dorothy Bohn TX
Dolly Bolton TX
Pauline Boyd OK
Mildred Brady TX
Marie Branch TX
LaDot Branch TX
Shirley Brasseaux TX
Sibyl Brian OK
Beverly Bright TX
Vida Brine TX
Patricia Brock TX
Judith Brombacher TX
Mrs. James Brooks TX
Lois Brown OK
Phyllis Brown TX
Jo Ann Brown TX
Jimmie Bryans TX
Alice Buckles OK
Betty Jo Burma OK
Laura Burnett TX
Betty Burnham TX
Ann Burton AR
Charlotte Butler TX
Linda Cain AR
Merlene Cain TX
Ann Callahan TX
June Cameron TX
Carol Campbell TX
Frances Caudill TX
Gayle Cavnar TX
Oma Cerceo TX
Joanna Chapman OK
Martha Chapman TX
Margaret Childers TX
Irene Childress TX
Barbara Christenson TX
Clara Clay TX
Billie Clements TX
Shirley Cmjdalka TX
Mary Cook TX
Audrey Covington TX
Doris Cowling TX
Velma Crenshaw OK
Ruby Crowell TX
Treva Cruse TX
Dolores Currie TX
Mrs. Wm. Dabney NM
Jeanne Dabney NM
Frances Dauner TX
Alice Davies TX

Willard Dawson TX
Nell Denman TX
Virginia Dennis TX
Letha Dent NM
Mrs. J. M. Dishongh TX
Shirley Drew NM
Sally Dubberley TX
Mrs. Roy Duhart TX
Mrs. Robert Durrett TX
Eagle Mt. Garden Club TX
Margie Eicke TX
Audrey Elkins AR
Margaret Ellis TX
Mrs. Prentis Ellis TX
Maye Ellison TX
Connie Elmore NM
Eulonda Everest TX
Oleta Faught TX
Helen Fear TX
Sandy Foote OK
Donna French TX
Frances Gardner OK
Joyce Garrett OK
Mrs. Lloyd Gary TX
Shirley Gibson TX
L. Gilligan TX
Jean Gipson AR
Betty Giroski TX
Melrose Goetz TX
Jeanette Golden AR
Rosalie Gooch TX
Alice Gowdey TX
Elizabeth Gresham TX
Maxcine Guffey TX
Mrs. R. D. Hall AR
LeVene Hankins TX
Analee Harper OK
Gaby Harris TX
Shirley Henderson AR
Rose Hendrick TX
Betsy Hendrix TX
Mrs. Wm. J. Hendy TX
Holly Henneke OK
Molindia Henson TX
Lillian Hestand OK
Carol Hickman TX
Viola Higginbotham OK
Billie Hildreth TX
Bettie Histand TX
Teena Holcombe TX
Odell Holdridge TX
Ella Mae Holland AR
Pat Holley TX
Elda Holt TX
Bettye Hopper TX
Judy Howeth TX
JoAnn Huckabee TX
Annie Jo Huffmon TX
Karin Jacobs TX
Mary Janson TX
Rose Jasick TX
Harriet Jeffers TX
Ruth Jenks TX
Wilma Jennings TX
Leslie Jobé NM

Jim Johnson TX
Vernada Johnson TX
Dolly Johnson TX
Kathleen Jumper TX
Mary Katherin OK
Geraldine Kautz TX
Elsie Kear NM
Louise Keith TX
Dana Kettle TX
Kay King TX
Shirley Kinworthy TX
Evelyn Kirkwood AR
Clara Klein TX
Barbara Kletke OK
Betty Kloesel TX
Mrs. Robert Knox TX
Pat Koppa TX
Miriam Kottle TX
Kathey Kranzthor TX
Anna Kubacak TX
Loraine Kuehn TX
Mrs. George Kush TX
Myra Ladra-Walton TX
Agatha Lapham TX
Mary Leatham TX
Diane Lester TX
Lewis Lewallen AR
Doyle Lewallen AR
Charlotte Long NM
Mrs. Stanford Long TX
Desma Lowry TX
Gloria Luckett TX
Mrs. Harry Luplow AR
Barbara Lutz TX
Mary Lyons TX
Mary Mallard TX
Ruth Marcotte TX
Ruhbye Martin TX
Dolores Matheny TX
Mrs. J. M. Matthews AR
Patsy Mayer TX
Geraldine Mayes OK
Mrs. E. M. McCarty TX
LaVerne McCloud TX
Carla McConnelee TX
Sherry McCrady TX
Vada McGill OK
Golda McGuire TX
Elane McIlroy NM
Marilou McKinney TX
Dana Mears TX
Janice Meissner NM
Mrs. J. M. Michie, Jr. TX
Imogene Miller AR
Patsy Ruth Miller OK
Ann Miller TX
Barbara Miller TX
Jo Moncrief TX
Gladys Moore TX
Marcia Moore TX
Ellen Morris TX
Geri Mullins TX
Ellen Musselman TX
Reta Neal TX
Henrietta Novotny TX

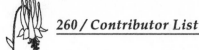
Jimmie Nutt TX
Doris Parker TX
Barbara Parker TX
Libbie Pavelka TX
Corene Pearce TX
Ruby Peck TX
Mary Perkins TX
Amali Perkins TX
Norlene Peterson OK
Mitch Peterson TX
Mrs. Oliver Pfeil TX
Nona Phillips TX
Scarlett Pickett TX
Sandra Pickett TX
Herminia Pipkin TX
Mrs. E. J. Pollock TX
Faye Potter TX
Mrs. George Poulos TX
Helen Power TX
Lois Poynor OK
Jean Prescott TX
Norma Preston TX
Helen Pugh TX
Lucy Rambo TX
Mary Redmond TX
Hazel Redmond TX
Peggy Redwine TX
Lucy Reed TX
Dorothy Reed TX
Betty Reinhardt TX
Lucinda Reynolds TX
Mary Robbins OK
John Rousseau TX
Janet Rund TX
Oleta Rurner TX
Virginia Russell TX
Sandy Russo TX
Dee Sanders TX
Mary Lu Sarkozy TX
Vera Sawyer AR
Sandra Schubert OK
Mrs. R. R. Scruggs TX
Joyce Searcy TX
Lucille Shamburger TX
Joan Shell TX
Nell Shimek TX
Eleanor Shipley TX
Brenda Shriver TX
Bettie Simmons TX
Tina Simon TX
Elizabeth Sinn NM
Ann Skok TX
Lea Slay TX
Hali Smith AR
Peaches Smith TX
Corrine Smith TX
Sue Smith TX
Liz Snider TX
Ann Sollers TX
Pat Spiller TX
Evelyn Splanow TX
Mrs. Moe Spradley TX
Mrs. I. B. Stafford TX
Mildred Stalnaker TX
Mrs. W. L. H. Stansfield TX

Mary Stark TX
Clara Stephens TX
Kathy Story TX
Mrs. N. J. Strasbaugh OK
Geraldine Suiter OK
Lee Sumpter OK
Carole Taylor TX
Alice Thomas TX
Betty Thomason OK
Elizabeth Thompson TX
Mrs. G. E. Thompson TX
Mrs. Vance Thompson, III AR
Jean Tripp TX
Mrs. H. D. Trippe AR
Judy Trowbridge TX
Helen Tullis TX
Oleta Turner TX
Betty Untermeyer TX
Myrtle Van Scoder OK
Danlyn Van Stone TX
Eileen Vela NM
Mary Vytopil TX
Portia Waddell TX
Carroll Wagner NM
Mrs. J. H. Wallace TX
Mary Walsh TX
Evelyn Wandell TX
Mollie Lou Warren TX
Ruth Webb TX
Jessica Webb TX
Dixie Webster TX
Mary Webster TX
Bernie Webster TX
Mrs. H. H. Wedeman TX
Lelia Wehner TX
Elzina Welch TX
Patty Welch TX
Hazel Wells AR
Helen Westpetal TX
Linda Whetsell TX
Patricia White TX
Hettie Whitfield TX
Kathryn Whitten TX
Pat Wight TX
Elizabeth Williams TX
Josephine Williams TX
Dee Williams TX
Helen Williams TX
Bitsie Williamson TX
Johnnie Wilson TX
Judy Winger TX
Lorene Wolf OK
Donna Womack TX
June Wood NM
Elauis Yantis TX
Marie Young TX

ROCKY MOUNTAIN
Mrs. Robert Robinson KS *
Mrs. Irwin Hoffman, Pres. CO
Mrs. Edgar Dies, Pres. KS
Mrs. Elden Jones, Pres. MT
Mrs. Fred Wesch, Pres. NE
Mrs. James Winter, Pres. ND
Mrs. Harold Buchheim, Pres. SD

Mrs. George Haddad, Pres. UT
Evelyn Kennedy, Pres. WY
Bonny Abboud NE
Willye Anderson CO
Marjorie Anderson MT
Lois Anderson SD
Sharon Andre NE
Marjorie Atkinson KS
Ruth Ballard NE
Amelia Banister KS
Mabel Barker KS
Iva Barkley KS
Sandy Bauer ND
Patty Bazil KS
Deanne Benish NE
Alice Blenheim SD
Marge Block NE
Armeade Bodenmiller NE
Bea Boory KS
Reta Bowen KS
Frances Brent KS
Gloria Broksle MT
Janice Brooks SD
Margaret Brown NE
Ruth Brown NE
Denise Brummer NE
Olga Bruntz NE
Bucklin Garden Club KS
Edna Bugner SD
Doris Burgess NE
Judith Burns MT
Twila Burwitz SD
Esther Bussell NE
Alma Caddy NE
Jeniece Cady NE
Catherine Cary KS
Vonda Chamberlain SD
Lucille Clark NE
Bonnie Cook WY
Sherry Corneliusen MT
Beverly Craddock SD
Helen Creasy KS
Elna Crick NE
Blanche Cruikshank NE
Ruth Darrough KS
Mrs. Wayne Dasher NE
Rosella Daugherty NE
Edith Davis KS
Donna Davis MT
Rosa Devier NE
Gladys Dirks SD
Mae Dowler KS
Connie Earley SD
Clara Eide ND
Agnes Einspahr NE
Marjorie Elliott NE
Florence Erickson NE
Chip Estes NE
Lorraine Fairchild KS
Lila Ferrell KS
Marjorie Finley NE
Melanie Fisher NE
Kathryn Foster KS
Phyllis Freeman NE
Lillian Gebhardt SD

Alyce Geiser NE
Ruth Gillock KS
Diane Gimber CO
Donna Goins KS
Golden West G C MT
Louise Greenberg KS
Daisy Greer KS
Marjorie Gunn SD
Betty Haas NE
Audrey Hallwachs SD
Verla Ham KS
Lesa Hamilton NE
Jeanette Hansen NE
Mary Hanson MT
Lois Hanson SD
M. C. Harberg NE
Mr. Ward Harrington ND
Velda Hatcher KS
Esther Hawley MT
Mary Lou Haywood WY
Alvina Heipler SD
Sherrie High MT
Diana Hill NE
Eunice Hill NE
Virginia Hilton NE
Catherine Hladky SD
Jane Hoeft NE
Jacquie Hoffman CO
Helga Hogness ND
Lydia Hove KS
Winifred Howley KS
Jim Hruska NE
Mrs. Tom Hudgens KS
Wynona Jacobson NE
LaVone Jelinek NE
Bernadene Jensan KS
Minnie Jensen SD
Jane Johnson CO
Dorothy Johnson KS
Junne Johnsrud MT
Dora Jones KS
Eilene Jones NE
Mrs. Oris Jorgensen SD
Bea Julson SD
Vera Kacirek KS
Alta Keating NE
Meta Keep NE
Irene Kehlbeck KS
Linda Keil MT
Joan Kilpatrick KS
Nadine Kiser CO
Erma Kivett KS
Elvera Klein NE
Viola Kloxin KS
Linda Knepp NE
Anna Marie Kolberg SD
Zaida Kraus NE
Irene Lahm NE
Patricia Langner SD
Betty Langston KS
Joyce Larkin WY
Eldora LaRoque CO
Wanda Larsen NE
Beatrice LeClair SD
Florence Lee SD

Mrs. Earl Lincoln NE
Shirley Lindekugel NE
Lucille Linstrom NE
Ratha Lea Loker KS
Dorothy Long SD
Lucille Lowe NE
Eleanor Lueck NE
Marjorie Lukanitsch MT
Wilhelmina Maassen NE
Mary Jeanne MacLaurin MT
Ileen Madsen SD
Ruth Magar UT
Fran Mallett CO
Enola Martin NE
Phyllis May SD
Leota Mayberry KS
Correne Mehrer CO
Pat Meiers SD
Marcella Melsted ND
Mrs. R. A. Mermis KS
Rev. Ken Mettler ND
Beth Miller NE
Charlotte Miller SD
Gwen Mitchell KS
Margaret Monson ND
D. J. Myers CO
Wanda Myers SD
Hazel Neff SD
JoAnn Newman KS
Joan Newman NE
Dottie Nieberding KS
Helen Nunn MT
Louise Oberfoell ND
Eunice Officer KS
Helen Olson NE
Delta Orthman NE
Alberta Parks KS
Ruth Parks NE
Paula Partsch NE
Helen Paulson NE
Norma Perkins MT
Shiz Peterson NE
Ilah Preitauer NE
Frances Prince NE
Betty Prochnow NE
Erica Putz ND
Lucy Raap SD
Jeanne Reints SD
Janet Remington NE
Eva Reyes KS
Grace Riley NE
Mrs. R. E. Robinson KS
Marjorie Roetinger CO
Neva Rogers WY
Carol Sue Roozen SD
Emil Rose SD
Lillian Rose SD
Eleanor Ruge NE
Beverly Savage UT
Bonnie Schaunama SD
Darlene Schick NE
Ella Schloss MT
Dollie Schroeder NE
Martha Schulz NE
Cindy Schutz SD

Lillian Schwab SD
Astrid Sebens ND
Camilla Seminara NE
Beulah Shaw SD
Lola Shellenbarger NE
Margaret Siek SD
Betty Sieps SD
Amelia Silve MT
Dorothy Sisson KS
Betty Smith KS
Ardelle Smith MT
Ardis Smith NE
Elizabeth Smith UT
Karen Smith UT
Beverly Sombke SD
Donna Stefanek CO
Mrs. James Stenslie MT
June Stohr MT
Shirley Stokka ND
Evelyn Swanson NE
Mary Swisher SD
Helen Templar KS
Frances Tomchak KS
Joan Tongish KS
Barbara Tucker MT
Donna Ulmer NE
Nellie Vigneri NE
Eva Votaw NE
Janet Waite
Pat Warsop WY
Nora Waterman KS
Lavina Waters KS
Esther Wedberg ND
Agnes Wells KS
LeVerna Wescost NE
Golden West MT
Mrs. M. G. Williams NE
Wilma Wilson KS
Edna Wilson KS
Linda Witt SD
Fran Wittgartner CO
Edna Woodman NE
Helen Wyckoff NE
Ethel Yax NE
Virginia Young NE
Margaret Zentz NE
Vera Ziebell NE
Carol Zilverberg SD

PACIFIC REGION
Mrs. Wil J. Tebo CA *
Della Colver Barry, Pres. AK
Mrs. John Colvin, Pres. AZ
Mrs. Mary Lou Van Deventer,
 Pres. CA
Mrs. Andy Antosik, Pres. HI
Mrs. E. C. Cleaveland, Pres. ID
Mrs. Steve Appel, Pres. NV
Mrs. Elaine Belts, Pres. OR
Mrs. Leslie Lothian, Pres. WA
Mary Ellen Ambuhl OR
Yvonne Augenstein AK
Janice Babcock AZ
Lillian Baca NV
Donna Balfrey CA

Mrs. Carl Bechtold AZ
Betty Belcher WA
Ruth Berger OR
Norma Berkovitz AZ
Ruth Blakeslee AZ
Ruth Byrne AZ
Beverly Cadman OR
Iva Clayton AZ
Mary Cochran AZ
Mary Ann Cooper AK
Maxine Cowie CA
Virginia D'Elia CA
Nan Dahlstet AZ
Fern Dawson AZ
Loretta Delk AK
Juanita Dootson WA
Elsie Dungan WA
Marie Dvorak OR
Lucille Ellwood AZ
Jane Ewaniuk AZ
Mrs. Clark Fee OR
Myrtle Findley CA
Dorothy Finger CA
Ethel Fox AZ
Mary Frey AZ
Harriet Funk AZ
Mrs. R. E. Garrison AK
Mazie George CA
June Gibbons AZ
Jean Gilbertson WA
Bunny Gladhart AZ
Betty Groves AZ
Peggy Hall AZ
LaRue Hall CA
Karen Hamball AZ
Helen Harrah NV
Pamela Hawkes OR
Bee Hawkins CA
Betty Hedtke CA
Roy Hedtke CA
Doris Helvig AZ
Teresa Henry AZ
Adelaide Heywood AZ
Marion Huddle NV
Madison Hunter AZ
Lucille Hurst AZ
Lucy Jacobson AZ
Hildegard Johnson AZ

Ima Johnson OR
Katherine Jordan AZ
Peggy Jordan AZ
Gladys Jurgemeyer AZ
Marian Kawulok AZ
Laurene Keltner AZ
Helen Kennedy AZ
Donna Kirts AZ
Carol Klingberg WA
Dorothy Knapp WA
Ruth Knutson AK
Clara Kuhfuss AZ
June Kuzminsky WA
Marianne Larson WA
Sue Lawrence CA
Sarah Lindsey HI
Roberta Love AZ
Jeanne Lundell ID
Frances Martinez AZ
Gloria Masser OR
Alvina McCullough AZ
Ruth McLaughlin WA
Mary Miller-Jones OR
Carmen Mitchell AZ
Shirley Mitsko HI
Beth Morris AZ
Pat Newcomb AK
Mary Newhouse HI
Ruth Nissly AZ
Lillian Norvell AZ
Mrs. Irvin Ogard CA
Miriam Owen WA
Jean Owens AZ
Ruth Parish NV
Edie Pate CA
Ruth Peake AZ
Evelee Pearns NV
Mary Pettigrew CA
Dell Poppenberger AZ
Joy Pound WA
Carol Reed AZ
Georgia Rehm AZ
Connie Riccio HI
Fran Robinson AZ
Julia Rolland ID
Nan Jean Roller OR
Jessie Rowland AZ
Emily Ruhlig CA

Madalynne Rutherford AZ
Louise Sabin AZ
Lee Sandor AK
Mildred Savage AZ
Evelyn Schenk OR
Gayle Schilling CA
Katy Schoenek ID
Ruth Schoonover AZ
Betty Shire AZ
Betty Siegfried AZ
Linda Silk AK
Virginia Smith AZ
Elizabeth Smith CA
Helen Sorkin NV
Viola Stansell AK
Dorothy Starek AZ
Lisa Stephens AZ
Loraine Stephensen AZ
Jean Stockwell ID
Ellen Swenson WA
Barbara Thomasson AZ
Phyllis Thompson AZ
Elizabeth Timmer WA
Frances Veach WA
Shirley Vigors AZ
Doris Walser AZ
Carol Wasieko AZ
Annette Weaver AZ
Betty Werschkull WA
Elizabeth Wilder HI
Elinor Williams ID
Janet Yamamoto HI
Irene Zani CA
Elinor Zappalo WA

**INTERNATIONAL
AFFILIATES**
Mrs. Wallace Barr, Chairman
Lillian Barlow, England
Maria Benjumea V., Colombia
Mrs. Wendell Cox, Mexico
Gilda de Garcia, Mexico
Emilia de Luna, Mexico
Anita de Moreno, Panama
Miradalva de Trejos, Costa Rica
Mrs. Kevin Finnerty, England
Isabel Ibarguen, Mexico
Anne Johnstone, Bahamas

Index

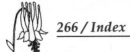

Nutritional Guidelines

The editors have attempted to present these family recipes in a form that allows approximate nutritional values to be computed. Persons with dietary or health problems or whose diets require close monitoring should not rely solely on the nutritional information provided. They should consult their physicians or a registered dietitian for specific information.

Abbreviations for Nutritional Analysis

Cal — Calories	Dietary Fiber — Fiber	Sod — Sodium
Prot — Protein	T Fat — Total Fat	gr — gram
Carbo — Carbohydrates	Chol — Cholesterol	mg — milligrams

Nutritional information for these recipes is computed from information derived from many sources, including materials supplied by the United States Department of Agriculture, computer databanks and journals in which the information is assumed to be in the public domain. However, many specialty items, new products and processed foods may not be available from these sources or may vary from the average values used in these analyses. More information on new and/or specific products may be obtained by reading the nutrient labels. Unless otherwise specified, the nutritional analysis of these recipes is based on all measurements being level.

- **Artificial sweeteners** vary in use and strength so should be used "to taste," using the recipe ingredients as a guideline.
- **Artificial sweeteners** using aspartame (NutraSweet and Equal) should not be used as a sweetener in recipes involving prolonged heating which reduces the sweet taste. For further information on the use of these sweeteners, refer to package information.
- **Alcoholic ingredients** have been analyzed for the basic ingredients, although cooking causes the evaporation of alcohol thus decreasing caloric content.
- **Buttermilk, sour cream** and **yogurt** are the types available commercially.
- **Cake mixes** which are prepared using package directions include 3 eggs and 1/2 cup oil.
- **Chicken**, cooked for boning and chopping, has been roasted; this method yields the lowest caloric values.
- **Cottage cheese** is cream-style with 4.2% creaming mixture. Dry-curd cottage cheese has no creaming mixture.
- **Eggs** are all large.
- **Flour** is unsifted all-purpose flour.
- **Garnishes**, serving suggestions and other optional additions and variations are not included in the analysis.
- **Margarine** and **butter** are regular, not whipped or presoftened.
- **Milk** is whole milk, 3.5% butterfat. Lowfat milk is 1% butterfat. Evaporated milk is whole milk with 60% of the water removed.
- **Oil** is any type of vegetable cooking oil. Shortening is hydrogenated vegetable shortening.
- **Salt** and other ingredients to taste as noted in the ingredients have not been included in the nutritional analysis.
- If a choice of ingredients has been given, the nutritional analysis reflects the first option.

THE NATIONAL COUNCIL OF STATE GARDEN CLUBS, INC.
4401 Magnolia Avenue
St. Louis, Missouri 63110

Enclosed is $_____ for _____ copies of
BLOOMING GOOD at $15.00 each plus
$2.50 postage and handling per book.
Please make checks payable to:

THE NATIONAL COUNCIL OF STATE GARDEN CLUBS, INC.

Name: _____

Address: _____

City/State/Zip: _____

For Information About STATE GARDEN CLUBS
Please Write To:
The National Council of State Garden Clubs, Inc.
4401 Magnolia Avenue
St. Louis, Missouri 63110
or CALL: (314) 776-7574